Joyce, Medicine, and Modernity

THE FLORIDA JAMES JOYCE SERIES

UNIVERSITY PRESS OF FLORIDA

Florida A&M University, Tallahassee
Florida Atlantic University, Boca Raton
Florida Gulf Coast University, Ft. Myers
Florida International University, Miami
Florida State University, Tallahassee
New College of Florida, Sarasota
University of Central Florida, Orlando
University of Florida, Gainesville
University of North Florida, Jacksonville
University of South Florida, Tampa
University of West Florida, Pensacola

Joyce,
Medicine,
and Modernity

Vike Martina Plock

Foreword by Sebastian D. G. Knowles

University Press of Florida
Gainesville / Tallahassee / Tampa / Boca Raton
Pensacola / Orlando / Miami / Jacksonville / Ft. Myers / Sarasota

Printed in the United States of America. This book is printed on Glatfelter
Natures Book, a paper certified under the standards of the Forestry Stewardship
Council (FSC). It is a recycled stock that contains 30 percent post-consumer waste
and is acid-free.

First cloth printing, 2010
First paperback printing, 2012

Library of Congress Cataloging-in-Publication Data
Plock, Vike Martina.
Joyce, medicine, and modernity / Vike Martina Plock ; foreword by Sebastian D. G.
Knowles.
p. cm.—(The Florida James Joyce series)
Includes bibliographical references and index.
ISBN 978-0-8130-3423-2 (cloth: alk. paper)
ISBN 978-0-8130-4226-8 (pbk.)
1. Joyce, James, 1882–1941—Criticism and interpretation. 2. Joyce, James,
1882–1941—Knowledge—Medicine. 3. Medicine in literature. 4. Literature and
medicine—Ireland—History—20th century. 5. Modernism (Literature)—Ireland.
I. Title.
PR6019.09Z7822 2009
823.'912—dc22   2009025058

The University Press of Florida is the scholarly publishing agency for the State
University System of Florida, comprising Florida A&M University, Florida Atlantic
University, Florida Gulf Coast University, Florida International University, Florida
State University, New College of Florida, University of Central Florida, University
of Florida, University of North Florida, University of South Florida, and University
of West Florida.

University Press of Florida
15 Northwest 15th Street
Gainesville, FL 32611-2079
http://www.upf.com

Contents

Illustrations

Foreword

Joyce had a pathological attraction to prescriptions of all kinds, especially medical ones. The rich and varied use of contemporary medical material in his work has not yet received its due, especially given Joyce's original aspirations as a "Trinity medical," in the disparaging terms of the Mabbot Street Bawd. In many respects, the "Ithaca" questioner is less a catechizer in the jesuitical tradition than he is a medical diagnostician, probing the body of a sick patient. The overarching paradigm for *Ulysses* is diagnosis: what ails Mr. Breen? What ails Stephen, or Bloom? More to the point, what ails Dublin and the modern world? Is *Ulysses* the "strong draught" that John Woolsey famously called it in his 1933 decision to permit the book's publication in the United States, or is the book itself a symptom of disease?

Vike Plock has the answers for us, and is especially good at the nosological classification of Joyce's various pathologies, from alcoholism (in *Dubliners*) to masturbation (in *A Portrait*), obstetrics (in "Oxen of the Sun") to neurasthenia (in "Eumaeus"). By linking Farrington's paralysis with the physiological theories of Cesare Lombroso and the psychological *dédoublement* of Pierre Janet, "Counterparts" acquires a depth of field it has previously lacked. In a synaptic reading of "Eumaeus," Plock maps out the nerve endings and neuroses of that episode, all carefully presented within the historical framework of the state of neurological science at the time. The work of Santiago Ramón y Cajal, arguing for contiguity rather than continuity in neural transfer, for which he won the Nobel Prize in 1906, becomes a crucial fragmentation to add to the collection of modernist crack-ups, along with the atom (Bohr), the psyche (Freud), time (Bergson), and the body (shrapnel). Plock's study of the state of contemporary gynecology places many of the book's curiosities in historical perspective: Mrs. Bellingham's remark, "Vivisect him!" can now be usefully connected to the rhetoric of the feminist and anti-vivisectionist Frances Power Cobbe.

What results is a gleaning of Joycean afflictions, and a book that clearly lays out, with surgical precision, the many ways in which Joyce's work is indebted to turn-of-the-twentieth-century medicine. One might call this book, after Rembrandt's study of Nicolaes Tulp, *The Anatomy Lesson of Dr. Plock*: like Rembrandt's painting, Plock's study of one man's revolutionary work with a scalpel is itself a work of art.

Sebastian D. G. Knowles
Series Editor

Acknowledgments

Over the years many friends, colleagues, and fellow Joyceans have helped me in dissecting James Joyce's works. During the project's embryonic stage at the University of York, Derek Attridge and Lawrence Rainey offered sound advice while Jane Moody's and Mary Luckhurst's passionate interest in drama, plays, and celebrity culture offered welcome distractions that kept me sane. In Matthew Creasy, Ulrika Maude, Stephen Regan, and Patricia Waugh I found like-minded Joyce enthusiasts at Durham University and I thank them for many fascinating discussions about Joyce, medicine, and physiology. During my appointment at University College Dublin I learned a lot about the Irish facets of Joyce's texts from working with John Brannigan, Anne Fogarty, and Declan Kiberd. It was also a pleasure to work with Laurent Milesi at Cardiff University, whose energy and incredible knowledge about Joycean matters proved to be particularly valuable. At a very crucial moment during the writing process, Richard Terry at Northumbria University encouraged me to make connections between Joyce and Laurence Sterne and generously shared his sources and ideas on eighteenth-century plagiarism.

In one way or another, a number of other Joyceans have had a strong impact on this project and made me feel at home in the Joyce community. Words cannot describe Fritz Senn's generosity in sharing his unfailing Joyce knowledge with newcomers. Two scholarships from the Friends of the Zurich James Joyce Foundation facilitated research trips to Switzerland, where I found two enthusiastic and knowledgeable discussion partners in Ruth Frehner and Ursula Zeller, who made me feel extremely welcome in Zurich. Warmest thanks are also due to Andrew Gibson, John Gordon, Sean Latham, John McCourt, Laura Pelaschiar, Tom Rice, Sam Slote, Michelle Witen, and especially Aida Yared, who generously provided the image from *Pearson's Weekly*, read my manuscript with surgical precision, and gave a physician's diagnostic approval. Any remaining medical blunders are my own. A very special "thank you" goes to my two wonderful and steadfast Joyce friends Valérie Bénéjam and Ariela Freedman.

Sebastian Knowles has been a fantastic series editor at the University Press of Florida. He took an early interest in this project and offered pragmatic advice at numerous stages in the production process. It was a pleasure to work with him. I would also like to thank Amy Gorelick at UPF, who is a model of efficiency and professionalism. I have never met anybody who responds so quickly to questions and queries.

Assistance, advice, and support have also been provided by many people who had absolutely nothing to do with Joyce. I do not know what I would have done without Keir Waddington, his wit and wisdom, and his expertise in nineteenth-century medical history. Carolina Amador, Nicole Devarenne, Monica Facchinello, Anthony Mandal, Becky Munford, Richard Sugg, and Rose Thompsom were equally important allies at different stages of the writing process. I have also been extremely lucky to have met Michael Whitworth, Martin Willis, and other members of the British Society for Literature and Science, and I thank them for many interesting discussions on this intriguing "interdiscipline." Finally, I would like to thank my family, my sister Nele and my mother Gabriele Plock, who offered encouragement and advice at crucial moments. This book is for Jason David Hall, who did the most.

Earlier versions of chapters in this book were published in the following collections and journals: a portion of chapter 1 in *Joyce in Context*, ed. John McCourt (Cambridge: Cambridge University Press, 2009); a shorter version of chapter 6 in *Journal of Modern Literature* 30.1 (2006), where it appeared as "A Feat of Strength in 'Ithaca': Eugen Sandow and Physical Culture in Joyce's *Ulysses*"; an earlier version of chapter 7 in *Joyce, "Penelope" and the Body*, ed. Richard Brown (Amsterdam: Rodopi, 2007), where it appeared under the same title. I would like to thank the editors and publishers of these journals and collections for permission to publish new versions of this material.

Abbreviations

D	James Joyce. *Dubliners*, edited by Terence Brown. London: Penguin, 1992.
FW	James Joyce. *Finnegans Wake*, edited by Seamus Deane. London: Penguin, 1992.
LI	*Letters of James Joyce*. Vol. 1, edited by Stuart Gilbert. New York: Viking, 1957.
LII	*Letters of James Joyce*. Vol. 2, edited by Richard Ellmann. London: Faber and Faber, 1966.
LIII	*Letters of James Joyce*. Vol. 3, edited by Richard Ellmann. London: Faber and Faber, 1966.
OCPW	James Joyce. *Occasional, Critical and Political Writing*, edited by Kevin Barry. Translated from the Italian by Conor Deane. Oxford: Oxford University Press, 2000.
P	James Joyce. *A Portrait of the Artist as a Young Man*, edited by Seamus Deane. London: Penguin, 1973.
SH	James Joyce. *Stephen Hero*, edited by John J. Slocum and Herbert Cahoon. New York: New Directions Books, 1955.
SL	*Selected Letters of James Joyce*, edited by Richard Ellmann. London: Faber and Faber, 1992.
U	James Joyce. *Ulysses: The Corrected Text*, edited by Hans Walter Gabler with Wolfhard Steppe and Claus Melchior. London: Bodley Head, 1993.

Introduction

I am nearly dead with work and eyes. (*LIII* 49)

The story of Joyce's creative labor is reminiscent of a medical case study. Gastric pains, rheumatism, and nervous collapses repeatedly interrupted the exasperated Joyce in his attempts to polish off his writings. In Joyce's case, art and debility continually overlapped. Particularly compromising in the extensive catalogue of aches and pains was, of course, the unpredictability of Joyce's "wretched eyes" (*LIII* 252). After the "rheumatic fever episode" in Trieste in 1907, iritis was Joyce's constant companion on the rocky road to publication, fame, and notoriety.[1] Over the next three decades, this particular disease, which left Joyce practically blind for a while and which required a cure with silver nitrate (Schneider 2001, 456), would continue to erupt.

Extremely troublesome were the years from 1917 to 1922, during which Joyce "suffered eight separate episodes of attacks in his eyes" (Gottfried 1995, 5). On April 22, 1917, Joyce reports, for instance, that he feels depressed about the duration of his eye attack and informs Harriet Shaw Weaver that work on *Ulysses* continues "at the usual snail's pace" (*LI* 102). A much dreaded operation seemed inevitable. So when Joyce collapsed with an attack of glaucoma on August 18, 1917, an iridectomy was the only possible solution, and Joyce went into surgery six days later. However, the operation resulted in the patient's "nervous collapse which lasted three days" and left Nora "too upset" to respond to a letter from Ezra Pound (*LII* 405).

After this first encounter with the oculist's surgical knife in 1917, Joyce's correspondence continues to parallel the writing process of *Ulysses* with references to his impaired vision and ocular troubles.[2] Roy Gottfried paints a vivid picture of a crippled Joyce writing and proofreading *Ulysses* with blurred and impaired vision, armed with a magnifying glass (Gottfried 1995, 6). Most infuriatingly for Joyce, though, doctors and eye specialists failed to agree on a consistent course of action. Whereas the 1917 iridectomy seemed inevitable, the infallible

Dr. Borsch, Joyce's Paris ophthalmologist, regarded it "a mistake" in 1923 (*LI* 201) and opted for a dionine treatment—although the consistency of Borsch's dionine solution differed significantly from the one prescribed by a Nice eye specialist (*LIII* 72). One can hardly blame Joyce for being pessimistic and for losing faith in doctors, medical research, and the art of healing. Frustrated by delayed recoveries and the conflicting opinions of his medical experts, he declared in 1923 that "[t]he question is almost as complicated as *Ulysses*" (*LI* 201).

Joyce, it seems, had ample reason to see analogies between the progress of his health and his avant-garde novel. Both troubled him exceedingly in the years from 1917 to 1922. But Joyce's statement also hints at another parallel between *Ulysses* and his physical condition. Joyce suggests that both his ocular troubles and his book are "complicated" and therefore elude analytical or diagnostic certainty. While Joyce's obstinate eyes refused to cooperate and while his doctors disagreed about nosological patterns and adequate cures, *Ulysses*, as a text, reads, in Joyce's eyes, like a stubborn patient, inviting analytical scrutiny but ultimately refusing to be diagnosed conclusively.

This book is an attempt to do a bit of diagnosing. Its focus is, as the title *Joyce, Medicine, and Modernity* suggests, Joyce's obsession with health, debility, and medicine—topics and subjects that crop up everywhere in his writing. Hence, while Joyce's physical body repeatedly made the acquaintance of the doctor's surgical knife and the question of his health remained "in the doctor's hands" (*LIII* 68), this study will dissect, analyze, and examine Joyce's textual corpus in search for medical references and intertexts. But it is an exploration of Joyce's aesthetics as well as a sociohistorical analysis. While it recovers a wide range of turn-of-the-century medical debates that were available to Joyce, it also investigates medicine's role and significance in Joyce's works.

Why was Joyce so fascinated by medicine, ailments, and imperfections? The first chapter, which chronicles the rise of medicine as a new cultural force in modern society, provides some answers to this question in its final section. Chapters 2 to 7 then present individual case studies by focusing on specific episodes and portions of Joyce's texts from *Dubliners* to *Ulysses*. They cover a wide range of material and include such unlike medical discourses as psychology, neurology, gynecology, and physical culture. But it is precisely this variety of medical references in Joyce's work that can illustrate the complexity of his stance toward modern medicine and its diagnostic practices. In *Ulysses*, Stephen's scorn for Buck Mulligan and the materialism of this "bonesetter" and "medicineman" (*U* 1.419), who sees "them pop off every day in the Mater and Richmond and cut up into tripes in the dissectingroom" (*U* 1.205–6), is matched by Bloom's assessment of doctors' compassionate and charitable nature: "Humane doctors, most of them" (*U* 8.400).

In what follows, we shall see that medicine had various and sometimes contradictory meanings for Joyce. He consistently traded on medical imagery and metaphors to enrich his aesthetic practices. John Gordon has fittingly noted that Joyce "constructed each of his four major books along developmental lines that became more and more explicitly biophysical" (Gordon 2003, 148). But Joyce also used his fiction to interrogate some of medicine's theories and to criticize medicine's cultural authority at the beginning of the twentieth century. Accordingly, chapter 2 on "Counterparts" shows how Joyce's text complicates a medico-pathological case story of chronic alcoholism. In Joyce's narrative, modern medicine's harsh analysis of inebriety is offset by an emphasis on the creative and rebellious potential of the alcoholic mind. Similarly, chapter 3 on sexuality and adolescent masturbation in *A Portrait of the Artist as a Young Man* examines how Joyce depicts medicine's regulatory power over Stephen's adolescent body. In depicting Stephen's frustrated personal and artistic formation, *A Portrait* shows that it is not Stephen but modern medicine and its analytical concepts that are dysfunctional and flawed.

Chapters 4 to 7 look at Joyce's appropriation of medical intertexts and imagery in *Ulysses*, the text that is, with its explicit references to body organs, most obviously connected to human physiology and medical themes. Medical allusions, references, and debates are scattered throughout the book. And although he certainly did not dismiss his critical stance toward modern medicine when writing *Ulysses*, it is with this text that Joyce's fascinated interest in medicine really comes to the fore. In my chapters on *Ulysses*, I am therefore interested, first of all, in exploring how Joyce's aesthetics developed alongside his synchronized interest in medicine: how his writing on the social body, Dublin, referenced or incorporated medical images and transformed them into narrative tropes. Turning to "Oxen of the Sun," chapter 4 thus shows how intimately Joyce's concept of writing and authorship relied on a creative and original interpretation of obstetrical metaphors.

Chapters 5 and 6 reinforce the suggestion that Joyce, in writing *Ulysses*, drew heavily on medical metaphors. The chapter on "Eumaeus" illustrates the episode's reliance on neurophysiologcal and ergographic vocabulary and argues that neuroscience provided modernist writers such as Joyce with an important new set of metaphors in their attempts to revolutionize literary conventions at the beginning of the twentieth century. This analysis of "Eumaeus," with its references to "hard sciences" such as neuroscience is followed by a lighter note. Chapter 6 demonstrates the influence, on the "Ithaca" episode, of physical culture and Eugen Sandow, the most famous and popular strongman at the turn of the century. In exploring the connections among Sandow's fitness cult, Zionism, racism, and eugenics, it shows how Joyce used some of physical culture's principles and guidelines in the characterization of Leopold Bloom. It also reconsiders the nature of the language in "Ithaca" by suggesting that the catechistical style, in spite of its distinctively surgical and diagnostic quality, foregrounds the power of the imagination.

The final chapter of this study, which discusses Molly Bloom's confrontation with modern medical authority and its pathologization of womanhood, returns to the topic of Joyce's critical assessment of medicine's cultural authority. In the Victorian era, gynecological theory and domestic medicine emerged as effective instruments in reinforcing conventional gender politics. Joyce, in proposing Molly's conflicting and kaleidoscopic image as a refutation of reductive representations of femininity, critically interrogates modern medicine's interventions in turn-of-the-century social and cultural politics.

All of these chapters chart, in one way or another, how Joyce's texts respond to specific theories about physical and psychological deficiency and disabilities, but given the variety and the complexity of this topic, my study on Joyce and medicine is intended to be read as a collection of essays organized around a specific theme. Its primary intention is to reopen the debate about the role of physiology, medicine, and the sciences in Joyce's works, not to offer conclusive or final remarks on any of these topics. This is why *Joyce, Medicine, and Modernity* ends its analysis with a prognosis on potential future work on Joyce and medicine, especially in *Finnegans Wake*. Medicine rearranged knowledge in the course of the long nineteenth century. It also analyzed and reorganized the social texture of the modern world. As we shall see, Joyce and his fiction were extremely responsive to this important historical process.

1

Joyce and Modern Medicine

I was interested to read what you told me in your last letter as I myself started
to study medicine three times, in Dublin, Paris and again in Dublin. I would have
been even more disastrous to society at large than I am in my present state had I
continued. (*LI* 137)

Joyce's ongoing fascination with medicine, health, and discourses on the human body is well known. His correspondence, interspersed with medical details and descriptions, distinctly reveals the particular interest that Joyce reserved from early youth for the art of healing. Well known, too, is the story
of his three failed attempts to study medicine. In October 1902 Joyce entered
the Catholic University Medical School in Cecilia Street only to drop out after
a month, daunted by the basic science lectures and unable to secure tutoring
to finance himself. After turning his back on Dublin on December 1, 1902,
the exiled Joyce attempted to get admission to the Faculté de Médicine at the
Sorbonne in Paris (Ellmann 1983, 106). Yet in a repetition of his Dublin experience, scientific inaptitude and financial problems forced Joyce to give up this
half-hearted attempt.

Having spent more time in the Bibiothèque Nationale and the Bibiothèque
Sainte-Geneviève reading Aristotle than in the lecture theaters, Joyce was then
called back to his mother's deathbed on April 10, 1903. Back home in Dublin he
made a last and even more unmotivated attempt to resume his medical studies.
Finally, after having dismissed the idea of a medical career for good, he could
be seen in the company of medical students such as Vincent Cosgrave, John
Francis Byrne, and, of course, Oliver St. John Gogarty, replacing serious medical scholarship for his friends' often raucous accounts of the hospital wards and
the dissecting room.

As J. B. Lyons's "clinical examination of the author's life" also shows, having
been the continuous object of medicine's scrutinizing attention, health and
medical treatment mattered to Joyce and distinctively influenced his works

(Lyons 1973, 9). An early example of medicine's impact on Joyce's writing is the 1900 unpublished and lost play *A Brilliant Career*. An homage to the much admired Henrik Ibsen, this early literary attempt follows the career of a young doctor, Paul, who sacrifices personal happiness for professional ambitions. Rejecting the woman he loves for a better match, Joyce's protagonist climbs the social ladder and is elected mayor of his hometown only to be confronted by an endemic outbreak of the plague. In due course the scourge is defeated, but the last scene of the play nevertheless forces Paul to recognize the futility of his juvenile ambitions.

Although certainly flawed in terms of plot, symbolism, and character development, as William Archer pointed out (Ellmann 1983, 79–80), the play touches upon many topics related to medicine, medical practitioners, and public health that occupied the public opinion at the turn of the century. Epidemics were a grim reality in Joyce's home country. Additionally, the ambitious young doctor's representation is a reflection on the changed status of medical practitioners in turn-of-the-century society. With medicine's emergence as a "political force" (Fee and Porter 1993, 250) in the Victorian period, especially in public health matters, and the growing specialization of its practitioners, doctors' social position improved significantly. Indeed, in the second half of the nineteenth century, medicine became a respected and politically influential profession. It promised an adequate income and social status and became "an occupation which gentry or ambitious parents could choose as a career for their sons" (Lane 2001, 11).

Although Joyce, after writing *A Brilliant Career*, never again chose medicine as a profession for one of his protagonists,[1] his works nevertheless resonate with medical imagery, allusions, and physical and pathological descriptions. Florence L. Walzl fittingly suggests that Joyce "absorbed clinical attitudes, which he carried into his fiction" (Walzl 1984, 159).[2] Especially *Dubliners*, with its case histories that depict the cultural stagnation in the Hibernian metropolis, uses the pathological expression "paralysis" as a metaphor for the Irish capital's social circumstances and therefore effectively appropriates medical terminology. Clinical observation and scientific diagnosis are therefore central conceptions in *Dubliners*. And in the schema that Joyce passed on to the Italian critic Carlo Linati in 1920, the episodes of Joyce's 1922 *Ulysses* are famously organized around a human body's organs, bones, nerves, locomotive apparatus, and blood circulation.[3] Although Joyce later dismissed the Linati schema as interpretative device for *Ulysses*, the novel nevertheless continues to accentuate his ongoing interest in exploring the analogies between the human body, the city as a social organism, and the corpus of his developing narrative.

In his texts Joyce also turned his "sharp pathological eye" (Walzl 1984, 159) to the workings of the medical profession and identified medicine as one of the dominant cultural authorities shaping the modern social landscape. As we shall see, the late Victorian period witnessed an explosive growth in medical theories, practices, and institutions, and medicine as a profession and an ideology attained the supremacy in modern society that had remained securely in the hands of the clergy for centuries. By the time Joyce, the one time medical student, was writing, medicine had emerged as an assertive progress narrative, energetically intervening in discussions about social and cultural improvement.

"Making mejical history all over the show!" (*FW* 514.2–3): Medicine, Progress, and Modernity

In 1890 the German bacteriologist Robert Koch unexpectedly announced the discovery of a cure for tuberculosis, one of the most devastating contagious diseases of the time.[4] This announcement was greeted with excitement and Koch's revolutionary finding swiftly promised to become a landmark in medical research. Arthur Conan Doyle, himself a doctor, visited Koch's laboratory in the same year and conveyed some of the ecstasy surrounding the event in an article in the *Review of Reviews*: "The stranger must content himself by looking up at the long grey walls of the Hygiene Museum in Kloster Strasse, and knowing that somewhere within them the great master mind is working, which is rapidly bringing under subjection those unruly tribes of deadly micro-organisms which are the last creatures in the organic world to submit to the sway of man" (Doyle 1890, 552).

Sadly, Koch's famous cure turned out to be ineffective after thorough trials. But Conan Doyle's account, unabashedly comparing the medical practitioner to an unflinching imperialist on his civilizing mission, nonetheless illustrates the unrelenting faith invested in medicine and medical research at the turn of the century. And modern medicine's achievements were indeed considerable. Due to improved technology and reformed analytical procedures, medical practitioners generated diagnostic labels for illnesses as diverse as hysteria and cholera and argued authoritatively about how to treat the pathological manifestations of modernity.

However, in the nineteenth century it was Paris rather than Robert Koch's Berlin that emerged as the first continental medical capital. Hence Joyce's decision to leave Ireland for the benefit of a continental medical education in 1902 cannot be regarded as entirely unreasonable. Although Dublin could look back proudly on a century of medical stardom—with medical coryphées such as the renowned ophthalmologist and census commissioner Sir William Wilde, the inventor of the hypodermic syringe, Francis Rynd, and the eminent physician Robert Graves, who introduced the continental system of "bedside teaching" in Ireland and secured international fame for the "elimination of starvation, purging and bleeding from the treatment of fevers" (Fleetwood 1951, 191)—the "heyday of the Dublin clinical school" was over by the 1870s (McGeachie 1999, 85). Although the Rotunda, the first British and Irish lying-in and maternity training hospital, was opened in Dublin by Bartholomew Mosse in 1745 and Dublin's surgical education had been superior to anywhere else in the United Kingdom at the beginning of the nineteenth century, Irish medicine now had to look abroad for the introduction of new and revolutionary medical discoveries. By 1900 "the Golden Age of Irish Medicine" had drawn to an end (Fleetwood 1951, 160).

Paris, in contrast to Dublin, continued to be a pulsating center for medical teaching and research. Throughout the nineteenth century, the French capital had developed its reputation as the heart of continental medicine, giving birth to innovative medical specialties. The case of Jean Martin Charcot amply illustrates this. From 1870 until his death in 1893, foreign visitors, laymen and medical experts alike, congregated in large numbers in the lecture theater of "the greatest neurologist of his time" (Ellenberger 1970, 89). Sigmund Freud, for instance, spent four months at the Salpêtrière during his stay in Paris in 1885 and 1886. And one of Charcot's most promising disciples, Pierre Janet, working in the Salpêtrière between 1893 and 1902, was to become the founder of modern experimental psychology. Another French medical luminary was, of course, the physiologist Claude Bernard, who revolutionized modern medicine by introducing a more experimental method in the study and practice of medicine. Paris in 1902, then, was a first-class choice for medical studies. Had Joyce pursued his endeavor with more zeal, his professional training would have been both solid and cutting-edge.

But since these innovative developments in modern medicine were the result of other fundamental cultural events stemming from the French capital, the emergence of Paris as medicine's continental center is not surprising. Indeed, medicine's appearance as a dominant cultural force in modern times can be traced back to the Enlightenment. And although the urge for medicine's reorganization and "academisation" (Ackerknecht and Fischer-Homberger 1977, 225) swept over different European countries at different times in the nineteenth century, it is vital to remember that the general spirit of reform dominating the medical profession at that time "was a European phenomenon in which, broadly speaking, the similarities between different countries were more striking than the differences" (Loudon 1993, 228). The late eighteenth and early nineteenth centuries, the "period of medical reform" (Loudon 1993, 219), systematically revolutionized the face of medical institutions, redefined medicine's role in modern society, and ushered in the age of modern diagnostic medicine as we know it today. As Michel Foucault argues, modern medicine "has fixed its own date of birth as being in the last years of the eighteenth century" (Foucault 1994, xii). Inspired by the Enlightenment's optimistic beliefs in man's rationality and by the democratic vista of the French Revolution, medicine all over Europe set out to reform itself in order to participate actively in the organization of the new social order. The century of democratic revolutions therefore initiated the consolidation of the medical practitioner's authority, replacing beliefs in feudal institutions and religion with those in science's teleological and progress-oriented philosophy.

It was in these turbulent times that medical practitioners finally abandoned Galen's theoretical heritage, one that had dominated medical scholarship since antiquity, and replaced his humoral theory with a "reductionist model which placed disease in organs, tissues and finally cells" (Brunton 2004, xii). No doubt, it was the evolving interest in and dominance of pathoanatomy in medical teaching and research that favored this reorganization of medical knowledge. The dissecting room's factual reality, the unearthing of localized and somatic changes in the opened corpse, effectively forced doctors to throw overboard the classical academic legacy of the body as a "holistic entity of fluids and energies" (Brunton 2004, xii). A new era of medical science saw the light of day: "hospital" or "clinical" medicine (Harrison 2004, 57). Hospitals emerged as the site of medical training, and the minute scrutiny of patient's pathological symptoms sanctioned the development of an objective nosological analysis. In the new and progressive medical training the practical experiences of the hospital's wards replaced the books, which had handed down traditional medical philosophy for centuries. It was during the Enlightenment, therefore, that doctors changed from wise healers into scientific experts. Although the example of Joyce's "A Painful Case," emphasizing Mr. Duffy's "saturnine" (*D* 104) disposition, conspicuously illustrates that Galen's vocabulary died a much slower death in quotidian usage, doctors had revolutionized their intellectual heritage by the beginning of the nineteenth century.

In the Victorian period the new understanding of localized diseases in the patient's sick body also brought about an epistemological change in the understanding of illnesses. Before the "clinico-analytical" method (Foucault 1994, 136) had gained its foothold in medical philosophy, practitioners had regarded illness as particular to an individual. But the minute scrutiny of patients' pathological symptoms now sanctioned the development of an objective nosological analysis. Whereas the "Hyppocratic consultation was a patient-oriented . . . form of diagnostic inquiry" and conferred importance upon the subject's individual description of the illness (Nicolson 1993, 802), the new clinico-analytical method developed generic disease entities that became independent of the patient's individual sufferings. Medical practitioners began to distinguish between "*symptoms* subjectively reported by the patient and *signs* registered directly in the body" (Rothfield 1992, 85). Epistemological priority was given to the doctor's physical examination whereas the patient's individual narrative became a negligible feature in the clinical case.

Consequently, under the new rule of empirical medicine the sick person was literally deducted from the pathological equation. Diseases became specific and separate entities, showing common traits, despite the patient's subjective sufferings and symptoms. This led to the attempt of classifying diseases and of creating accurate illness directories. For instance, one of the most influential directives came from the Edinburgh professor of medicine, William Cullen, who published his decisive nosology in the 1778–79 best-selling *First Lines of the Practice of Physic* (Porter 2001b, 165).

Together with this epistemological revolution modern medicine also radically changed the face of its institutions. Before the industrial revolution medicine's influence on people's lives had been marginal. Most illnesses were treated at home in the family, assisted by midwives or the occasional philanthropic support of ministers and "ladies of the manor" (Loudon 1997, 82). Professional medical assistance was only available to the very prosperous, whereas hospitals carried a charity stigma, treating only the "deserving poor" (Granshaw 1993, 201). The medical profession itself, being organized in a firm hierarchical order, lacked unity. No structured medical education or official medical registration that distinguished between regular and irregular practitioners was available. Medical practitioners were therefore constantly threatened by the competition with Grub Street quackery. Besides, only the university-trained physicians, attending to the physical needs of the upper classes and charging high fees for consultations, were in possession of the MD degree. The apprenticed surgeons who were in charge of emergency amputations and the apothecaries who sold medicines lacked both social status and a recognized degree and qualification.

Interestingly, by the end of the nineteenth century the situation had changed radically. In the nineteenth-century spirit of "self-governing professionalism" (Parry and Parry 1976, 117), the different medical professions joined hands, combined their interests, and metamorphosed into a unified corporation with representative bodies. Consequently, the newly organized medical profession gradually developed into an influential body in nineteenth-century politics. This was especially evident in the emerging public health sector. Confronted by the results of growing industrialization, urbanization, and the problem of the "great unwashed," who perished in large numbers in urban quarters and workhouses, state intervention had become inevitable. Statistics effectively highlighted the "remarkable gulf in life expectancy between various classes" (Wohl 1984, 5). Subsequently, sanitary officers, philanthropic institutions, and medical practitioners formed an alliance to combat the appalling sanitary conditions in Europe's urban slums.

With the dawn of the public health movement, it was no longer regarded as sufficient to alleviate the population's immediate distress only during the recurring ordeals caused by epidemics. Instead preventive medicine aimed at the elimination of epidemics' causes. While urban developers and sanitary reformers designed plans for improved sewage systems, waste disposal, street paving, and ventilation, doctors commented on overcrowding, poverty, water supply, and the inhabitants' poor diet and wretched living conditions. In fact miasmatism, the prevailing mid-nineteenth-century theory of disease, went as far as correlating foul smells and places with disease.[5] Disease became synonymous with poverty, and reformers believed that the abolishment of pauperism would eventually result in the triumph over epidemic and endemic diseases. In "Telemachus" Buck Mulligan temporarily adopts the public health officer's role: "—If we could live on good food like that, he said to [the milkwoman] somewhat loudly, we wouldn't have the country full of rotten teeth and rotten guts. Living in a bogswamp, eating cheap food and the streets paved with dust, horsedung and consumptives' spits" (*U* 1.411–14). The milkwoman's admiration for Mulligan emphasizes both medicine's incessant impact on the turn-of-the-century public health movement and the medical student's social prestige. Like so many of her contemporaries she regards the medical man, Buck Mulligan, as a decisive authority on the country's well-being.

By the end of the Victorian period, and even more so in Edwardian society, the medical profession had thus gained a certain public status while its practitioners distinguished themselves in numerous medical specialties. Accumulated medical knowledge required a new form of scientific expertise that the regular general practitioner (GP) could no longer guarantee. The result was an explosive growth of new medical subjects that provided patients with a wide range of experts, specializing in specific disease entities or particular human organs (oncologists treating cancer and cardiologists treating diseases of the heart, for example). A good example of the increase of medical specialization is the rapid development of Harley Street as a fashionable consultants' quarter in London's West End: here the number of specialists rose from 36 in 1873 to almost 150 in 1900. Likewise, in 1860, the English capital could claim to be the host of a total of 66 specialist hospitals and dispensaries (Porter 1999, 350 and 386).

Unsurprisingly, in the 1931 collection of essays known as *Doctors' Delusions*, Joyce's compatriot, George Bernard Shaw, therefore answered the question of whether or not modern society had lost its religious faith with the polemic statement: "Certainly not; but we have transferred it from God to the General Medical Council" (Shaw 1950, i). Undeniably, in many European countries, medicine had effectively replaced the church's authority at the beginning of the twentieth century. Great Britain is a particularly noteworthy case in point. Here, the institutionalization of the General Medical Council, the medical profession's "ethico-legal watchdog" (Porter 1999, 355), was one of the principal legacies of the 1858 British Medical Act—one of the most important landmarks in medicine's rise to institutional authority.

"[W]ith their medical assassiations all over the place" (*FW* 146.14): Modern Medicine in Britain and Ireland

Although medicine was taught at Oxford and Cambridge in the nineteenth century, many English would-be medical practitioners were trained in Scotland. After the foundation of its medical school in 1726, Edinburgh University soon became the preeminent British center for medical education. By the 1780s around 200 medical students received their degrees there and by the 1820s even twice as many medical apprentices frequented its lecture theaters (Porter 1999, 291). Englishmen, interested in a first-class medical education, flocked to the Scottish capital in order to benefit from the unique training in scientific medicine. Yet Edinburgh trained its students in more than just medicine. Influenced by new continental developments emanating from medical centers such as Leiden and Paris, the Scottish university "offered a medical education of a type quite new in Britain involving the integration of a wide range of medical and allied subjects" (Parry and Parry 1976, 105). As early as 1739 subjects such as pharmacy, surgery, anatomy, botany, chemistry, and midwifery formed part of the medical student's general syllabus in Edinburgh.

The discrepancy between an English and a Scottish medical degree shows the extent to which the British medical profession lacked unity before the nineteenth century. No "structured system of medical education and official medical registration" (Loudon 1995, 230) was available. And as early as the eighteenth century the obvious differences between a degree offered by Scottish universities and one granted by the Royal College of Physicians in London became a significant source of dispute among the different medical corporations. In short, the quality of a medical education varied extremely from place to place. To make matters worse, without a national register the distinction between the "regular" and the "irregular" practitioner remained shockingly imprecise.

The Irish situation was further complicated by religious divergences. Although the Royal College of Surgeons in Ireland offered from 1785 onward a surgical diploma that did not require a religious test, Trinity College Dublin (TCD), then the only Irish institution granting a medical degree, "discriminated until 1873, and severely until 1783, against members of churches not in communion with the Church of Ireland, while aspiring licentiates of the College of Physicians in Dublin had to be TCD matriculates or hold a degree in arts" (Froggatt 1999, 61). Accordingly, the Catholic University of Ireland's foundation in 1854, with its Medical School premises opening in Cecilia Street in 1855, served one purpose in particular: it created "an institution run by catholics for catholics and (largely) of catholics, and under episcopal control" (Froggatt 1999, 68).

Add to all this the medical profession's complicated hierarchical division into physicians, surgeons, and apothecaries, the limited legal power of their respective representative bodies (Royal College of Physicians, Royal College of Surgeons, and the Company of Apothecaries), whose structure was based on the guild tradition, not to mention the tensions between the metropolis and the provinces, and we get an impression of the chaotic circumstances that governed the British medical profession at the end of the eighteenth century. Reform was necessary, but reform was also a precarious political issue since it threatened to overthrow the medical profession's long-standing hierarchical order, which was carefully guarded by the high-status physicians. It is also vital to remember that, despite various important milestones in the reform of medicine, the nineteenth-century British medical revolution was characterized by many setbacks and disappointments. The medical order's emergence as the most prestigious and influential profession at the turn of the twentieth century was a long and complicated process, incorporating both revolutionary and reactionary elements in its development.

Not surprisingly, the first attempt at reforming the medical corporations in 1794 came from the medical pecking order's lower end, the apothecaries, who formed the core of the emerging new medical profession, the general practitioner. With the lowest social status among medical professionals, general practitioners were constantly being threatened by the competition with druggists and chemists. As a result several leading London apothecaries founded the General Pharmaceutical Association. It was the first attempt of a group of general practitioners to voice common interests. In 1806 the Royal College of Physicians, dreading the potential rivalry with the general practitioner, answered with the proposal of a bill extending "its powers of control over all types of medical practice in England and Wales" (Parry and Parry 1976, 110). Although the bill was never passed, it strikingly emphasized the internal confrontations and the political struggle governing the relationship between the different medical institutions at the turn of the nineteenth century.

In July 1812 the foundation of the Association of Apothecaries and Surgeon-Apothecaries was yet another effort of the surgeon-apothecaries/general practitioners to be "in sole charge of the selection, examination, and certification of those who chose their branch of the profession" (Loudon 1995, 238). Naturally, the College of Physicians refused its support. Similar internal conflicts overshadowed the introduction of the 1815 Apothecaries' Act. Although the Act established the Apothecaries' Company as the qualifying association for England and Wales and as general practitioners' licensing body, it did not manage to dissolve the colleges' rigid structure in favor of a unified governing body.

Under these wedged circumstances the *The Lancet*'s launch as the medical profession's organ in 1823—conveying "to the Public, and to distant Practitioners as well as to Students in Medicine and Surgery, reports of the Metropolitan Hospital Lectures" (Anonymous 1823, 1)—proved to be a crucial event. In creating a representative journal for the whole medical profession, *The Lancet*'s conception was an important attempt at unifying its disparate branches. Founding the Irish Medical Association in 1839, Richard Carmichael and Arthur Jacob pursued similar efforts in Dublin. Earlier that year they had already founded *The Dublin Medical Press*.

In spite of these early attempts, a real breakthrough in unifying the medical profession did not occur until the introduction of the 1858 Medical Act, which legally consolidated many of the reform efforts that had proved to be so challenging in the medical profession's attempted homogenization. This act finally established a General Medical Register for England and Wales, created the General Medical Council, responsible for "jurisdiction over malpractice and 'infamous conduct' including advertising and collaboration with irregulars" (Porter 1999, 356), and began to rescue the apothecaries, surgeons, and general practitioners from low social status and their tradesman stigma.

The recently joined medical orders were now concerned with one question in particular, that of a unified medical education. By the time the 1858 Medical Act was introduced, only physicians benefited from the privileges of a university career. Surgeons and apothecaries were still apprenticed. This internal clash in medical training weighed heavily on the mind of the General Medical Council, whose explicit aim was to raise not only the general practitioner's educational standards but also the medical profession's social status. The following declaration, made by one of its members in 1868, shows that in comparison with other professions the Victorian doctor's social rank lacked the prestige that a Buck Mulligan can, in 1904, take for granted: "[A]s regards position we may remark that the gentry look upon the clergy as their social equals, that they look upon members of the bar as their social equals, nay more that they regard a certain portion of our profession in the same light. Which portion then? and why not all of our members?" (Ashe 1868, 146 cited in Parry and Parry 1976, 132–33).

As much as the medical profession itself, the medical practitioner's public image required reforming. This was achieved by celebrating the doctor's assimilation into "the cult of the gentleman" (Parry and Parry 1976, 131). The Victorian media did its share in assisting the aspiring medical profession in its effort, setting "the profession on a pedestal, as is further evident in the handsome and flattering caricature portraits of society doctors which appeared in *Vanity Fair* and elsewhere" (Porter 2001a, 262). No wonder that a university degree became the required standard examination for doctors. It signified social status. With her character Tertius Lydgate in *Middlemarch* (1871–72), George Eliot was already beginning to indicate the Victorian practitioner's changing socioprofessional constellations. The recently fashioned gentleman-doctor, whom Victorian gentry such as the Vincys could receive in their parlors in the 1830s, did therefore as much in reforming the medical profession's public image as the obligatory national registration of its practitioners.

With medicine thus becoming a learned profession and its practitioners being transformed into respected and well-educated gentlemen, the medical order turned to the demanding problems of one of the nineteenth century's most significant medical branches: public health. In Britain, the first European country facing industrialization's consequences, the deteriorating sanitary conditions in large urban centers urgently demanded medical and sanitary reformers' attention. Paradoxically, although the national death rate constantly declined during Victoria's reign, a growing number of her subjects were forced to endure the squalor and the resulting diseases such as tuberculosis and typhus controlling Britain's slums. While paupers succumbed in large numbers to contagious diseases at the beginning of the nineteenth century, the British poor relief system was hopelessly out of date and unable to cope with the dirt, the poverty, and the inevitable deaths.

Extremely grim was the situation in Ireland. At first glance this must seem surprising, because a relatively small proportion of Ireland's population lived in towns. Whereas in England 56.3 percent of Victoria's subjects lived in big urban centers by 1881, the figure for Ireland reached only 16.3 percent in the same year (Wohl 1984, 201). However, the wretched living conditions of Ireland's peasants made life in the Irish countryside equally unbearable. Sanitary offenses such as domestic pig-keeping, overcrowding, and unwholesome diet had reduced the Irish peasant's resistance to infectious diseases since the beginning of the nineteenth century. At the same time, Ireland's population mushroomed exorbitantly. "[T]he potato island had become one of the world's most densely populated places" (Porter 1999, 29). Shortly before the famine Ireland's population had reached a figure of 8,295,061, having increased by over one-and-a-half million within a quarter of a century (Fleetwood 1951, 198).

The 1845–47 potato crop failure and resulting famine hit the already enfeebled Irish peasantry with full force. In point of fact, the famine reduced the Irish population to half its size. Poverty-related diseases such as typhus, relapsing fever, and dysentery raged unrestrictedly, claiming the lives of around one million people. Especially typhus struck the Irish population with incomparable harshness so that this scourge became widely known as the "Irish fever," an association perilously connecting pathology with race. Even at the turn of the twentieth century infectious diseases still "accounted for one-third of all deaths in Dublin" (O'Brien 1982, 104). The Joyce family was not exempt from these terrible scourges. In 1902 George Alfred Joyce, James's fourteen-year-old brother, contracted typhoid fever and succumbed to his illness (Ellmann 1983, 93–94).

Unsurprisingly, therefore, descriptions of the grim sanitary conditions in the Hibernian metropolis find their way into Joyce's texts. In a Dickensian passage in "A Little Cloud," Little Chandler is walking "swiftly down Henrietta Street" and here encounters a "horde of grimy children" who "stood or ran in the roadway or crawled up the steps before the gaping doors or squatted like mice upon the thresholds" (*D* 66). Although Little Chandler gives "them no thought" while he is making "his way deftly through all that minute vermin-like life" (*D* 66),[6] Joyce's text does register the poverty, the dirt, and the squalor that characterizes the lives of many Dubliners. Likewise Bloom, in "The Lotus-Eaters," observes "a boy for the skins" with "his bucket of offal linked, smoking a chewed fagbutt" and a "smaller girl with scars of eczema on her forehead" "listlessly holding her battered caskhoop" (*U* 5.5–7)—an equally grim depiction of Dublin slum life. Urban poverty is also a pressing topic in *Finnegans Wake*. Scholars such as James Atherton and Jean-Michel Rabaté (Atherton 1974, 76–78 and Rabaté 2001, 190) have shown that Joyce used Benjamin Seebohm Rowntree's 1901 *Poverty: A Study of Town Life* for the depiction of the "fair home overcrowded" (*FW* 543.22) in chapter 3.3 where the text suggests that slum inhabitants should receive "calories exclusively from rowntrees and dumplings" (*FW* 544.34–35).[7]

Many million Irish chose emigration over starvation and disease, leaving their homes behind to flee to the already densely populated urban centers of Britain and the United States. Naturally, their ordeal was not over in their new homes. Poor living conditions and contagious diseases continued to ravage their numbers. Furthermore, the swarm of Irish immigrants was blamed for the importation of infectious diseases. Especially in the New World during the 1832 and 1849 cholera epidemics, the Irish were singled out as scapegoats for bringing this scourge to the shores of the United States. Well known is also the case of "Typhoid Mary," the Irish-born cook Mary Mallon, who, in spite of being asymptomatic, infected almost fifty people with typhoid fever in New York at the turn of the century (Porter 1999, 424). But the stereotypical association of the Irish with disease gained an equally strong foothold in England. As the historian Mark Harrison argues: "Protestants claimed that Catholicism bred poverty, corruption and disease" (Harrison 2004, 139).

Accordingly, the Irish Poor Inquiry of 1836 heard many witnesses asserting the role of the Irish in spreading diseases.[8] In his 1845 study *The Condition of the Working Class in England*, the young Friedrich Engels, in describing the

Irish as barely human, being "comfortable only in the dirt" (Engels 1999, 46), further consolidated this persisting stereotype. Indeed, Engels's rhetoric shows the full extent to which the Irishman had, in the popular nineteenth-century imagination, not only become a medical but also a social and economic source of contamination: "[T]he Englishman who is still somewhat civilized, needs more than the Irishman who goes in rags, eats potatoes, and sleeps in a pigsty. But that does not hinder the Irishman's competing with the Englishman and gradually forcing the rate of wages, and with it the Englishman's level of civilization, down to the Irishman's level" (Engels 1999, 88–89). No doubt, these and similar images of Irish filthiness, as well as the perceived causal connection between Irish immigration and infectious diseases, hastened the sanitary reform process at home. Back in Dublin a number of sanitary improvement works were carried out. A General Board of Health was created in 1820 and from 1850 onward the Irish capital benefited from various sanitary measures such as drainage, street paving, erection of public privies, and the appointment of Medical Officers of Health.[9]

However, as the causal connection between poverty and an exorbitant death rate began to penetrate the awareness of nineteenth-century social reformers everywhere, the question of pauperism obtained top priority. One man in particular advocated the "sanitary idea" with almost religious zeal: Edwin Chadwick, lawyer, English civil servant, and former secretary of Jeremy Bentham. Influenced by the latter's utilitarian philosophy, Chadwick, in his role as secretary to the Poor Law Commission, first sketched out the modalities of a new Poor Law. Initiated in 1834, it was based on the premise of "less eligibility." In other words, the workhouses were meant to be repellent locations, forcing laborers to combat their poverty by their own force of labor instead of relying on charitable institutions. While the grim reality of Chadwick's new pauper legislation is very vividly depicted in Charles Dickens's 1838 *Oliver Twist*, the number of paupers, to Chadwick's great disappointment, did not decline under the new Poor Law's regime. It was only then that the "correlation between dirt and disease" was firmly grasped (Chadwick 1965, 21). However, in order to facilitate the work of the sanitary reformers, detailed demographical information on the laboring poor had to be made available. In England this was achieved in 1837 when the Registrar General's Department was established, providing for the first time precise birth, marriage, and death rates. In contrast, Ireland had to wait until 1864 for the establishment of an Irish Registrar General.

The increasing interest in the nation's health statistics and demographical surveys facilitated Chadwick's 1842 *Report on the Sanitary Condition of the Labouring Population of Great Britain*. With the help of three doctors—Neil Arnott, James Philip Kay-Shuttleworth, and Thomas Southwood Smith, all of whom shared his enthusiasm for sanitary reform—Chadwick produced an extensive study on the appalling hygienic conditions of Britain's rookeries. The report "concerned itself entirely with technical details concerning sewerage, water supply and drainage: the holy trinity of Chadwick's 'Sanitary Idea'" (Harrison 2004, 113). The repeated advent of epidemic and endemic diseases thus no longer appeared to be a social but primarily an engineering problem, one which could be remedied by extensive urban reorganization.

Chadwick's *Sanitary Report* eventually initiated the 1848 British Public Health Act, which created the General Board of Health as central authority for the sanitary reform movement. It was a first attempt to bring public health and preventive medicine under central control. The Board could enforce the Act on local communities with a death rate exceeding 23 per 1,000 (the average national death rate). The local boards of health were then put in charge of sanitary supervision and inspections and were held responsible for the improvement of municipal hygienic conditions.

Interestingly, the Public Health Act's introduction in England coincided with an important historical event. In 1848 a revolutionary tide once more swept across Europe. Insurgencies, ignited by the Parisian February Revolution, temporarily threatened to overthrow the social order of many major European countries. This apparent menace for the establishment made the question of the laboring poor even more pressing. Clearly, reform was seen as a means to prevent revolution, and subsequently Chadwick's sanitary vision obtained immense political significance. Especially the new French emperor, Napoleon III, an enthusiastic supporter of Chadwick's public health reform, adopted the imperative task of urban improvement. Under his direction Baron Georges Haussmann redesigned Paris's urban grid, separating the working classes' quarters by his magnificent new boulevards. From 1854 onward the Parisian sewerage system also grew from 143 km to 773 km (Harrison 2004, 115). And although these reconstructions might appear merely a result of the popular sanitary spirit of the day or a general philanthropic gesture, they nevertheless had political significance.

The Parisian sewers, having been used as a hiding place for revolutionists in the past, had long been associated with insurgencies and their extension and

modernization was therefore meant to be cleansing in a twofold way. Haussmann's new architecture thus emphasizes the alliance between the sanitary
movement and reactionary politics. Cutting through areas densely populated
by the poor, the newly constructed grand boulevards were aimed at inhibit-
ing communication and thus preventing revolutionary gatherings or further
insurrections. But Haussmann's urban reorganization of Paris is just an early
example of medicine's intersection with social politics. With the close of the
nineteenth century and during Joyce's lifetime this interaction had gained both
in force and candor.

Back in England Chadwick's labors on the General Board of Health were
greeted with widespread hostility. His attempt to bring public health matters
under centralized control opposed the general laissez-faire spirit dominating nineteenth-century British society. "We prefer to take our chance with
cholera and the rest rather than be bullied into health," declared *The Times*
in response to Chadwick's ongoing efforts (quoted in Porter 1999, 412). The
public was not prepared to be subjected to the new public health movement's
centralizing tendencies. The unpopularity of Chadwick's General Board
eventually led to its liquidation in 1854. However, the sanitary idea did not
die with Chadwick's dismissal. With his successor it only acquired a different
orientation.

From 1858 onward the functions of the General Board of Health were
taken up by the newly created Medical Department of the Privy Council and
a medical man, John Simon, was appointed as Britain's first medical administrator. More diplomatic than Chadwick, he considered "sanitary progress"
chiefly as an "educational matter" and granted local authorities the right of
regulating sanitary inspections and reforms (Simon 1887, 483). For Simon "as
for so many other officials of the time, knowledge and persuasion, the exposure of abuses and the provision of advice, seemed infinitely more preferable
than coercive sanctions as means of administration" (Lambert 1963, 264).
With this new administration, Britain's public health movement reached an
important turning point. Under John Simon's careful supervision, medical expertise gained unforeseen prominence. Simon himself produced a number of
Blue Books investigating, with the help of scientific empiricism and statistical
evidence, all relevant features of Britain's health situation. Eventually, the new
clinico-analytical method, which had governed empirical medicine since the
Enlightenment, was now applied to the ailments of society at large. Simon and
his supporters regarded the precise scientific examination of sanitary condi-

tions as the first step to introduce a successful preventive health administration.

In his role of chief medical administrator, Simon finally introduced new sanitary legislation, culminating in the 1875 Public Health Act, which instituted the appointment of a medical officer of health for every sanitary district in England and Wales. An Ireland Public Health Act was introduced three years later with dispensary doctors being appointed as medical officers of their respective districts. Public medicine had now effectively organized British and Irish society into manageable units, optimizing its effectual impact on individuals' lives. Moreover, Simon's sanitary legislation concretized medicine's supremacy in the public health movement. Although the administrative power was firmly placed in the hands of local governments and remained no longer in those of a centralized body, the sanitary movement continued to rely on medicine's scientific evaluations and opinions regarding preventive methodologies. By linking medical knowledge to administrative authority, it created a new social elite in the form of the medical expert. Consequently, by the end of the nineteenth century, medicine had finally advanced from its early nineteenth-century marginal position to one of crucial social and political importance.

No doubt, medicine's involvement in the public health movement served its purpose, sparing many lives with the introduced reform measures. In the secularized late nineteenth-century climate medicine did do the great work of the future. Yet much of the medical research undertaken by Victorian scientists was not just confined to laboratory work. Instead, medicine's scientific parameters were freely applied to the analysis of the social context. Public concerns such as teenage masturbation, insanity, or alcoholism, which had been regarded as moral problems for centuries, were scrutinized in a novel, scientific light. And although medical research into such matters did not replace moral unease about recurring social problems, it helped significantly to reinforce prevailing social opinions in providing nineteenth-century morality discourses with a more rational and objective undercurrent.

Setting new scientific standards, medical practitioners argued persuasively on the question of cultural and social acceptability. They established firm guidelines for what was to be regarded as normal, healthy, or sane, while they conducted at the same time sustained studies of social irregularities and abnormalities that could take on distinctively discriminative undercurrents. Examples of such late nineteenth-century medical projects are as far-reaching as they are colorful: phrenology or the anthropological studies of the Italian anthropologist and criminologist Cesare Lombroso, who, in his study *L'Uomo Delinquente* (1876), argued forcefully for biological determinism in the behavior of criminals.

Late nineteenth-century medicine's most pessimistic predictions came to the fore with emerging degeneration theories. Writers such as the English psychopathologist Henry Maudsley or the French alienists Benedict Augustin Morel and Valentin Magnan established pathological taxonomies of alleged hereditary diseases such as alcoholism or insanity. No doubt, degeneration was the most aggressive medical evaluation of the social context. For not only did this pseudomedical theory single out specific disease patterns, but it also equipped individuals with decisively pathological labels. Furthermore, its alleged scientific and objective stance made it difficult to refute hostile conclusions as irrelevant and insignificant. However, it is with degeneration's rise to intellectual prominence at the end of the nineteenth century that Joyce's own debate with medicine becomes of interest.

"[D]osed, doctored and otherwise" (*FW* 438.36–439.1): Medicine and Joyce

What was it that intrigued Joyce about modern medicine? As we will see in more detail in the next chapter, Joyce was intrigued by degeneration and its studies of human pathologies. Lombroso is mentioned several times in his correspondence with Stanislaus in 1906 (*LII* 151, 157, 190), where Joyce's casual remarks about "Lombrosianism" (*LII* 151) are linked to comments about socialism and continental theories on Jewishness and anti-Semitism. But this fascination with degeneration and its pathological configurations has to be seen in the context of his wider interest in medicine and its preoccupation with human debility, diseases, and ailments. As Rick Rylance notes, the nineteenth-century discourse of medicine "emphasized the diagnosis not of ability but of debility." Medicine was therefore associated with the idea of "correction or management of potential or actual dysfunction" in both a physiological and psychological sense (Rylance 2000, 112). It is per se a scientific practice interested in finding remedies, cures, and treatments for specific human deficits, unfitness, and disorders. In other words, it is a scientific discourse about lack and improvement. It is hardly surprising, then, that Joyce took an interest in such matters. While he worried excessively about his own failing health and collapsing body, medicine with its corrective urges and didactic agenda started to occupy a central place in his writing, which aimed to expose and criticize the unhealthy and stagnant cultural conditions in the Irish metropolis—a city that was as much in need of medical care and attention as one of its famous offspring.

As this chapter has shown, medicine was regarded as a significant and influential cultural force at the turn of the century and during the years in which Joyce wrote *Dubliners*, *A Portrait of the Artist as a Young Man*, and *Ulysses*. Medicine was associated and became synonymous with modernity and modernization. For Joyce, a historically conscious writer, medicine therefore formed part of the phenomenology of modernity that was the reference point for his experimental modernist writing. More important though, if medicine was associated with progress, improvement, and above all modernity, Joyce in writing *Ulysses*, the quintessential modernist novel, would not have hesitated to trade on medicine's cultural capital.[10]

Yet Joyce's relationship with modern medicine was by no means straightforward. In his informative study *James Joyce and Sexuality*, Richard Brown asserts that medicine and medical lore "offered [Joyce] a more satisfactory way of understanding his human nature than the Church" (Brown 1985, 52). It seems, of course, very compelling to suggest that Joyce, in his analysis of modern culture, and modern Irish culture in particular, regarded medicine's scientific rationalism as a welcome alternative to the stifling religious doctrine of the Catholic Church. He certainly included numerous references to medical debates and contexts in his works in order to illustrate his enthusiastic interest in modern medicine, and some of my chapters on *Ulysses* show explicitly that Joyce was seduced by the image of medicine as a modern progress narrative. But did he really regard medicine as intellectually liberating? Is it not more likely that his upbringing in Catholic Ireland would have made him extremely receptive to the workings of dominant cultural politics?

Joyce's critics have frequently emphasized his diagnostic talent for sensing social inequities. Indeed, having grown up in a country that remained captivated in the sway of orthodox Catholic authority, Joyce developed, from early youth, a keen sense for the complex workings of dominant cultural politics. Recent studies such as Andrew Gibson's *Joyce's Revenge* (2002) and especially Katherine Mullin's *Joyce, Sexuality and Social Purity* (2003) have brought welcome attention to Joyce's productive struggle with the regulatory social politics of his time. Within this cultural matrix, modern medicine played an especially prominent role. What I want to suggest in this study is that Joyce's intellectual dependence on medicine's vocabulary and imagery did therefore go beyond a complacent acceptance of medicine's demand for cultural authority at the beginning of the twentieth century.

Science's (and medicine's) cultural dominance in turn-of-the-century culture is most vigorously attacked in Joyce's 1899 essay "The Study of Languages," in which he uses vivisection as an example of modern "heartless science" that leads "only to inhumanity" (*OCPW* 14). But Joyce, who states in "The Study of Languages" that "science may improve yet demoralize" (*OCPW* 14), also used some of his other texts to critically interrogate the prevalent claim that medicine should be regarded as a satisfactory modern progress narrative preferable to religious dogmas. While medical specialists and doctors undoubtedly helped to improve living standards at the turn of the century, they also assisted in formulating scientific designs about cultural and social norms and standards. Medicine, as some of Joyce's texts show very well, was therefore instrumental in producing prejudiced readings of the modern cultural context. This is why medicine was, for Joyce, not simply a liberating alternative to the church. Conversely, he would have noticed that medicine produced—not unlike theological practices—a set of powerful and instructive arguments that actively regulated and changed the cultural politics of his time. As the next chapter will show, "Counterparts," written in 1905, is an early example of Joyce's critical assessment of medicine's role in the modern world.

2

"Alcoh alcoho alcoherently"

Alcoholism and Doubling in "Counterparts"

Dubliners, the book Joyce liked to call his "nicely polished looking-glass" for the Irish people (*LI* 64), draws heavily on medical terminology in the analysis of the Irish capital's citizens. Well known is the fact that Joyce employed the neuropathological term "paralysis" in order to comment on the cultural stasis in his home city: "My intention was to write a chapter of the moral history of my country and I chose Dublin for the scene because that city seemed to me the centre of paralysis" (*LII* 134).[1] In using this particular medical term, paralysis, in his statement Joyce already suggests that his narrative perspective relied, in an almost Flaubertian manner, on scientific analysis and clinical observation.

What Joyce seemed to be most interested in, in writing *Dubliners*, is a diagnostic approach to the many ailments that paralyze his home town. To that purpose Joyce's first book displays a wide variety of pathologies and illnesses and it is certainly no accident that the collection opens with a reference to a "third stroke" (*D* 1). However, as J. B. Lyons notes, drunkenness is identified as the predominant disease in the Hibernian metropolis (Lyons 1973, 85). Almost every story in *Dubliners* depicts and discusses alcoholism and its devastating consequences: Mrs. Sinico in "A Painful Case," Mr. Kernan in "Grace," Eveline's father in the eponymous story, and finally Freddy Malins in "The Dead," to name just a few examples. But the story that examines the effects of a drinking disorder in detail is "Counterparts."[2] It vividly illustrates the household disturbances of the clerk Farrington, who, after a long humiliating day at work, a pawned watch, and a long night with drinks in Dublin's public houses, releases his built-up aggression by assaulting his son at home.

Oppression and tyranny are central themes in "Counterparts." Farrington, a copy clerk in a law firm, is enmeshed in the world of modern office politics that heartlessly mechanize human labor. Similarly, Joyce makes the oppressive dominance of English colonial power an important subtext of the story. Mr. Alleyne, Farrington's despotic boss, is from the North of Ireland and Weathers, who beats Farrington in the arm-wrestle match, stems from England—like many other pub frequenters who join Farrington during his night out. On his way home Farrington also has to pass the British Military Barracks on Shelbourne Road (*D* 93), a very definite marker of British colonial presence in Ireland.

Among the many oppressive forces that determine Farrington's depressing day is also medicine as a practice that resolutely pathologizes him as a clinical case of chronic alcoholism. Even a reader not trained in medicine would have no problems identifying Farrington's clinical picture as a prototypical alcoholism case, one of professional and personal disintegration. It seems therefore as if Joyce's character is not only trapped in his alcohol addiction, but "Counterparts" also illustrates that Farrington is subjected to a medico-pathological examination. He becomes the subject of a case study that aims to evaluate him according to degeneration's classificatory system. Yet while Joyce seems to confirm the medical theories on chronic alcoholism that were fashioned under degeneration's leadership in the outgoing nineteenth century, "Counterparts" also resists such a smooth interpretation as case history. As readers of Joyce's story will remember, Farrington's only rebellion against the crushing circumstances of his professional life lies in his unexpected "retort" to Mr. Alleyne:

> —*You - know - nothing.* Of course you know nothing, said Mr Alleyne. Tell me, he added, glancing first for approval to the lady beside him, do you take me for a fool? Do you think me an utter fool?
>
> The man glanced from the lady's face to the little egg-shaped head and back again; and, almost before he was aware of it, his tongue had found a felicitous moment:
>
> —I don't think, sir, he said, that that's a fair question to put to me. (*D* 87)

Although turn-of-the-century psychological experts would certainly have classified this anomalous behavior as distinctively pathological, it is worth noting that Joyce's text associates Farrington's surprising outburst with ingenuity, rebellious cerebral activity, and disobedience.

Although Farrington goes home defeated, confirming the prototypical image of the aggressive alcoholic in beating up his son, there are glimpses of rebellion against the many oppressive forces that determine his monotonous and disheartening life. In this chapter we shall see how a "pathological" character trait of the chronic drinker becomes the means to facilitate Farrington's very brief moment of rebellion and disobedience in the face of oppression and the "alcoh alcoho alcoherently" (*FW* 40.5) case story that is simulated by Joyce's short story.

.

Alcoholism and drinking disorders were prominent markers in nineteenth-century medical directories. But it is interesting to see that medical theory underwent a significant change in its approach toward alcohol-related disorders in the course of the Victorian age. In fact, it would not be wrong to state that alcoholism, as we know it today, was invented during the "period of medical reform." Hence, it was in 1849 that Magnus Huss, a Swedish physician, coined the term. In classifying the somatic and mental damages caused by regular alcohol consumption, he was the first practitioner to identify alcohol's physiological and psychological effects as a form of poisoning (Sournia 1990, 46). However, even before Huss published his groundbreaking study *Alcoholismus Chronicus,* this epistemological change in the knowledge of alcohol and alcohol abuse could be universally noted.

Like many other maladies created in the nineteenth century, alcoholism had been understood, prior to its official elevation into modern medicine's pathological catalogue, as an exclusively moral vice. Whereas religious authorities had always frowned upon the repeated consumption of alcoholic drinks, the new scientific understanding of this condition identified alcoholism primarily as a disease and thus as a decisively medical subject. While physicians started to enter the overcrowded mental asylums of the nineteenth century, chronic alcoholism became one of its most studied pathologies. Eminent writers such as the French neurologist Jean Martin Charcot, the Victorian psychopathologist Henry Maudsley, and the Italian criminologist Cesare Lombroso all introduced discussions of chronic alcohol abuse into their works.

At the same time, alcoholism was increasingly seen in connection to pressing social problems such as public disorder, crime, and degeneration. And through their sustained interest in and scrutiny of alcoholism, doctors also aimed, with increasing persistence, to influence and restrict drinking habits. In this attempt they joined hands with temperance or social purity movements and promoted teetotalism while pointing to alcohol-related organic and cerebral damages. In the case of absinthe, the medical order's labor was eventually greeted with a widely celebrated success. Although it was a popular beverage at the turn of the century and one of Joyce's favorite drinks (Ellmann 1983, 455), medical men gave testimony to the serious somatic damages resulting from its consumption and in 1915 the "green fairy" was banned from the French market (Harris 1989, 252).

In the clinical analysis of alcohol-related disorders no aspect of the newly discovered disease was left unobserved. Whereas physicians studied the organic damage caused by drinking, psychologists and especially the French alienists concerned themselves with alcoholism's resulting mental aberrations. Newly coined expressions such as delirium tremens (shaking hands, hallucinations, and circulatory disturbances in alcoholics) or dipsomania (temporary and compulsive craving for alcohol) found their way into medical language to distinguish different degrees of intoxication or addiction. But among the wide range of classified mental pathologies a special place was reserved for chronic drinking. It soon became the equivalent of hysteria—a significant connection that will be explored later in this chapter.[3]

Viewed in this new medical light the alcoholic became a fixed pathologic entity in the nineteenth century's wide topography of degenerate phenomena, whose somatic characteristics and psychical disturbances could be unmistakably recognized. According to Lombroso, for instance, the alcoholic exhibits visible signs of an acquired degeneracy: paresis (slackness) especially of the face, hyperaesthesia (increased sensitivity of any of the sense organs, especially of the skin), and alphagesia (sensation of pain at contact with painless bodies) (Lombroso-Ferrero 1911, 82). Predominant, however, is the changed condition and expression of the eyes. In his numerous case studies Lombroso noticed a distinctive inequality of the pupils or a slight exophthalmia (abnormal protrusion of the eyeballs)(Lombroso-Ferrero 1911, 82).

Interestingly, some of those Lombrosian symptoms and signs reemerge in Joyce's "Counterparts" in the first description of Farrington.[4] At this point it is, of course, important to recall that Joyce was familiar with the name Lombroso. He read or at least heard of Lombroso's work in Trieste. Writing to Stanislaus in 1906, he mentioned a fellow office worker who "was ridiculing Lombrosianism" (*LII* 151). Joyce also expressed an apparent interest in the fact that Lombroso "is a Jew" (*LII* 190). Moreover, it seems as if the composition of "Counterparts" and Joyce's interest in the Italian criminologist coincided.[5] For this reason it is not surprising that the larger part of "Counterparts" could have easily been found among the many cases that nineteenth-century psychologists and anthropologists had collected. At the beginning of the short story the reader is introduced to the protagonist, his "dark wine-coloured" "hanging face" (*D* 82), and his "heavy dirty eyes" (*D* 90) that "bulged forward slightly" (*D* 82). Not only is Farrington classified as a pathological type according to Lombroso's theories but "Counterparts" itself also appears almost like a scientific case study on chronic inebriation.

In addition to meticulously charting the addict's somatic alterations, Lombroso also stressed the connection between alcohol consumption and various mental disorders. He mentions delusions, hallucinations, apathy, and criminal impulses as alcoholism's most frequent psychological manifestations.[6] But doctors not only suggested that the alcoholic's chronic symptoms were similar to those of many mental illnesses ("The insanity produced by alcohol is instructive, for it exhibits in more rapid sequence a train of symptoms very like those of ordinary idiopathic insanity" [Maudsley 1886, 487]), they also established a causal relationship between alcohol consumption and insanity. Henry Maudsley, for instance, stated in 1886 that: "Persons who have been previously insane, or who have suffered an injury to the head which produced severe symptoms at the time, or who have had a sunstroke, or who have inherited a strong disposition to insanity, or who are epileptic—persons in fact who have a natural or acquired undue irritability and instability of the brain—are liable to have their irritable and unstable brains upset by slight alcoholic excesses and to do very strange and eccentric things in consequence, or even to compromise themselves by some act of impulsive violence" (Maudsley 1886, 483).

In the eyes of many nineteenth-century medical specialists such as Lombroso and Maudsley, alcohol consumption produced mental illness in individuals with a predisposition to insanity. Since it was common knowledge that the temporary taste of alcohol might alter a person's character so that an "honest, peaceable individual is transformed into a rowdy, a murderer, or a thief" (Maudsley 1886, 80), alcohol addiction was seen to result in permanent brain damage. The pathological character alterations are thus irreversibly imprinted onto the sufferer's personality. No wonder, then, that nineteenth-century medical celebrities such as Lombroso strengthened this associative connection so that the alcoholic metamorphosed into a mentally handicapped person.

Farrington suffers from all these predicted afflictions. His ability to concentrate has been severely damaged. He is no longer able to perform his workload, because his "mind wandered away to the glare and rattle of the public-house" (*D* 86). Reflecting on his financial situation, he completely forgets his whereabouts until Mr. Alleyne throws him out of his office (*D* 83). Joyce's text thus distinctively stresses Farrington's tendency for daydreaming and his vivid imagination, which remove him from reality into an illusionary realm mainly characterized by one thing: alcohol. "He knew where he would meet the boys: Leonard and O'Halloran and Nosey Flynn. . . . His imagination had so abstracted him that his name was called twice before he answered" (*D* 86).

However, above all other disturbances, it was the alcoholic's violent mood changes that were identified as the most critical symptom. In fact, Lombroso's observations show that chronic drinkers often rush from states of deepest melancholy and gloom to a "fit of mad energy, often of a homicidal or suicidal nature" (Lombroso-Ferrero 1911, 83). Both pathological character alterations and morbid mood changes were an established facet of the alcoholic's clinical picture. Medical theorists thus saw themselves justified in establishing a distinctive connection between alcoholism and involuntary criminal behavior. If alcohol was identified as a factor in the perpetration of offenses, convicted criminals could escape harsh sentences. Between 1880 and 1910 25 percent of all murder cases reported in Paris were related in some way to the perpetrator's falling prey to the evil influence of alcohol (Harris 1989, 243). Alcoholics could now, like insane criminals, advantageously claim diminished responsibility for their illegal and offensive behavior. During the trial, it was, of course, the indispensable medical advisor who ultimately decided about the perpetrator's clinical record and consequently about their juridical destiny. In *Stephen Hero* Joyce explicitly refers to "Lombrosianism" and its legal and social consequences when noting that: "Italy has added a science to civilization by putting out the lantern of justice and considering the criminal in . . . production and in action" (*SH* 186).

"Counterparts" picks up the theme of alcoholic violence. Not only the final attack on his son Tom, but also the minute description of Farrington's emotional thermometer gives evidence to his disturbed psychological nature: "He was so enraged that he wrote *Bernard Bernard* instead of *Bernard Bodley* and had to begin on a clean sheet" (*D* 86); a "spasm of rage gripped his throat" (*D* 83); "He felt strong enough to clear out the whole office single-handed" (*D* 86); "He felt savage and thirsty and revengeful" (*D* 88); "He was so angry that he lost count of the conversation of his friends" (*D* 91); "He was full of smouldering anger and revengefulness" (*D* 93); "His heart swelled with fury" (*D* 93). Even the weather description seems to reflect Farrington's mood: the gloomy, foggy February evening is not only a counterpart to his occasional melancholic state, but it also recalls a specific literary genre: gothic literature or sensation fiction. On leaving the office for a quick drink Farrington encounters a very gothic scenario: "Darkness, accompanied by a thick fog, was gaining upon the dusk of February and the lamps in Eustace Street had been lit" (*D* 84).[7] The fog, the darkness, indeed everything in this scene is not just set for "a night for hot punches" but also "for a spell of riot" (*D* 86).

Not surprisingly, therefore, Farrington assumes selected character traits of one of the late nineteenth century's most notorious villains: Robert Louis Stevenson's hideous Mr. Hyde. To be sure, certain similarities between the two characters can be observed. Stevenson's 1886 murder scene is set in a foggy night, with Hyde breaking out "in a great flame of anger" (Stevenson 1998, 25) before murdering his helpless and innocent victim with violent cane blows. Furthermore, an evident atavistic predisposition seems to disfigure Stevenson's Mr. Hyde: "Evil besides (which I must still believe to be the lethal side of man) had left on that body an imprint of deformity and decay" (Stevenson 1998, 63). The relationship between savage behavior and atavism is even more evident in the description of Mr. Hyde's hand, the agent of so much viciousness: "lean, corded, knuckly, of a dusky pallor and thickly shaded with a swart growth of hair" (Stevenson 1998, 67).

Correspondingly, "Counterparts" makes repeated references to Farrington's savage nature (*D* 88), suggesting that drinking has distinctively lowered his position in the evolutionary hierarchy. And although Farrington's offense is certainly not comparable with the deeds of Mr. Hyde, it is important to remember that his aggression toward his son, which also involves a walking stick, violates a fundamental convention cherished in all Western societies: the father's duty to protect his offspring. The end of Joyce's story shows the devastating consequences of Farrington's alcoholic character alteration. The protagonist's reversal of character is further suggested by another revealing text passage: "[Farrington's] wife was a little sharp-faced woman who bullied her husband when he was sober and was bullied by him when he was drunk" (*D* 93). The usual domestic routine, although not necessarily pleasant, is interrupted, reversed, and turned on its head by Farrington's recourse to the bottle.

This suggestion that alcoholism transforms the afflicted into a negative characterological copy is vividly illustrated by a very specific and very curious mid-nineteenth-century study. In his 1853 *Comparative Physiognomy or Resemblances between Men and Animals*, the American physician James Redfield points to the damaging effect of alcohol consumption on the inhabitants of the Irish isle. Redfield's analysis, which is probably one of the saddest chapters in medical history, compares characteristics of the Irish race with those of dogs. However, this is not to say that other races get treated less severely. Other peculiar passages conflate the English with bulls and compare the French to frogs or to alligators (Redfield 1853, 11). But what is of interest here is not this amalgamation of human and animalistic features, but Redfield's resolute assumption that the Irishman is, in an intoxicated state, transformed into a perverted counterpart.

In this alcoholic distortion of character, positive traits such as sensitivity, hospitality, conviviality, domestic affection and neighborly love are, as Redfield attests, altogether wiped out (Redfield 1853, 255). In Redfield's words: "But there is a way in which [the Irishman] can submit to the operation of having the ties which bind him to his kindred and country rent asunder, and his heart taken from him as if it were a fungous excrescence—and that is, to be made *drunk*" (225). This "perversion" of truth (261) by the demon drink changing the "genuine coin" into "its counterfeit" (261), reverses the Irishman's character and turns him into his distorted copy, into a version of Stevenson's Mr. Hyde.

At this point it is worth recalling, as David Lloyd does, that the title of Joyce's story ("Counterparts") refers to a duplicate of a legal document, another "double" (Lloyd 2000, 145). The trope of the double that is central in the analysis of its protagonist is thus already identified by the story's title. And predictably, "Counterparts" is indeed a story of doubles and copies. Farrington is a copy clerk. But "Counterparts" also doubles Mr. Alleyne's assault on Farrington with the scene of domestic violence at the story's end in order to emphasize Farrington's doubled role as a victim and a victimizer.

Finally, Joyce's story exhibits a curious narrative duplication. "Counterparts" integrates two different narrative strands. In the story's opening paragraphs a clinical observer identifies "the man" Farrington more as a case than as an individual: "The man muttered *Blast him!* under his breath"; "The man entered Mr Alleyne's room" (*D* 82); "The man recognised the sensation"; "The man walked heavily towards the door" (*D* 83). But whereas this first narrative strand observes Farrington with a detached clinical eye that is reminiscent of medical case studies on pathological alcoholism, the second describes the scene in the public house in terms that are undoubtedly much more inviting. In this passage the narrator also greets Farrington with his name: "Farrington stood a drink in his turn" (*D* 89); "Much to Farrington's relief he drank a glass of bitter" (*D* 91); "Farrington pulled up his sleeve accordingly" (*D* 92). The final section of "Counterparts" then reverts back to the narrative perspective used at the beginning of the story—that of the clinical, detached observer: "A very sullen-faced man stood at the corner of O'Connell Bridge" (*D* 92–93); "The man sat down heavily on one of the chairs" (*D* 94). This narrative duplication that opposes the scientific analysis of "the man" Farrington with that of the public house's conviviality is certainly the most explicit example of the story's obsession with doubles. It is also an astute textual repetition of Farrington's pathological double nature in "Counterparts."

The concept of the double was, independent of Redfield's curious claims, also a central feature of the nineteenth century's scientific understanding of alcoholism: according to prevalent psychological theories, alcohol consumption resulted in a pathological doubling or "delirious incoherence" (Maudsley 1886, 485) of the drinker's mind. Within this theoretical framework one man is of particular importance: the French psychologist Pierre Janet, who undertook extensive studies into the psychological manifestations of hysteria and trauma and who was universally regarded as the founder of dynamic psychiatry at the threshold of the new century. Although his name is almost forgotten today, Janet was in his time an energetic opponent of Freud's psychoanalysis and coined the term "subconscious," a commonplace expression in today's cultural vocabulary. He was further responsible for identifying a particular form of pathological character dissociation, a psychological state that he called "doubling" ("dédoublement de la personnalité" [Janet 1889, 365]). Janet's doubling theory is, as we shall see, of vital importance for both Joyce's text and its cultural background.[8]

The work that is most significant for the present discussion of the late nineteenth century's perception of alcoholism is Janet's 1889 *L'Automatisme psychologique*.[9] In this study, which Janet submitted as his doctoral thesis in philosophy, the French psychologist showed his sustained indebtedness to the French alienists, who had a fundamental influence on nineteenth-century European medical philosophy and who emphasized hereditary factors in a person's physiological and psychological composition (Bynum 1984, 60). In arguing that pathologies were inherited from previous generations, Jean Etienne Dominique Esquirol and his followers laid the foundation stone for much of what was to become the late nineteenth-century concept of mental pathologies.

The newly coined disease, alcoholism, was hereby greeted with particular concern. And again, as with Henry Maudsley, we find an unambiguous comparison between alcohol addiction and mental diseases at the heart of this important nineteenth-century medical theory (Sournia 1990, 81). In fact, the alienists assumed that intoxicants such as opium, phosphorus, and alcohol were likely to cause the degenerate symptoms scrutinized with such vehemence. Although drinking was regarded as the outcome of the alcoholic's lamentable social circumstances, it was believed that the resulting changes in the physiological makeup would be transmitted to the offspring, plunging them deeper into the inescapable misery of progressive degeneration.

Among the alienists it was Benedict Morel, who advocated this pessimistic theory of hereditary and human regress and decline with specific zeal. In his 1857 *Traité des dégénérescences physiques, intellectuelles et morales de l'espèce humaine* he connects the human race's course toward psychological and somatic doom with the damaging influences of inebriety. According to Morel, its extreme version, dipsomania, irreversibly turns a mentally healthy person into a raving criminal (Sournia 1990, 62). Dipsomania found equal attention in the works of Valentin Magnan, who injected dogs with alcohol and other toxic substances in order to demonstrate their damaging effects for the animal organism. In 1874 he summarized his findings in the study *De l'Alcoolisme, des diverses formes du délire alcoolique et de leur traitement*. Not only did this influential book offer a new nosology of alcoholism that was to replace Magnus Huss's, but it further enforced the connection between alcohol and mental disorders. As the director of a mental asylum Magnan was able to survey many patients hospitalized for alcohol-related disorders (Sournia 1990, 85). His extensive experience with patients' cases thus provided the basis for his theoretical association of alcoholism and insanity.

Another very radical test series was undertaken by the French physician Jacques-Joseph Moreau (de Tours), who examined the effects of intoxicants through a series of self-tests with hashish in order to investigate the origins of insanity (Moreau [de Tours] 1845, 30). According to Moreau (de Tours), it was an excellent experimental method to explore the world of mental illness, which he firmly associated with dreams and hallucinations, radically dissociated from reality: "[I] had to concede that the regular delirium was a psychological condition not only analog but *absolutely identical* with that of dreams" (Moreau [de Tours] 1845, 31).[10] In Moreau (de Tours)'s theory, perfect moral and psychological health is characterized by the separation of the two distinct realms, a separation achieved by dreams as a mental barrier. A "normal" or mentally "healthy" person would exhaust his or her desire for the fantastic during the night. Crucial is only the conflation of the two realms. Once the boundaries are broken down and the two fuse, the unavoidable result is mental illness and alienation from the real world.

Alcohol, Moreau (de Tours) believed, had an extremely violent effect on the disintegration of the two psychological realms: through its modification of the psychological makeup a person's intellectual functions can be severely damaged so that the afflicted becomes incapable of distinguishing between the "real" and the imagined: "[U]nder the growing influence of alcoholic excitation, the drunkard passes from the real world into an imagined one, from a state of awareness into one of dreams. And it is when a form of fusion between the two states is achieved, when the individual fails to distinguish between phenomena that belong exclusively to one or the other, that he has to be considered insane" (Moreau [de Tours] 1845, 199).[11] In other words, mental illness is an analytical failure. The sufferer cannot discriminate between real, external stimulations and imagined experiences. Although Janet himself preferred to subject his patients to induced somnambulism rather than undergo self-tests with hashish, Moreau (de Tours)'s mental illness concept had, as we shall see, a crucial influence on his own work (Janet 1889, 6).

Janet, in his early study *L'Automatisme psychologique*, devotes himself to the analysis of what he calls "simplest" and "rudimentary human activities": "automatisms" (Janet 1889, 1).[12] He defines these automatisms as reflexes, as movements of the muscles, or as simple emotional reactions that are the expressions of a basic form of the human's psychological system. They are opposed by the higher ones defined by Janet as the perceptive faculty, the power of judgment, and the human will. In other words, automatisms are learned reactions to environmental stimulations. In the case of new or unexpected external challenges, a higher mental function, which Janet calls the function of synthesis, combines the so far learned with the new experience so that the person can react accordingly. Once this is achieved, the individual is left with a pleasing sense of completeness (Janet 1889, 336). In leaning on Moreau (de Tours)'s theories, Janet defines the state of perfect health as the moment when these two psychological phenomena, automatism and the synthesis function, operate in perfect harmony (Janet 1889, 486). This, however, is not always the case.

During his long years of research and through the constant observation of his four most outstanding patients, Marie, Léonie, Lucie, and Rose, Janet had the opportunity to observe the results of a damaged relationship between the two psychological components, automatisms and synthesis function. His hysteria patients showed unmistakable symptoms of personality disintegration ("l'état de désagrégation") (Janet 1889, 337). Janet explained this psychological aberration by pointing toward the disturbance of the synthesis function. Through shock or a traumatic experience its smooth operation can be upset. Consequently, perceptions cannot, as under normal circumstances, be united into a single consciousness (Janet 1889, 364). Instead, they are separated and incorporated into one or several incomplete psychological groups that start to lead an existence beyond the consciousness's awareness.

Eventually, in especially severe cases, the so-created psychological groups give birth to a second, subconscious personality within the primary psyche. This is the state that Janet calls "doubling" ("dédoublement de la personnalité") (Janet 1889, 365). The second, subconscious personality then expresses itself through psychological irregularities such as incoherent and compulsive movements or desires that are at odds with that of the primary personality. Janet was able to observe this phenomenon among his hysteria patients during their seizures or during induced hypnosis.[13] A psychological war breaks out between the different mental identities and the observed uncontrolled automatisms are unmistakable signs given by the second personality hidden somewhere in the hysteric's subconscious. In Janet's words: "one forms the normal personality, the other, susceptible to further subdivisions, establishes itself as an unnatural and different one from the first who completely ignores it" (Janet 1889, 366).[14] This leads not just to the development of uncontrolled automatisms, but to potentially more disastrous consequences. If the second, pathological person has, for instance, criminal aspirations, the primary person might be forced to commit accusable actions against his or her own will.

When we return to Joyce and "Counterparts" we can see that Janet's theoretical definition of personality "doubling" is an adequate medical description of Farrington, the pathologically "doubled" character in Joyce's text. First, it is noticeable that his synthesis function is fundamentally damaged. The result is Farrington's inability to concentrate: "He was so angry that he lost count of the conversation of his friends" (*D* 91). Farrington's mind absorbs unimportant details, so that he is no longer able to discriminate between various environmental challenges. He fails to perceive reality clearly. Even the mechanical task of copying manuscripts becomes impossible: "He stared intently at the incomplete phrase: *In no case shall the said Bernard Bodley be* . . . and thought how strange it was that the last three words began with the same letter" (*D* 86). Farrington has temporarily lost the ability to synthesize experiences. Consequently, he lacks a sense of completeness. Both the copied document and Farrington's psychological experiences remain incomplete.

Second, Farrington's behavior shows identifiable signs of automatisms that are foreign-controlled. In fact, Joyce makes it clear that there is an evident discrepancy between Farrington's will and his automatic behavior, between his mind and his body's reaction to the environment. Whereas Mr. Alleyne "shook his fist in the man's face" (*D* 87) and demonstrates that his actions are in complete harmony with his intentions, Farrington's agency is fundamentally disturbed. He seems to have lost control over his own body, which functions independently of Farrington's will: "The tirade continued: it was so bitter and violent that the man could hardly restrain his fist from descending upon the head of the manikin before him" (*D* 87); "His body ached to do something, to rush out and revel in violence" (*D* 86); "He felt his great body again aching for the comfort of the public-house" (*D* 88).[15]

Furthermore, Farrington's mental dissociation is supported if not initiated by his heated emotional state. His anger and rage are responsible for his mental distraction and the disturbance of his synthesis function. In his *L'Automatisme psychologique* Janet points to the precarious effect that emotions exercise on the mind's ability to synthesize experiences. Often they are responsible for the resulting "misère psychologique" (Janet 1889, 444): "To sum up, an emotion has a dissolving influence on the mind, diminishing its synthesis and leaving it miserable for a moment" (457).[16] But according to Janet, who followed his intellectual precursors, the alienists, in firmly associating chronic drinking with mental disease, alcohol had a similar effect on the human mind in that its consumption produced, like violent and strong emotions, mental and psychological dispersion.

What is of interest at this point is that Janet was a supporter of the so-called "continuity model," the theory that mental aberrations were only an exaggeration of psychological circumstances found in a healthy mind. Indeed, the French psychologist argued that "the principles of a malady are the same as those of health and they are nothing but an exaggeration or diminution of certain phenomena already present there" (Janet 1889, 5).[17] Accordingly, the mental abnormalities that Janet observed among his hysteria patients were, in his view, only an exaggeration of symptoms displayed to a lesser extent by the so-called healthy. Janet was therefore able to use his personality doubling hypothesis to explain the similarities between chronic alcoholism and hysteria: "Certain intoxications such as alcoholism, saturnism or poisoning through carbon sulphur . . . can produce symptoms that one can confound with those of hysteria" (Janet 1889, 449).[18]

The symptoms displayed by chronic drunkards that he observed during his career as a doctor confirm his hypothesis. Janet reports, for instance, the case of a young man, P., who enters his ward in Le Havre one evening, displaying all the apparent symptoms of delirium tremens. He is haunted all night by hallucinations, in which he visualizes his participation in terrible massacres. Even when returning to his normal and sober state the next morning, he is still troubled by imaginary vermin.[19] P. also shows surprising somnambulist signs, reacting to Janet's commands in the way his hysteria patients do, purely automatically (Janet 1889, 171–72). Reporting this crucial observation and supporting his theory with that of Moreau (de Tours), Janet now deduces: "alcohol intoxication . . . renders a man more suggestible and more automatic than a somnambulist" (450).[20] In other words, the symptoms of the hysterical somnambulist and the chronic drinker can be strikingly similar.

As John Gordon has already pointed out (Gordon 2003, 165), "Counterparts" presents Farrington in an advanced state of uncontrollable automatisms. His extremities lead a life of their own. Moreover, his behavior toward Mr. Alleyne shows signs of strong suggestibility. Paul Lin argues that Mr. Alleyne has incorporated the workings of modern technology into his behavior, reacting mechanically like an automaton through his repetitive exclamations: "—*Mr Shelley said, sir*"; "*Mr Shelley says, sir*" (*D* 83); "Do you hear me now?"; "—Do you hear me now?" (*D* 83); "—*You - know - nothing*. Of course you know nothing" (*D* 87); "—You impertinent ruffian! You impertinent ruffian!" (*D* 87); "You'll apologise to me"; "you'll apologise to me" (*D* 87); "you'll quit the office instanter! You'll quit this" (*D* 87) (Lin 2001, 39). However, given the story's psychopathological intertext, it seems more likely that Alleyne's conduct resembles in some ways that of an exasperated therapist communicating with his somnambulant patient. His comments are mostly suggestions and commands responding to Farrington's hypnotic state. The fact that Farrington is, like Janet's hysteria patients, captured in a state of somnambulism is also indicated by Alleyne's comment: "I might as well be talking to the wall as talking to you" (*D* 83). Unfortunately, Alleyne's violent attempts to bring Farrington back into the real world do not have the desired effect. Instead, they appeal to another part of Farrington's fractured personality, the one that reacts with the desire for drinks and violence. Ironically, in infuriating Farrington further, Alleyne's remarks increase the dissociation of his personality.

What should be remembered at this point is that Joyce's "Counterparts" is by no means the only literary text that shows an indebtedness to Janet's theory of doubling or split personality. Janet's character model had far-reaching consequences for cultural and especially literary conventions and was, in turn, also heavily influenced by them. The nineteenth century and especially its last years were obsessed with theories and images of the double (Miller 1985, 331). Joyce would have been able to find this trope in many nineteenth-century texts and contexts. E.T.A. Hoffmann's 1815 *Die Elixiere des Teufels* (*The Devil's Elixirs*) is a very early example of this particular genre. The text relates the story of the monk Medardus, who consumes a magic elixir transforming him secretly into a criminal double. And despite the text's metaphysical argument, a medical subtext is introduced early on in the book, which explicitly suggests that Medardus's father lost his fortune through an unnamed sin that has been inherited by the son (Hoffmann 1815, 11). A medically trained eye would have no problem uncovering the latent alcoholism tale that lurks in the novel's background and an alienist would certainly have suggested the following diagnosis: the father's intemperance is responsible for the son's advanced stage of degeneration, while the son's mental illness is responsible for the experienced hallucinations and criminal proclivities.

A later variant of the same literary theme is, of course, the already mentioned *The Strange Case of Dr. Jekyll and Mr. Hyde*. Interestingly, in both Hoffmann's and Stevenson's tale, the personality change occurs after the protagonist drinks a mysterious substance: the elixir in Medardus's case and the brewed potion in Dr. Jekyll's. In admitting that he performed his experiment with the single intention to dissociate the two conflicting natures captured in his conscious-ness—"I stood already committed to a profound duplicity of life" (Stevenson 1998, 60)—Stevenson's troubled protagonist also indicates the theme of split personality. Even before he takes the mysterious substance, Jekyll is aware of being a profound "double-dealer" (60).

Less mysterious but no less significant is a novel by the French writer Léon Hennique, *Minnie Brandon*, a bestseller upon publication in 1899. It tells the story of a young woman, admired by many suitors, who has the unfortunate habit of turning into a repulsive shrew whenever she is given the smallest amount of alcohol. Expectedly, in the course of the novel her second, alcoholic self gains control (quoted in Ellenberger 1970, 166). Joyce himself explores this popular theme in "Circe" where the two Siamese twins, Philip Sober and Philip Drunk, fight for hegemony over Stephen's mind (*U* 15.2512–39). Whereas Philip Sober reminds Stephen of all the money he has been spending on ale, his drunken counterpart reflects unambiguously on the possible "[r]eduplication of personality" (*U* 15.2523).

Returning to "Counterparts" we can now understand why Joyce's text re-peats this doubling of Farrington's personality on a textual level. Whereas nine-teenth-century medical specialists regarded personality doubling as one of the chronic drinker's most prominent disorders, Joyce's text adopts this fundamen-tal pathological symptom when presenting his clinical case study on alcohol-ism. As we have seen, one narrative strand evaluates Farrington as a clinical case whereas the other one warmly welcomes him in addressing him with his name. The majority of the story assumes the medical and clinical perspective but the pub interludes provide temporary interruptions. In this, Joyce's narra-tive might comment on alcohol's addictive qualities, tempting Farrington to further excesses. In simulating the public house's and alcohol's seductive nature by the more inviting narrative elements, Joyce, it could be suggested, demonstrates how intrinsically Farrington remains trapped by his alcohol addiction and consequently by the medical case story.

While only the increased alcohol consumption can free him temporarily from the unsympathetic, clinical eye of the detached observer, Farrington, in consuming more alcohol, irretrievably increases his dependence on the very substance that has turned him into such a desirable object for the medical analyst. His story is thus one of successive addiction, decline, and deterioration. However, in spite of this pessimistic suggestion there are specific subversive resonances in Joyce's text that associate the alcoholic's pathological character traits with originality, ingenuity, and with the imagination. But to fully appreciate this unexpected link between pathology and the imagination we have to return, for a moment, to the nineteenth-century medical understanding of alcoholism and mental illness.

An essential part of Janet's *L'Automatisme psychologique* is dedicated to the comparison between the symptoms of the hysteria patient and the role of the psychic medium in spiritualism. In both cases, manifestations of the paranormal or the pathological are associated with automatic writing. Whereas the second, subconscious personality in Janet's patients uses automatic writing as communicative device, this specific "psychic gift" achieved a vital importance in spiritual séances and especially in theosophical circles.[21] But as Janet's analysis shows, while this unnatural talent for receiving messages from the beyond was celebrated in spiritual circles, nineteenth-century doctors regarded it as part of the widely contemplated "misère psychologique." According to *L'Automatisme psychologique*, the celebrated abilities of the so-called spiritual mediums were, in fact, nothing but the manifestations of mental dissociations commonly found in the inmates of the mental asylum (Janet 1889, 401). Observed more carefully, Janet suggests, the mediums all showed signs of abnormal delicacy and nervous energy, symptoms of Janet's favorite study object: hysteria (405).

Janet's colleague and teacher Charcot went even further in his assault on spiritualism. In his 1887 *Les Démoniaques dans l'art* he establishes a firm connection between religious iconography and hysteria. As Charcot points out, images of religious ecstasy commonly found in medieval depictions of Christian saints all show a remarkable resemblance to his own photographic images of "la grande hystérie." Yet Charcot did not only use religious iconography to explain hysteria. Instead, in following the alienists, who had identified religious enthusiasm as a monomania (Harris 1989, 204), he heretically interpreted the depicted religious scenes as hysterical manifestations and erotic deliria (Didi-Huberman 1982, 148).

In Janet's psychopathological theory, alcoholism is, like its neurotic counterpart hysteria, intrinsically linked to abnormal forms of mental activity. From here it is only a small step to causally link drinking and alcoholism to creativity or the overstimulated imagination. And Janet was by no means the only person to make this connection between psychopathology and the creative imagination. The *Oxford English Dictionary* (OED), for instance, lists very different entries for the English expression "spirit." A first one defines "spirit" as "the animating or vital principle in man (and animals); that which gives life to the physical organism, in contrast to its purely material elements; the breath of life." Another entry understands it as "a being essentially incorporeal or immaterial" whereas a later one gives a radically different interpretation: "a liquid of the nature of an essence or extract from some substance, esp. one obtained by distillation; a solution in alcohol of some essential or volatile principle." This doubled connotation of the word "spirit" indicates the associative connection between animism and alcohol consumption. It almost suggests that alcohol can function as a form of mental stimulant in invigorating the vital principle in the human organism.

Joyce's works dynamically apply these overlapping meanings of the concept "spirit" as vitalistic or volatile. In "Grace" Tom Kernan's infatuation with alcoholic beverages is, during the retreat, solemnly replaced by a more worthy spiritual devotion. Moreover, the decision for the pledge is formed during a discussion of Catholicism and popes generously heated by stout and "special whisky" (*D* 166). Other Joycean texts associate artistic creation directly with alcohol consumption. Stephen's Shakespeare theory, developed in the National Library, is preceded by the liquid luncheon to which he had treated the "Gentlemen of the Press" (*U* 7.20). Mulligan, too, suggests that Stephen cannot "manage it under three pints" (*U* 1.551). And Mulligan's own play *Everyman His Own Wife or A Honeymoon in the Hand*, that he produces in "Scylla and Charybdis," is certainly not the outcome of the Lord's communication as Mulligan insists (*U* 9.1056), but rather of his stopover in the "Ship," eagerly awaiting Stephen's "school kip," "[f]our shining sovereigns" (*U* 1.293, 295). The same applies to Hynes's elegy for Parnell in "Ivy Day in the Committee Room," which is delivered after significant alcohol consumption. Even Mrs. Sinico's painful case shows that her "temperament of great sensibility" (*D* 105) and her refined taste for music and literature, which enables her to act as Mr. Duffy's spiritual muse, is offset, after his cruel rejection, with her dependence on another form of "spirits" (*D* 111). Finally, the many stories and parables that are recited in Earwicker's pub in *Finnegans Wake* are also the product of intemperance.[22]

"Counterparts" develops this Joycean interpretation of alcohol as mental stimulant. The second narrative strand that focuses on the public house is said to become "theatrical" (*D* 90). Although the expression refers to the subject of the conversation—the men talk about the theater—the passage also alludes to the mode of discourse in the pub. While Farrington and his work colleagues delight in rhetorically decorating his retort to Mr. Alleyne, Joyce's text also suggests that it is with the prospect of drinks, that Farrington and "the boys" (*D* 89) start to "exchange stories" (*D* 90). Mark Osteen, in using Marcel Mauss's theory on gift exchange and potlatch, has written illuminatingly on Irish drinking habits that are undermined by a subtle economy of exchange, which forces its participants to progressive financial extravagances and which is informed by a sense of latent hostility and aggression (Osteen 1995, 250–79).[23]

Whereas "Counterparts" picks up those themes of financial excess, rigid exchange regulations, and resulting aggression when the Englishman Weathers complains that "the hospitality was too Irish" (*D* 90) and when the virtually penniless Farrington "cursed his want of money" and "particularly all the whiskies and Apollinaris which he had stood to Weathers" (*D* 91), Joyce's story also demonstrates that alcohol and narratives are both worthy stakes in the pub's heartless exchange game. Farrington therefore carefully rehearses his show: "As he walked on he preconsidered the terms in which he would narrate the incident to the boys:—So, I just looked at him - coolly, you know, and looked at her. Then I looked back at him again - taking my time, you know. *I don't think that that's a fair question to put to me*, says I" (*D* 89). Generally, it seems that everybody's creativity is encouraged by the reward of more liquor: "The men asked [Higgins] to give his version of it, and he did so with great vivacity for the sight of five small hot whiskies was very exhilarating" (*D* 89).

Even Farrington's clever and unexpected retort, which is motivated by a glass of porter, is in itself a witty remark worth being considered creative. Joyce's text certainly indicates that much when identifying Farrington as "the author of the witticism" (*D* 87). Moreover, "Counterparts" recognizes Farrington's surprising reaction as an uncontrolled automatism. This time it is the tongue that spins out of control: "and, almost before he was aware of it, his tongue had found a felicitous moment" (*D* 87).[24] And although he pays dearly for his rebellious outburst, this brief rhetorical riot remains Farrington's only personal victory throughout his long humiliating day. By beating up his son at home he confirms the pessimistic construct of the chronic drinker. But while "Counterparts" ends on this gloomy and desperate note, Joyce's story indicates, by underlining the connections between alcoholism and mental agility, that the straightforward clinical interpretation of alcoholism is, in many ways, reductive and flawed. As Farrington's "pathological" outburst illustrates, the depressing picture of the degenerate drunkard incorporates rebellious and, unexpectedly, resourceful possibilities. By introducing this diagnostic complication, "Counterparts" challenges medicine's aim to rigorously pathologize its objects of study.

3

"The Heinous Sin of Self-Pollution"

Medicine and Morals in *A Portrait of the Artist as a Young Man*

At first glance, Joyce's first novel, *A Portrait of the Artist as a Young Man*, seems to depart from *Dubliners* in its lack of concern for medicine's corrective interventions. By focusing on the formation and early adulthood of a young Irish artist in Dublin, Joyce, in *A Portrait*, decided to follow a certain European literary tradition in constructing his novel in the form of the bildungsroman or *künstlerroman*. But in spite of appearances, *A Portrait* shares with *Dubliners* a keen interest in diagnostics and social analysis. Like *Dubliners*, *A Portrait* provides its readers with a detailed character study that includes pathological components. Considering its ending, however, the novel's interest in pathology and debility might not be so noticeable. In fact, Joyce's examination of Stephen's formative years results in an optimistic final score, seeing Stephen actively renounce the restrictive conditions of the Irish social order in favor of artistic nonconformity and continental liberalism. Stephen, it seems, is able to cast off his ties to Irish Catholicism and, at the end of the novel, the spiritual freedom suggested by intellectualism and artistic creativity replaces the moralistic essence of his Catholic upbringing.[1]

However, such optimistic readings of *A Portrait*—which argue that Stephen, at the end of the novel, casts aside his emotional baggage by choosing the career of the artist—fail to see how rigorously a set of culturally dominant medico-moral discourses pathologized teenage artistic activities. As Hugh Kenner pointed out long ago, Stephen's character remains static in *A Portrait*: he is the "egocentric rebel become an ultimate. There is no question whatever of his regeneration" (Kenner 1955, 112). This is precisely why Joyce would eventually lose interest in Stephen as a character. But as we shall see in this chapter, Stephen's character formation, his spiritual and emotional stasis, and his reinvention as an egocentric aesthete are the response to a powerful medico-moral discourse that produced strictly determined recommendations on the normative development of teenage sexuality. Paradoxically, it is because Stephen decides to choose the career of the artist that he remains a fixed component on modern medicine's pathological index. Medicine is, in fact, the one dominant cultural force that Stephen, in recasting himself as an aesthete, is unable to negotiate successfully at the end of *A Portrait*.

.

Medical scholarship has a long history of linking artistic creativity to pathology. Long before Joyce wrote his *künstlerroman*, medical practice had started to relate the artist and artistic creativity to specific diseases and pathological configurations. In the analysis of "Counterparts," I have already illustrated that nineteenth-century medical practitioners linked alcoholism, hysteria, and other mental illnesses to spirituality and a "pathologically" stimulated imagination. And whereas Susan Sontag has shown persuasively that a nineteenth-century Romantic understanding associated tuberculosis with artistic temperaments (Sontag 1978, 32), Kirstie Blair has recently demonstrated that Victorian poets also linked cardiac diseases to emotional sensitivity (Blair 2006, 11). However, in the medical literature of the nineteenth century, the pathologization of the young male artist as a teenage masturbator had equally strong resonances. Henry Maudsley, for instance, spotted an underlying connection between Edgar Allan Poe's degenerate writing and his deviant solitary sexual practices. Although he never explicitly identifies Poe's "pathology" as masturbatory insanity, Maudsley speaks euphemistically of Poe's "faculty for self-indulgence" and "perverted self-feeling," which, at least in Maudsley's eyes, explain both Poe's social inaptness and his writing's "madness, horror and sin" (Maudsley 1859, 351, 356).

   Joyce himself was certainly never prudish when it came to sexual matters, and the "solitary vice" played an especially important role in his life and works: his obvious delight in learning that Nora was guilty of "the gentle art of self-satisfaction" (*LII* 72), the "dirty letters" of 1909 that served a clearly onanist purpose, Leopold Bloom's self-gratification at the glimpse of Gerty's drawers in "Nausicaa," and Jarl van Hoother's crime of "laying cold hands on himself" in the Prankquean episode in *Finnegans Wake* (*FW* 21.11) all reveal Joyce's ongoing fascination with the "private sin"—and its centrality in his oeuvre.[2] Nowhere else is this theme more visible than in *A Portrait of the Artist as a Young Man*. The reference to schoolboy "smugging" (*P* 42) in the first chapter might already introduce the topic of masturbation paranoia developed explicitly in the novel's later chapters. The second part of the text then illustrates very well that Stephen's adolescence is marked by one central conflict: the incompatible demands of his teenage body and the omnipresent moral dogmas of the church and turn-of-the-century antimasturbation propaganda.

Recently, Katherine Mullin has noted the importance of "the secret sin" to *A Portrait*'s structural progress. Her 2003 study *James Joyce, Sexuality and Social Purity* scrutinizes the impact of the social purity movement on masturbation's moral condemnation and carefully traces the ways in which a dominant Irish-Catholic chastity discourse complemented the cry for "true manliness" issued by the Protestant vice crusaders (Mullin 2003, 83). But in focusing foremost on constructions of masculinity, Mullin's argument sidesteps the artist theme, the most important one for Joyce's first published novel and one so intrinsically linked to the late nineteenth-century masturbation panic. As we shall see, at the turn of the century, medical theory created pathological directories that allied the degenerative figure of the teenage masturbator and the adolescent artist. Medico-moral debates suggested that the young masturbator's specific pathology resembles psychological and physiological traits attributed to the would-be teenage artist. The adolescent masturbator's image in late nineteenth- and early twentieth-century medical descriptions, his illnesses and his character traits, therefore recall that of the excessively committed scholar. His disturbing and off-putting clinical figure is constructed as the evil twin or the negative copy of the sensitive and creative adolescent artist.

Medicine is therefore an important controlling force in the life of young Stephen Daedalus and one that is intimately connected to the structural development of Joyce's *künstlerroman*. Indeed, the following reading of *A Portrait* will show how much material a suspicious medical reader such as Henry Maudsley might find in the pages of Joyce's first novel that could indicate sexual transgression on the part of its protagonist. However, before we turn to Joyce's text, masturbation's career as the most feared and condemned modern sexual disease has to be surveyed. From our modern point of view, and especially after the advent of psychoanalysis, this particular sexual practice is understood as a common and almost ordinary stage of the individual's sexual and personal development. Yet recently cultural historians have excavated a wide range of eighteenth- and nineteenth-century discourses produced by medical men, ministers, and social purity pamphleteers that surrounded this adolescent sexual practice and its ostensible health risks.[3]

Masturbation's history as a modern disease entity started explosively in the early eighteenth century. Indeed, its rise to prominence and fall into oblivion was confined to the 200 years between 1710 and the 1930s. In the interwar years, the "secret vice" then slowly vanished from its prominent place in medical discussions. Prior to the eighteenth century, the concept of masturbation as disease was virtually nonexistent. Then, around 1710, an English pamphlet entitled *Onania, or the Heinous Sin of Self-Pollution* revolutionized laymens' conceptions of solitary sexual practices (MacDonald 1967, 423). Before the publication of this anonymous treatise, which advocated a quack remedy for this newly created ailment, masturbation had been understood only as a moral or theological problem. Grouped with other impurity sins such as marital excess, fornication, or homosexual activities, masturbation's alleged dangers for the individual's physical constitution had so far been ignored. This all changed with *Onania*'s claims. While it was the first time that a medical manual attributed somatic illnesses to sexual excess and masturbation in particular, the list of the masturbation-related illnesses was extensive and included "thin and waterish seed, fainting fits and epilepsies, consumption, loss of erection and premature ejaculation, and infertility" (MacDonald 1967, 425).[4]

But despite its popularity in lay circles, *Onania*'s medical sermons might have been forgotten today if it had not been for the famous Swiss physician Samuel Tissot and his 1758 book *Onanism or A Treatise upon the Disorders Produced by Masturbation*.[5] Although Tissot clearly distinguishes his work from *Onania*'s "chaos" (Tissot 1985, x and 21), he acknowledges the accuracy of its central thesis: masturbation results in constitutional damages for the addicted sufferer. In doing this, Tissot elevated the discussion of masturbation as a disease from Grub Street quackery to the world of serious medical scholarship. With his acclaimed book, he put masturbation on the map of modern sexual disorders.

Tissot's book further offers the first attempt to explain masturbation's etiology. It identifies seminal fluid as vital life force whose loss deprives the man of essential vigor, literally draining him of his stamina. The indispensable outcome is physical and mental decay. Tissot's famous statement that "the loss of an ounce of [the seed] would weaken more than that of forty ounces of blood" (Tissot 1985, 2) was persistently preserved and became a commonplace in many turn-of-the-century medical treatises and purity pamphlets on masturbation.[6] Henry Varley could thus open his 1884 *Lecture to Men* with the words: "Gentlemen, [i]n a very important sense the seed is the life. Without doubt it is one of the most vital forces of man's physical constitution" (Varley 1884, 5). In addition to seminal loss, Tissot saw the dangers of sexual indulgence mainly in its destabilizing effect on the nervous system. According to his physiological model, an augmented quantity of blood rushes to the brain during the sexual act and causes the nervous disorders that doctors allegedly observed in the committed onanist. And again, Tissot's reasoning proved to be extremely persistent. Late nineteenth-century medical men still argued that the "irritability of the nerve centers is remarkably increased in all onanists" (Howe 1883, 97).[7]

Nineteenth-century medicine continued to pathologize the "private sin," resolutely replacing what was left of the moralistic eighteenth-century tone with a more firmly orientated medical point of view. But whereas both the English author of *Onania* and Tissot had concentrated their efforts mainly on pointing out masturbation's resulting somatic damages, nineteenth-century doctors were increasingly interested in the connection between "self-abuse" and mental or nervous disorders. The alienists on the Continent emerged as particularly active spokesmen for the causal relationship between "over-indulgence" and mental ailments (Hare 1962, 4). Jean Etienne Dominique Esquirol stated, for instance, that "masturbation is recognized in all countries as a common cause of insanity" (quoted in Porter 2006, 206). The reasons for drawing this connection are easy to recapitulate. The observation of many asylum inhabitants' unashamed sexual indulgences prompted the alienists to confuse cause and effect. They failed to regard masturbation as a clinical symptom and instead located the reason for mental degeneracy in the patient's "genital abuse" (Gilbert 1980, 273).

Victorian Britain, despite being the home of masturbation's first medical analysis, was surprisingly slow in appropriating contemporary, continental interests in sexual matters. In the light of "repressed" Victorian attitudes toward sex, open discussion of its pathologies remained for a long time unthinkable. So at least remarked William Acton in 1857 by complaining that the "necessary regulation of the sexual feelings or training to continence, is what hitherto no one has dared to advocate" (Acton 1857, 9). Acton's own book, *The Functions and Disorders of the Reproductive Organs*, a work regarded as representing "the official views of sexuality held by Victorian society" (Marcus 1967, xv), marked in many ways a turning point in the British medical attitude toward sexual passion in its manifold and diverting forms.

Notably, this Victorian sex revolutionist betrayed a specific interest in his voluminous study: although he promoted the ideal of the "sexless passivity of the Victorian female" (Hall 1991, 16), Acton's principal aim was the examination of male sexuality. Taking the physiological dangers of "over-indulgence" for granted, he advocated merciless spermatic economy and masculine self-discipline.[8] For Acton the sexual drive can become dangerous, and the failure to keep it under control inevitably results in the individual's social irresponsibility. Accordingly, Acton also argues that the sexual appetite is incompatible with the "intellectual ratio" (Acton 1857, 16). In claiming that "some of the ablest works have been written by bachelors" (16), Acton even establishes a subliminal relationship between sex and intellect. In other words, he believes it possible to channel sexual energy into socially beneficial cerebral activity.

The fatal consequences of juvenile masturbation in Acton's model lie in the initiation of sexual passions.[9] Once the indulgence is gratified, the delinquent is doomed to repeat the vicious act until it becomes habitual and the sufferer's health and social progress are irreparably destroyed. That Acton was increasingly concerned with the "solitary vice" can be seen in the development of the masturbation topic throughout the different reprints of *Functions and Disorders*. Whereas Acton treated "self-pollution" more or less en passant in the first edition of 1857, he devoted an entire chapter of the sixth edition, published in 1875, to its different forms and pernicious health outcomes (Acton 1875, 38–70). And whereas he had previously concentrated his explanations mainly on masturbation's physiological effects, the later edition explicitly linked the "secret vice" to mental illness. As Acton at this point boldly states: "[t]hat insanity is a consequence of this habit is now beyond a doubt" (62).

But Victorian medical attitudes toward masturbation were not always based on exclusively scientific standards and parameters. Indeed, as cultural perceptions of the "secret sin" changed over the course of the nineteenth century, masturbation became less a medical and once more a social and moral problem. When the medical belief in masturbation's catastrophic consequences for the human constitution waned, another cultural force took up the responsibility of combating the "secret vice," adopting the medical terminology previously used and forcing medical men into an unsettling alliance (Hunt 1998, 593). From 1880 onward, masturbation's history as a medical disease became linked to that of the social purity movement. Once more, the battle against this medical pathology was couched in a predominantly moralistic terminology. The movement's campaign for a new form of uncorrupted masculinity, one that stressed sexual continence and chivalry, insisted in an almost Actonian fashion on adolescent masturbation's corrupting effects on male sexuality and character development. Once released, male sexual passion would become uncontrollable. The explosion of advice manuals, medical treatises, quack advertisements, and social purity pamphlets that swamped the late nineteenth-century literary market testified to this renewed moral interest in "self-abuse."

In accordance with these new and dominant cultural politics, purity activists reproached medical men for false delicacy, for promoting tolerance and what we would today call a more liberal or modern attitude toward diverging sexual activities (Barker 1888, 8). And if doctors went as far as to "counsel immorality" (Varley 1884, 47) and advise fornication or an occasional visit in nighttown as a remedy for spermatorrhea and nocturnal emissions, they openly jeopardized both the moral standards of the social purity movement and the reputation of the medical profession. Medical men were thus confronted with an obvious choice: either join forces with this culturally dominant moralistic movement or risk public defamation. This dilemma faded only with Havelock Ellis's 1899 publication *Auto-Eroticism*, a work openly challenging the common assumption that sexual "misconduct" equaled social transgression and arguing for a "liberal toleration of difference" (Hall 1991, 22). Yet before the general acceptance of Ellis's assertions, the two "solitary vice" discourses mutually reinforced each other and expressed themselves in a renewed medico-moral rhetoric that became a characteristic of many of the late nineteenth-century antimasturbation pamphlets and treatises.

James Barker's 1888 *A Secret Book for Men* is a good example of this uneasy conflation of medicine with morals: whereas the author identifies himself as a phrenologist, claiming to be up to date with the medical avant-garde, his treatise's style and argumentation are oddly reminiscent of Father Arnall's retreat sermon in *A Portrait* (P 126–46), attacking the "appalling evils" that wreck "with a blight and withering curse the foundation principles of our English and Christian manhood and physique, both in the Church and the world" (Barker 1888, 3). In his advice manual *Facts for Men*, Alfred Dyer, one of the founding members of the White Cross League (a social purity group), used well-known medical terminology for a different end. Dyer explains that exposing the somatic stigma common to the "pampered passion" (Dyer 1884, 6) serves to publicly denigrate the sinner's concealed and secret breaches against sexual and moral purity. Masturbation is in most cases a secretive and solitary activity. But, as Dyer suggests, whereas the individual's moral flaws remain invisible for everyone except God, the physical marks on the culprit's body plainly expose his addiction to the "secret vice."

But social purity activism did not just repeat established medical insights into pathological "self-abuse." Instead, the movement's emphasis on the disease's universality radically changed contemporary conceptions of the masturbator. In light of the late nineteenth-century purity rhetoric, he was no longer a pathological individual. Masturbation was, on the contrary, a universal problem that threatened the nation's healthy growth. Naturally, the universality of the vice/disease made a medical intervention even more indispensable, and medical men voluntarily embraced their new responsibility: references to masturbation's generic nature can be found everywhere in the vast amount of late nineteenth-century medical literature on sexual excess and chronic "self-abuse" (Howe 1883, 62; Varley 1884, 8).

Childhood and teenage "self-abuse" became the main expression of this collective disease or cultural vice, and for the first time the new medico-moral advice literature in Europe and the United States included the pubertal and prepubescent male and his sexuality's regulation in their analyses. Indeed, reformers faced a controversial situation. Whereas the purity and innocence of the child had been taken for granted, the devastating statistics of boarding school sexual transgression supplied considerable evidence for the schoolboy's moral corruptibility. This new understanding of youth and infantile sexuality generated an intense masturbation panic, visible in the amount and nature of advice literature on "self-abuse." The case of the American physician J. H. Kellogg, founder of the Battle Creek Sanatorium and author of various purity manuals, illustrates the rigorous control machinery that subjected masturbation to professional management. His 1894 *Man, the Masterpiece* promises "plain truths plainly told, about boyhood, youth and manhood" (Kellogg 1894), acknowledging the responsibility to reform not just a corrupted fraction of modern masculinity but manhood in its universal nature.

Sylvanus Stall's Self and Sex Series (1897–1901) makes this endeavor even more transparent. The titles of this series include *What a Young Boy Ought to Know*, *What a Young Man Ought to Know*, *What a Young Husband Ought to Know*, or *What a Man of 45 Ought to Know*. No aspect of male sexuality was to remain unmediated. And whereas other antimasturbation texts "were beset by persistent euphemisms" (Hunt 1998, 568), the language of *What a Young Boy Ought to Know* is surprisingly straightforward. Although he introduces the unpleasant topic with a general synopsis of procreation in the animal kingdom, Stall does not avoid calling masturbation by its proper name, identifying information and knowledge as the best safeguard against solitary sexual deeds (Stall 1897, 99).

And, indeed, at times social purity campaigners and medical practitioners vividly described the pathological formations resulting from obsessive "self-abuse": a suspicious "roundness of the shoulders, or stooping posture in sitting" or "an unnatural stiff, wriggling gait" are only two of the many alleged physiological damages resulting from excessive "venery" (Barker 1888, 7; Acton 1857, 63–64). This list of physical deformations, which focuses mainly on the masturbator's bad posture, can be explained with the belief in the semen's vital physiological connection to the sinews of the spinal column and the bone marrow. Other unpleasant side effects causally linked to the "secret vice" are epileptic seizures, pain in the back, palpitations, and an uncomfortable "twitching of the muscles" (Kellogg 1894, 380). It seems as if the orgasm's spasmodic quality is the reason that epilepsy and excessive masturbation were linked. When repeated excessively, masturbation inevitably activates its unpleasant twin to exhibit the sexual culprit's secret guilt. Definite local and organic irregularities such as abnormal development of the penis or the testicles can equally be found in this register of woes as the well-known weakness of the teenage eyes that requires the "almost universal use of eye glasses and spectacles" (Barker 1888, 7 [quoted in Mullin 2003, 100]).

This reference to myopia is particularly interesting when turning to Joyce's *A Portrait*. No doubt, a suspicious medical observer such as Henry Maudsley might read very much into Stephen Dedalus's first experience with schoolboy flogging at Clongowes. As readers of Joyce will remember, Stephen is punished for breaking his glasses. And whereas and unsuspecting reader would assume that the prefect of studies canes Stephen simply for being a "[l]azy idle little loafer" (*P* 51), a Maudsleyan reader might come to a very different conclusion, especially because this particular event occurs almost simultaneously with the discovery of the "smuggers." Sexual transgression and schoolboy masturbation therefore provide the narrative background for Stephen's humiliating experience. To a suspicious medical observer, Stephen's impaired vision might therefore turn him into a suspect not only for laziness but also for sexual indulgences. The fact that Joyce comes back to the topic of Stephen's "weak eyes, tired with the tears" (*P* 55) after the pandybat scene, certainly lends credence to the cultural significance attached to myopia in the masturbation-haunted late nineteenth century.

In addition to all those well-known physiological defects, the "private vice" was at the turn of the twentieth century held responsible for almost every sign of physical and psychological infirmity. Doctors were enthusiastic in attributing diseases with unknown causes to solitary sexual practices. When in doubt, masturbation was a welcome scapegoat, accountable for various inexplicable illnesses. One example is the common, late nineteenth-century belief in "insanity of self-abuse" raving among teenagers and young adults (Maudsley 1886, 452). The accepted belief in masturbation's causal link with juvenile insanity only faded when the German psychiatrist Emil Kraepelin's dementia praecox concept, introduced in 1893, slowly superseded this dated disease model.

Overall, an astonishing aspect of the history of masturbation's nosology is the persistence with which the alleged symptoms continued to terrorize generations of teenagers after Tissot. Already in 1758 Tissot had subdivided

Figure 1. "The Physiological Results of Masturbation." An image from R. J. Brodie. 1845. *The Secret Companion,* 19. London: The Author. © British Library Board. All Rights Reserved. Shelfmark 1172.c70.

masturbation's varying disease symptoms into the categories: "depraved diges-tions, weakness of the brain, and of the nervous system, and irregular perspi-ration," and he concluded, no doubt, convincingly, "that there is no chronic disorder which may not be deduced from this triple cause" (Tissot 1985, 62). Nineteenth-century antimasturbation activists voluntarily embraced Tissot's suggestions, displaying even more imagination than the masturbation bible's author in detecting suspicious illness symptoms. One of the most striking examples comes from an 1847 German antimasturbation pamphlet, which, after listing commonplace symptoms, also refers to the increased number of "doubly or multiply splitted hair tips" that an attentive observer was to detect with the help of a magnifying glass (Andresse 1847, 86). This truly hair-splitting argumentation shows how nineteenth-century masturbation theorists continued to embellish Tissot's intellectual legacy.[10] A very dramatic illustration of this degenerate and ghoulish nightmare describing the onanist can be found in the typographical depiction in R. J. Brodie's 1845 quack pamphlet, *The Secret Companion* (figure 1). What this image conspicuously highlights is that the onanist has squandered his masculinity with the amount of semen he has so imprudently wasted. The depicted masturbator's feminine facial features and dress style effectively demonstrate the nineteenth-century fear of degraded virility associated with the "secret vice" and other "sins of impurity."

When we return to *A Portrait*, we can see how many references to the "solitary vice" an apprehensive and concerned turn-of-the-century medical observer can detect in the novel's first pages. The already mentioned "smugging" episode that could indicate schoolboy masturbation and Stephen's perturbed conflation of the words "cocks" and "suck" (*P* 8), followed by the comment, "That was a very queer thing" (*P* 8), might all testify to the possible reality of Stephen's premature sexual knowledge.[11] Nothing, then, can stop the adolescent Stephen's inevitable plunge "into the abyss" (Brodie 1845, 12) of "savage desire," "dark orgiastic riots" (*P* 105), and "wasting fires of lust" (*P* 106). It is only Father Arnall's hell sermon that marks the turning point in Stephen's young life: if he had before "cared little that he was in mortal sin" (*P* 105), then the preaching of eternal damnation rouses his troubled awareness of and resistance to "those things" (*P* 148). But interestingly, although the initial inducement to resist indulging in those "secret riots" (*P* 105) comes from the Catholic Church's authority, Stephen's ensuing administration of self-discipline has its source in the antimasturbation literature provided by such social purity activists as J. H. Kellogg or Sylvanus Stall.

Katherine Mullin has shown explicitly how well the older Stephen has incorporated the control mechanisms that trace masturbation's suspicious marks on his adolescent body (Mullin 2003, 100–101). His self-image, distinguished by his "cold and damp" hands (*P* 147) and "bodily weakness" (*P* 96), is not so much the product of Stephen's own mind, but of antimasturbation propaganda's predictions for the "self-polluting" addict. To combat the desire for "his own mad and filthy orgies" (*P* 96–97), Stephen subjects his body accordingly to a rigid regime of self-control, following the approved advice in every detail.

Attracted by the appeal of the recommended "hydropathic treatment" (Barker 1888, 34), Stephen envisages his Jesuit masters—these "serious priests, athletic and highspirited prefects"—as "men who washed their bodies briskly with cold water and wore clean cold linen" (*P* 168). The model character of the priests, those embodiments of chastity, is extremely troublesome in light of the direc-tor's suggestions for Stephen's clerical career (*P* 170). Through Stephen's vision, Joyce emphasizes the disturbing difference between the priests' imagined vir-tue and Stephen's own "monstrous reveries" (*P* 95). Not only have Stephen's "masters" (*P* 168) successfully managed their spiritual growth, but also they have, through a meticulous regime of cold-water appliances, efficiently sedated their bodies' luring turmoil. In Stephen's imagination the cold water and the cold linen of the priests become a counterpoint to his own "cold and cruel and loveless lust" (*P* 102), which irreversibly disqualifies him for priesthood.

Stephen nevertheless enforces his own hydropathic treatment, leaving "parts of his neck and face undried so that air might sting them" (*P* 163), attempt-ing to subject his senses to "a rigorous discipline" (*P* 162). Stephen also might have heard of so-called "night chains" that render "the wearer uncomfortable when asleep should he turn on to his back" (Jimison 1912, 13). Imposed sleep-ing positions—"[i]t is always advisable to sleep on the right or left side. The former is the best" (Howe 1883, 238)—are part of a carefully established agenda for monitoring the patient's sleeping rhythm. Stephen, who in this attempt at self-mortification "never consciously changed his position in bed" (*P* 163)[12] and who rises early for mass in the "raw morning air" (*P* 159), surrenders temporar-ily to the regime of uncompromising self-surveillance. Furthermore, Stephen's intense Mariolatry follows, as Mullin shows, another of social purity's advices to the young sinner: to visualize an idealized female figure when the urge to masturbate threatens to be overwhelming (Mullin 2003, 103). These "moral gymnastics" (Acton 1857, 94), together with regular physical exercise and the right diet, were supposed to lead the falterer back onto the path of virtue and health.

All this demonstrates how thoroughly the adolescent Stephen is tormented by his guilt about solitary sexual practices. However, so far Stephen's confron-tation with his own sexuality and the institutional and cultural restrictions that make his sexual experiences so disturbing does not in any way render his situation exceptional. The universality of the "secret vice" in young teenagers had in Stephen's adolescence been widely acknowledged, and what the young Irishman has to endure only resembles the fate of innumerable other adoles-cent transgressors. But interestingly, in Joyce's *A Portrait* the depiction of this generic teenage disease is complicated by references to Stephen's professional aspirations, the artist's career, which tie Joyce's protagonist even more explicitly to the pathological portrait of the adolescent "self-abuser." As we shall see, turn-of-the-century antimasturbation propaganda developed a specific clinical profile for the teenage masturbator that focused specifically on the young person's psychological and characterological peculiarities.

Late nineteenth-century antimasturbation literature assumed that the chronic genital abuser exhibited a prominent antisocial disposition. "The vile habit" irreversibly transforms the culprit into a "solitary, cowardly, morose and pessimistic" individual (Jimison 1912, 5). Guilt-ridden and self-obsessed, "[t]he sufferer retires from the notice of strangers and has a taste for seclusion, liking to lie awake in bed, always with the hands under the clothing and upon the sexual parts" (Hall 1907, 15). Signs of the future development of solitary sexual practices are detectable early in childhood. An obvious symptom, in addition to the already noted "taste for seclusion," is a marked change in the young sufferer's character: "the bright, frank, happy, and obedient boy has become the fretful, irritable, stolid, and reticent boy" (Stall 1897, 102–3). "Precocious development" is equally suspect: "[l]ittle boys who show a decided preference for the society of little girls need careful watching" (Kellogg 1894, 380) because they are likely to turn into teenage "genital abusers."

In *A Portrait* Joyce equips his young protagonist with many of these suspicious characteristics: the singing and dancing "baby tuckoo" (*P* 3) is transformed into a child full of "embittered silence" (*P* 69). Moreover, Stephen's early intimacy with Eileen, whose "cool and thin and soft" hand exerts a troubled fascination on Stephen, especially when it finds its way into his pocket (*P* 43), could yet be another example of Stephen's sexual prematurity. Knowing other Joycean texts such as "Sirens," readers are bound to notice a certain erotic undertone in the passage describing the two playing children: while Eileen's hand is fingering in Stephen's pocket, "a fox terrier was scampering to and fro on the sunny lawn" until "all of a sudden she had broken away" (*P* 43, 72–73).[13] It seems as if Joyce wrote this overdetermined passage exclusively for the eyes of the antimasturbation censor. A nineteenth-century moral reformer or medically trained observer reading *A Portrait* would probably jump to strong conclusions regarding Stephen's future sexual development.

The suspicious love of solitude as one of the juvenile masturbator's predominant traits can equally be noted early on in *A Portrait*. Naturally shy, Stephen dreads physical contact during recreation at Clongowes, longing for the quietness of the study hall (*P* 6) and even more for the comfort and seclusion of his bed (*P* 9). The detailed description of "the yellow curtains round and before his bed that shut him off on all sides" (*P* 16) reveals that the young Stephen is painfully aware of the surveillance system in Clongowes, from which only his bedtime hours are exempt, assuring a minimum of privacy. Joyce further illustrates his young protagonist's social exile in the description of the Harold's Cross children's party: "when he had sung his song and withdrawn into a snug corner of the room he began to taste the joy of his loneliness" (*P* 71), suggesting that Stephen finds comfort only in the two extremes: center of attention or gloomy solitude.

But Stephen's frustrated childhood and adolescent existence becomes even further entangled with the presuppositions of the interfering antimasturbation propaganda. As the narrative develops, Stephen matures more and more into the categorized teenage "self-abuser." In fact, social purity activists and medical men had singled out a certain type who was especially prone to fall victim to his stirring sexuality. As William Acton observes, "it is not the strong athletic boy, fond of healthy exercise, who thus early shows marks of sexual education—it is your puny exotic, whose intellectual education has been cared for at the expense of his physical development" (Acton 1857, 7). Acton's remark shows that even in early childhood, sexual activity and masturbation are supposedly diseases of scholarly mindsets.

Not surprisingly, nineteenth-century reformers therefore employed the image of the Boy Scout as bogus remedy for the "solitary vice." The scout's uniform symbolized his carrier's "loyalty, chivalry, discipline, courage and truthfulness," "the bed-rock of a good character" (Fowke n.d., 4), and turned him into the masturbator's glowing and esteemed foil. The intellectual boy was, "because of a more highly wrought nervous organization and because of keener sensibilities" destined to become addicted to the "secret vice" (Stall 1897, 99). In the eyes of medical reformers, masturbation became the disease of "high-society teenagers, who were allowed to loll on sofas reading lubricious romances" (Porter and Hall 1995, 102). And although he is subjected to considerable running exercises (*P* 63), Stephen is certainly more the intellectual type, the preferred subject of medical antimasturbation treatises. Bullied at school, weak and sickly, but "leader of the Yorkists" (*P* 53), he is the model type for medicine's clinical attention.

That studiousness and reading were essentially linked to the threats of "self-abuse" can also be seen in the clinical symptoms ascribed to chronic masturbation. The weak eyes, bad posture, porous bone marrow, in fact the whole figure of the crippled, degenerate onanist is a thinly disguised description of the solitary scholar. The masturbator's clinical symptoms are therefore firmly associated with the ailments of excessive reading and writing. Even in the cases of insanity and pulmonary consumption, the two most extreme results that medical men identified as consequences of obsessive masturbation, a link between the masturbator and the artist can be established. Whereas insanity is a disease of the imaginative and sensitive mind, we have already noted Susan Sontag's argument that tuberculosis was, in the Romantic imagination, intimately connected to the artist's image.

Madness and consumption are not accidentally the two illnesses Stephen has to confront on the way to a university lecture: the mad nun's shrieks and the "doll's face" of the "consumptive man" (*P* 191) are both graphic illustrations of what might await Stephen should he give way to his sexual cravings again. Buck Mulligan's verbal assault on the scholarly Eglinton in "Scylla and Charybdis" follows a similar line: "*Magee that had the chinless mouth. / Being afraid to marry on earth / They masturbated for all they were worth*" (*U* 9.1150–52). In Mulligan's mocking hymn, the assiduous bachelor is, unlike in the Actonian model that associates spermatic economy with successful scholarship, identified as a convicted onanist. Even antimasturbation propaganda's most fervent advocates had to acknowledge that "overstudy and overwork may produce the same" symptoms as chronic "self-abuse" (Kellogg 1894, 377; Dyer 1884, 20). The artist's image thus incorporates the masturbator's traits and vice versa.

Since intellectual work and "overstudy" were deemed unhealthy for the adolescent's sexual continence, antimasturbation campaigners carefully monitored the reading habits of turn-of-the-century teenagers. The question of how much and how long children were allowed to read was fiercely debated. Moreover, doctors also gave advice on the suitability of particular reading material. Suitable subjects of "wholesome reading" were "histories and biographies," "the sciences and arts," "travel and exploration," but certainly not novels and romances (Stall 1897, 147). Novels, in particular, were regarded as particularly corruptive. But this prohibition is hardly surprising. Masturbation is "the creature of the imagination" (Laqueur 2003, 21). It is the one sexual act that does not require a foothold in the real world. Instead, the physical processes are exclusively the products of fantastic ravings. In the eyes of many turn-of-the-century medical men, reading novels was also regarded as extremely provocative for the imagination because it "nourishes nothing but illusions" and, "by bringing into yet more definite contrast what might be and ought to be," renders the individual unfit for social interaction (Austin 1874, 253).

So according to the medical experts, the two activities, reading novels and solitary sex, resemble each other. Both activities are dangerously hedonistic, and, since they are the result of too much leisure, they threaten to be socially harmful. However, it was not only "the vile French photos and novels" that the tempted teenager is asked to avoid. Surprisingly, penny magazines, smutty photos, and lowbrow sensationalist novels, although dangerously corruptive, did not offend antimasturbation propagandists most. Instead, it is the "gilded vice" of "wicked artists with depraved genius" that is particularly destructive and corrupting (Barker 1888, 32). Masturbation's adversaries therefore launched an organized attack on both the reader and the producer of contaminating highbrow novels. Romantic poets and the writers of romances were also at the top of the censor's index. Unsurprisingly, the "queer old josser" (*D* 18) in "An Encounter," who seems to be an embodiment of the crippled, degenerate masturbator, alludes to both Sir Walter Scott and Lord Lytton, the author of sensational romances when he distinguishes himself as a "bookworm" (*D* 17). And while he asks the boys who has "the most sweethearts" (*D* 17)—a question that indicates his interest in the boys' sexual prematurity—he also identifies the narrator as studious and intellectual while simultaneously suggesting that Mahony "is different; he goes in for games" (*D* 17). "An Encounter" thus explicitly links bookishness and a liking for romantic novels to the "secret sin."

Having been removed from Clongowes, Stephen enters exactly the kind of "long spell of leisure and liberty" (*P* 74) that medical advisors so explicitly warned against, since it leaves the youngster enough time to discover his sexual organ and its potential (Dyer 1884, 22). And indeed, in Stephen's case, a medical advisor might have ample reason to be concerned. Stephen's reading list includes Lord Byron and Alexandre Dumas's *The Count of Monte Cristo*, texts that represented an explicit offense to the moral censor.[14] Worse still, Joyce seems to confirm antimasturbation propaganda's worst fears when illustrating Dumas's poisonous effects on Stephen. Deeply affected by the story's plot, Stephen recreates its setting, living "through a long train of adventures, marvellous as those in the book itself" (*P* 65), and searching for his own Mercedes, whose image produces "a fever gathered within him," forcing him to "rove alone in the evening along the quiet avenue" (*P* 67). An alert medical reader might suggest that the novel's romantic plot is responsible for Stephen's admittance into the allied world of daydreams and solitary sex.

Stephen himself certainly notices his damaged reality concept. He becomes, with Emma's entrance into his world, painfully aware of the inconsistency between reality and idealizing fantasy. Recalling Eileen and his first experience with sexuality and sexual matters, Stephen uses Emma's seductive advances on the tram's steps as fodder for his imagination: "I could hold her and kiss her" (*P* 73). Reality, with all "which he deemed common and insignificant" (*P* 74), here gives way to an idealized or romanticized version of the incident. This shows that Stephen's imagination, which according to late nineteenth-century moralists, plays an important part in the "suicidal business" (Barker 1888, 17), has already taken control of the situation. Emma's physical presence is only the stage setting for another, more optimistically romantic plot, taking place in Stephen's head and occupying him for two years (*P* 81). And according to the late nineteenth-century moral police, it is only a small step from "hyper-sentimentality to gross lust" (Barker 1888, 17). As William Acton states: "[A]ided by [the imagination] the present hour is peopled by delicious forms, which the eyes can feast upon, the lips embrace, and the arms enfold. Graceful phantoms, combinations of real and ideal loveliness, may at her bidding plunge the soul and the senses into the most complete voluptuous ecstasy of love" (Acton 1857, 5–6).[15] With the suggestion that Stephen has given himself over to the "company of subversive writers whose gibes and violence of speech set up a ferment in his brain before they passed out of it into his crude writings" (*P* 82–83), Joyce again seems to repeat antimasturbation propaganda's standardized opinion of literature's infective potential—that the reading of subversive material inevitably produces subversive writing and encourages solitary sexual practices.

Equally strong is the suggestion that Stephen has plunged into a world of phantoms and phantasmagoria. Not surprisingly, he is only happy when "alone or in the company of phantasmal comrades" (*P* 89). In acknowledging that, "[b]y his monstrous way of life he seemed to have put himself beyond the limits of reality. Nothing moved him or spoke to him from the real world unless he heard in it an echo of the infuriated cries within him" (*P* 98), Stephen also connects his sexual excesses explicitly to his mind's pathological withdrawal from reality. Nothing is sacred. In "his monstrous dreams, peopled by apelike creatures and by harlots with gleaming jewel eyes" (*P* 124), even Emma's "innocence" is "trampled upon" with "brutelike lust" (*P* 124).

For this offense Stephen is punished by a "flood of shame" (*P* 124), which shows that his internal censor's agency is still intact, aware of the uncomfortable discrepancy between reality and fiction, and that Stephen's glide "into the deep, dark vortex of unknowable and unutterable doom" (Barker 1888, 4) is still reversible. And the agents of the exterior moral censor do not remain immobile. Stephen is confronted with Father Arnall's impressive hell sermon, which uses, interestingly, the young masturbator's alleged weakness, the imagination, in producing the deterring image of "the material character of that awful place and of the physical torments which all who are in hell endure" (*P* 137).

Indeed, the textual proximity between Stephen's sexual reveries and the disciplinary hell sermon is noteworthy. Joyce here emphasizes the similarity between the rebellious and the sanctioned fiction, between the teenager's sexual fantasies and Father Arnall's sermon: both rely on the producer's imagination. In this context it is worth remembering that the image of the masturbator's alleged clinical symptoms is remarkably graphic—a figure coming straight from the culprit's worst or most hellish nightmares.[16] In juxtaposing Stephen's sex fantasies with Father Arnall's theological ejaculations in *A Portrait*, Joyce therefore underlines the obvious weakness in antimasturbation propaganda's moral logic: its use of and reliance on the imagination's pathological stimulation, the characteristic that antimasturbation rhetoric had singled out as one of the most distinctive ones in the chronic teenage masturbator's clinical picture.

But while doctors and moral advisors eagerly referenced the self-destructive aspects of the onanist's secretive habits, they also noted his manifest lack of social responsibility. Strikingly, the turn-of-the-century understanding of the masturbator's "gloomy misanthropy" and social indifference that is "the result of his own vicious conduct" (Brodie 1845, 16) demonstrates a certain resemblance to our modern-day understanding of the incurable drug addict. Their respective addiction habitually leads them into a vicious circle of moral corruption, "producing a tendency to steal, lie, cheat, swear, be indecent, cruel and generally corrupt" (Barker 1888, 10). However, the apparent difference between the two is the masturbator's predominant autoerotic inclination. The subject of his monomania is his own body as a site of sexual pleasure. But precisely this unrestricted autarchy in securing unlimited sexual pleasure was the reason why the teenage masturbator was regarded as utterly corrupting and despicable by the Victorian medical profession: "[B]ecause everything required—the desire and its satisfaction—was securely lodged within the individual" (Laqueur 2003, 52), no limits were set for the masturbator's sexual excesses. His autonomy is total—a fact that can be seen in the choice of the many euphemisms for "genital abuse": "*self*-pollution," "*self*-abuse," "*self*-indulgence," "*solitary* sex," or "*solitary* vice."

No one was more aware of this precarious state than Henry Maudsley, who, in his influential and already much quoted work, *The Pathology of Mind*, launched an organized attack on the masturbator's degraded moral nature. Interestingly, when describing the juvenile masturbator, Maudsley's language is

surprisingly passionate and betrays the condemnation that this medical observer reserved for the "secret vice," "its socially disruptive qualities," and its
"violation of normative expectations for 'productive' or 'industrious' middle-
class male behaviour" (Cohen 1987, 184):

> The most striking features in this variety of mental derangement are the
> intense selfishness and self-conceit that are shown. The patient is com-
> pletely wrapped up in self, egotistically insensible to the claims of others
> upon him and of his duties to them, hypochondriacally occupied with his
> sensations and his bodily functions, abandoned to indolent and solitary
> self-brooding; he displays a vanity and self-sufficiency quite unbecoming
> his age and position; exacts the constant indulgence of others without
> the least thought of obligation or gratitude, and is apt, if he gets not the
> consideration which he claims, to declare that his family are unfeeling
> and do not understand him, or are actually hostile to him. (Maudsley
> 1886, 452–53)[17]

Since in this short passage the word "self" is mentioned five times and the word
"solitary" is referred to once, Maudsley seems to identify the masturbator's
central pathology as a morbid selfishness. Masturbation was, in Maudsley's
eyes, the "supreme narcissistic act, the retreat into selfish enjoyment of one's
own body without reference to the social order" (Gilbert 1980, 278).

It is certainly not difficult to establish, once again, an analogy between this
sexual pathology and Stephen Dedalus when we look at his refusal to participate in his friends' parallel political projects, advocating alternatively Irish na-
tionalism, feminism, or "*Pax super totum sanguinarium globum*" (*P* 214). In *A
Portrait* it is mainly MacCann, who, struck by his friend's political indifference,
has taken on the role of teaching Stephen the rules of social conduct, employ-
ing hereby an almost Maudsleyan rhetoric: "—Dedalus, you're an antisocial
being, wrapped up in yourself" (*P* 191); "—Dedalus, said MacCann crisply, I
believe you're a good fellow but you have yet to learn the dignity of altruism
and the responsibility of the human individual" (*P* 215). To a medical observer
MacCann's well-meant rebukes would certainly be very suggestive when ana-
lyzing Stephen's case.

But if Joyce shows how Stephen fits neatly into the medical category of
the teenage masturbator, *A Portrait* also illustrates that many of Stephen's actions to rid himself of his unpleasant and sinful habit trap him further in the
masturbator's pathological pattern. Even the rigorous and self-disciplining regime that follows antimasturbation propaganda's strictest advices reconnects

him irrevocably with the onanist's image. For instance, Joyce's text states that "[i]n order to mortify the sense of sight [Stephen] made it his rule to walk in the street with downcast eyes, glancing neither to right nor left and never behind him. His eyes shunned every encounter with the eyes of women" (*P* 162–63). Ironically though, Stephen, in his attempt to battle the "secret vice," repeats the behavioral pattern of the chronic masturbator, who is, apparently, notably shy in the presence of women and whose eyes "seldom meet yours, but steal side-long glances, when your attention is drawn in another direction" (Howe 1883, 67). In fighting his morbid pathology, Stephen unconsciously reaffirms it.

His preference for the artist's career is, unfortunately, the best example of this unfortunate development of events. In choosing this particular profession, Stephen becomes, once more, entangled with the masturbator's pejorative clinical picture, especially since he decides to base his artistic creed on "silence, exile, and cunning" (*P* 269), characteristics that, according to the medical literature, firmly belong into the psychopathological range of the teenage masturbator. That the artist and the onanist are indeed connected in medical antimasturbation propaganda is nowhere more noticeable than in Maudsley's 1868 article "Illustrations of a Variety of Insanity." The young and aspiring artist's projects are here identified as one of the clinical picture's most notorious symptoms: "He often talks in high poetical or idealistic style, speaks of absurdly exalted plans, but is entirely unpractical; he does not find sufficiently exalted feelings and high aims in the world, and cannot sympathise with, but is distressed by, its low aims and rude ways. He has great projects, but no resolves; abundant self-conceit, but no self-knowledge; a spasmodic sort of self-will, but no true will" (Maudsley 1868, 157).[18] What characterizes the teenage masturbator's artistic ambitions is therefore their pointlessness and futility. They remain unfulfilled and are, according to Maudsley, just another demonstration of the patient's tendency for self-indulgence and narcissistic fixations.

Needless to say, the artistic aspirations of Joyce's protagonist remain thwarted throughout *A Portrait* and *Ulysses*. Unfortunately, Stephen, despite his intellectual competence, remains an unpublished poet at the end of *Ulysses*, and Mulligan might well be right with his suspicion that Stephen "is going to write something in ten years" (*U* 10.1089–90). Stephen's only literary product in *Ulysses*, the Shakespeare theory, is a classic example of his "futile enthusiasms" (*P* 96). Eglinton's frustration with the "French triangle" (*U* 9.1065) is understandable, especially in light of Stephen's disbelief in his own brainchild. Joyce's text, it seems, confirms with startling analogy Maudsley's pejorative opinion of the teenage artist's lack of professional determination—a pathological character formation, which medical practitioners firmly associated with the teenager's corrupted sexual practices.

Stephen's artistic productivity in *A Portrait* that parallels the development of his "snobbish individuation" (Latham 2003, 143) is also less than impressive. Alongside the villanelle and the aesthetic theory, the diary entries at the end of the novel are the only real proof of Stephen's writerly productivity. Among those artistic outputs, the villanelle, Stephen's "Frenchified verses" written "in bed in an erotic swoon" (Kenner 1955, 112), provides, of course, the best opportunity to think about Stephen's art as a sterile form of autoeroticism. Considering his own aesthetic theory, which prescribes a continuous process of artistic depersonalization for the creation of "the highest and most spiritual art" (*P* 232), it is, of course, surprising that Stephen produces this poem, which is, according to his own standards, as a representative of the "lyrical form," "the simplest verbal vesture of an instant of emotion" (*P* 232), hardly an artistic masterpiece.

Joyce critics have noted, with a certain embarrassment, that this poem is certainly not worthy of Stephen's high artistic aspirations. Sean Latham notes, for instance, that Stephen's "composition of his villanelle seems ridiculously out of place, a throwback to an earlier period of his life" and that "this short poem suggests a primitive talent still mired in the impressionistic language and Symbolist imagery that seemed to collapse in the wake of Stephen's encounter with the girl on the beach" (Latham 2003, 146). Whereas Stephen's artistic theory demands the impersonality of the artist, the villanelle is embarrassing as an artistic product because its focus is the self, the artist's persona, who is here a far cry from being "behind or beyond or above his handiwork, invisible, refined out of existence, indifferent, pairing his fingernails" (*P* 233). However, the production of the villanelle, a poem with a distinctive personal touch, can appear as less of an artistic anomaly when we consider it in the context of the teenage masturbator's clinical picture as it has been described by Henry Maudsley. If we remember that prominent features of this pathological configuration were the sufferer's self-obsession and his narcissistic fixations, the villanelle becomes a more than appropriate artistic output.

Indeed, the passage describing Stephen's "dewy wet" (*P* 235) epiphany is rife with expressions suggesting that the villanelle can be read as the product of a wet dream: "A gradual warmth, a languorous weariness passed over him" (*P* 241); "A glow of desire kindled again his soul and fired and fulfilled all his body" (*P* 242); "Her nakedness yielded to him, radiant, warm, odorous and lavishlimbed, enfolded him like a shining cloud, enfolded him like water with a liquid life" (*P* 242). The text's emphasis on body temperatures and liquids, especially water, makes obvious Stephen's attention to body fluids and his physical response to the imagined sexual union with Emma. But when "the letters of speech" that form his villanelle become, in Stephen's mind, themselves liquefied and "flowed forth over his brain" (*P* 242), Joyce's text also suggests that Stephen's poem is not only the product of but also the source for further auto-erotic pleasure. Although Emma's picture has doubtlessly still a strong hold on Stephen's imagination, he is solipsistically in love with his own artistic creation. Text and sex become intertwined while erotic energy is turned inwards to satisfy Stephen's narcissism.

Given the fact that Stephen is (in many ways) turning upon himself in this scene, the closed-off, inward-looking form of the villanelle is therefore an appropriate poetic expression of the aspiring young artist's egotistic self-absorption. Built on its two rhymes and the two refrains ("Are you not weary of ardent ways" and "Tell no more of enchanted days"), Stephen's poem is stuck on the same sound, "ways, days, blaze, praise, raise" (*P* 236). As a lyrical form, the villanelle is a text without real sonic development—a text that is repetitive, static, and refuses to move on. It represents narrative sterility par excellence and is therefore synonymous with the intellectual infertility of Joyce's artist hero. But by undercutting narrative development, by preferring sound and rhythm over sense and content, the villanelle is also a poetic form most evidently in love with its own technical skill and its own complex structure. Like its producer, young Stephen Dedalus, the villanelle thus advertises self-obsession and a snobbish solipsism.

Viewed in this light, the composition of the villanelle represents more than an artistic relapse. It advertises Stephen's ongoing obsession with his own body and person and places him once more right in the center of Maudsley's pathological chart. More important, though, we have seen earlier on how diligently Stephen tries to fight his fascination with the "secret vice" and to free himself from his vile habits. If a morbid self-interest is the predominant characteristic of the teenage masturbator, Stephen's artistic theory, prescribing the depersonalization of artistic creation, could then almost be read as another of his ongoing attempts to rid himself of more than just an aesthetically unsound practice. Aiming to get away from a pathological preoccupation with the self, the artistic theory appears to be an important element in Stephen's self-diagnosis and self-cure strategy. Because it brings Stephen's personality and his obsession with his own emotions back into the picture, the villanelle, it must be said, represents a much more drastic setback than critics have so far suspected.

But the composition of Stephen's "Frenchified verses" is by no means the only time when Stephen's writerly outputs signal his inability to put a distance between his own person and the pathological picture of the chronic masturbator. With its last pages, which contain Stephen's diary entries, the novel itself turns against its protagonist's ongoing efforts. If Stephen singles out "that old English ballad *Turpin Hero* which begins in the first person and ends in the third person" (*P* 233) as a good example of a narrative that is "no longer purely personal" (*P* 233), *A Portrait*, with Stephen's diary entries in its final pages, undergoes the opposite transformation from third-person to first-person narrative. It is true, we have no way of finding out how long Stephen has kept his diary, but the important thing is that Joyce's novel starts to represent Stephen's entries only in its last pages. These diary entries chronicle Stephen's last month in Dublin, before his well-anticipated departure from Ireland. They are, therefore, a record of personal and emotional experiences. Moreover, they do show how thoroughly Stephen is "wrapped up in self": "[T]he world precipitously collapses into the singularity of Stephen's consciousness," writes Sean Latham, and the "conflicts with E. C., Cranly, Davin, and his mother . . . are each suddenly resolved in the diary, and all in Stephen's favor" (Latham 2003, 148). Stephen records a "[l]ong talk with Cranly," for instance, accusing him of "grand manner" but describing himself as being "supple and suave" (*P* 270). Likewise, the public park, Stephen's Green, is appropriated and transformed into "my green" (*P* 271), showing how much Stephen's consciousness has started to take possession of the world around him.

Michael Levenson, after drawing attention to the "sentimental reading" of the novel's final passage, that regards it "as a decisive expression of revolt" (Levenson 2003, 184), also shows how the style at the end of Joyce's novel contradicts the optimistic tenor of Stephen's account: "A space opens between the self and its form of representation" (194). Stephen might think that he can escape the confines of his social environment, but the novel questions this possibility by its formal appearance. As Levenson points out, *A Portrait* contains an "elegantly disguised chiasmus" (199). It ends on a sequence of events that parallels and inverts incidents at the novel's beginning (compare "father telling a story, mother putting on the oil sheet, Charles and Dante, the fantasy of marrying Eileen, Dante's threat, the eagles" to "'terrible queer creatures,' E—C— and Dante Alighieri, the 'kinsmen,' mother putting his clothes in order, old father, old artificer") (199). Like the villanelle, *A Portrait*, a text that is in a sense closed-off, looks inwards and refuses to let Stephen move on. So if Stephen is in revolt against his social environment, the language of *A Portrait* creates its own insurgent energies and turns against him to contradict his aims and hopes. But this inward turn, suggested by the changed style at the end of Joyce's novel, also underlines that Stephen continues to be preoccupied with his own person and that he remains confined in the clinical picture that the medico-moral masturbation discourse has generated. Sex and text, once again, entrap and restrain him.

At the end of *A Portrait* we see Stephen renounce his hometown, his spiritual upbringing, and Irish social structures. He becomes a snobbish, cold aesthete. Ironically, though, even this final rejection of the culture that produces the restricting doctrine he intends to cast off, ultimately reinforces his connection to its most despised morbid outcast. In exiling himself from the social order, Stephen categorically confirms the medical prophecies that link the chronic masturbator to a social pariah—a person who shuns social contacts and encounters. Whether or not he leaves Ireland, Stephen never manages to escape the specifically designed medical category of the convicted masturbator. Physiologically and characterologically he verifies its notorious characteristics.

However, it was certainly not Joyce's aim to pathologize Stephen and to repeat, with creative fervor, the prejudiced readings of late nineteenth-century medico-moral debates. Instead, *A Portrait* illustrates medicine's complex interaction with social politics and shows its responsibility in first creating and then enforcing its own pathologies. We see this when Stephen, even in the moments when he is trying to fight his assumed pathology, remains trapped in its clinical picture. So if we want to read Stephen's case and that of his artistic aspirations as one of failure and inefficiency, we should remember that *A Portrait* indicates that Stephen's social and artistic paralysis is at least partly the outcome of a domineering medico-moral discourse that determines a sensitive and imaginative Irishman's adolescence.

Medicine and medical debates form a very specific imperious force in Stephen's life. Hence Joyce writes Stephen's case not to confirm the medical prophecies of the domineering antimasturbation context. Conversely, he suggests that Stephen's presumably morbid character and his failed artistic career are partly the products of this all-invasive medico-moral discourse. Whereas medical practitioners hoped to assist modern progress and improvement politics, *A Portrait* holds a specific medical debate responsible for personal and professional stasis. In thus describing Stephen's rocky road to adulthood, Joyce effectively turns his critical attention to the question of how medicine's analytical interpretations helped to reorganize the cultural fabric of the modern world.

4

"The True Purefoy Nose"

Medicine, Obstetrics, and the Aesthetics of Reproduction
in "Oxen of the Sun"

With *Dubliners* and *A Portrait of the Artist as a Young Man* published in 1914
and 1916 respectively, Joyce now turned his energies toward his next task: writing *Ulysses*. In this new text Joyce's interest in debility and medicine's diagnostic practices continues to be noticeable. However, it is offset by a corresponding
fascination with medicine's metaphorical potential. Although Joyce had already
employed the paralysis metaphor in *Dubliners*, he would use medical imagery
much more resolutely in *Ulysses* to create a conceptual scaffold. Famously, *Ulysses* is organized around the organs of the human body. With the exception of
the first three chapters in the "Telemachiad," every episode is linked to a body
part with specific physiological functions—a fact that makes explicit the novel's
connection to physical topography. At times Joyce's text thereby simply establishes links between the activities in "the Hibernian Metropolis" (*U* 7.1–2)—the
city as a social organism—and the physiological processes in a human organism. This can be seen in the "Wandering Rocks" episode, one of the busiest in
the novel, where the buzz and commotion of Dublin city life is mirrored in the
physiological image of blood circulation. Elsewhere, the assigned body parts
allow a much more critical evaluation of individual chapters. The allusion to
the "lungs" as the organ emitting discarded, superfluous air offers a suggestive
reading of the workings of the "Gentlemen of the Press" (*U* 7.20) in "Aeolus"
and casts doubt on the political merits of excessively reiterating rhetorically
heavyweight oratories and speeches.[1] When we turn to *Ulysses* we must therefore note that Joyce's critical evaluation of medical practices and discourses is
balanced by his artistic reliance on medicine and its metaphors.

Joyce's aesthetic interest in medicine becomes very apparent in the "Oxen
of the Sun" episode. This chapter, which Joyce wrote between February and
May 1920 (Norburn 2004, 91), cultivates associative readings of the text as a

physical organism and the human body as a text. "Oxen" takes place in the National Maternity Hospital on Holles Street and indirectly indicates the birth of Mortimer Edward Purefoy. It is the first time, therefore, that Joyce chooses a medical institution as a geographic backdrop for an episode. Both the Linati schema and the Gilbert-Gorman plan also designate "medicine" as the episode's art and "the womb" as its organ. In a 1920 letter to Frank Budgen, Joyce also suggested that the episode's individual parts are linked "with the natural stages of development in the embryo and the periods of the faunal evolution in general" (*LI* 140). It has therefore been suggested that "Oxen" adopts Ernst Haeckel's recapitulation theory—the idea that the ontogeny (the origin and the development of the individual organism) recapitulates the phylogeny (the evolutionary development of a species or other group of organisms through a succession of forms) (Gordon 1979, 158). In this theory, Haeckel proposed that the fetus in its embryonic development parallels and repeats the evolutionary progress that produced the human race.

As so often, Joyce liberally adjusts this medical axiom for artistic purposes. In "Oxen" the fetus's genesis is not associated with the evolution of the human race, but rather, as Joyce himself explains in a letter to Frank Budgen, with the development of the English literary canon, represented by an anthology of Joyce's literary precursors:

> Technique: a nineparted episode without divisions introduced by a Sallustian-Tacitean prelude (the unfertilized ovum), then by way of earliest English alliterative and monosyllabic and Anglo-Saxon ('Before born the babe had bliss. Within the womb he won worship.' 'Bloom dull dreamy heard: in held hat stony staring') then by way of Mandeville ('there came forth a scholar of medicine that men clepen, etc') then Malory's *Morte d'Arthur* ('but that franklin Lenehan was prompt ever to pour them so that at the least way mirth should not lack'), then the Elizabethan chronicle style ('about that present time young Stephen filled all cups'), then a passage solemn, as of Milton, Taylor, Hooker, followed by a choppy Latin-gossipy bit, style of Burton-Browne, then a passage Bunyanesque ('the reason was that in the way he fell in with a certain whore whose name she said is Bird in the hand') after a diarystyle bit Pepys-Evelyn ('Bloom sitting smug with a party of wags, among them Dixon jun., Ja. Lynch, Doc. Madden and Stephen D. for a languor he had before and was now better, he having dreamed tonight a strange fancy and Mistress Purefoy there to be delivered, poor body, two days past her time and the midwives hard put to it, God send her quick issue') and so on through

Defoe-Swift and Steele-Addison-Sterne and Landor-Pater-Newman until it ends in a frightful jumble of Pidgin English, nigger English, Cockney, Irish, Bowery slang and broken doggerel. (*LI* 139–40)

As we can see, in "Oxen" Joyce's parodistic take on English literary styles deliberately follows a reproductive writing methodology. In fact, Mark Osteen has suggested that, in "Oxen," "because he borrows not only the styles of his predecessors but also their words, [Joyce's] strategy may be described as bold plagiarism" (Osteen 1995, 228).

What I want to show in this chapter is that "Oxen," although it draws extensively on contemporary medical debates such as embryology, birth control, imperialist population controls, Darwinism, and eugenics, links its reliance on medical imagery to these intertextual strategies.[2] Indeed, what has so far passed unnoticed is that among the many literary texts that provide the base for Joyce's episode is one that most notably brings the reproductive practices of "Oxen" into play. Moreover, it shares with "Oxen" a thematic and structural interest in medicine, especially obstetrics, and its metaphorical connection to reproduction aesthetics. "Oxen" establishes an intertextual dialogue with the first three volumes of Laurence Sterne's 1759–67 *The Life and Opinions of Tristram Shandy, Gentleman*. And, as I will show, the textual interactions between Joyce and Sterne, both metafictional texts born out of sophisticated intertextual practices, confuse and contaminate what both "Oxen" and *Tristram Shandy* seem to be most unrelentingly insisting upon: unambiguous notions of origin *and* originality. Although Joyce's interest in the human body, debility, and contemporary medicine becomes in no way submerged in "Oxen,"[3] it is by means of a suggestive overlap of the episode's verbal imitations and its debate of physiological reproduction, that "Oxen"—the episode in *Ulysses* most obviously concerned with the relationship between literature and medicine—turns medicine into an aesthetic principle—or, as Joyce called it, an "art."

.

If Joyce's "Oxen" establishes an intertextual relationship with Sterne's *Tristram Shandy*, what, then, are the essential thematic links between the two texts? "Oxen" opens with a review of the halcyon days of Irish medicine, stating that "among the Celts, who nothing that was not in its nature admirable admired, the art of medicine shall have been highly honoured" (*U* 14.34–35). Then, with its specific allusions to the National Maternity Hospital, "[o]f that house A. Horne is lord. Seventy beds keeps he there" (*U* 14.74),[4] and explicit references to its historical backdrop, "Oxen" provides a swift but accurate survey of Irish medicine's status quo in 1904.[5] What follows is well known: Mina Purefoy, who is "three days bad now" (*U* 8.282), as Josie Breen tells Bloom in "Lestrygo-nians," eventually gives, after a painful and prolonged labor, a "weary weary while both for patient and doctor" (*U* 14.1311–12), birth to another Purefoy: "if ever there was one, with the true Purefoy nose" (*U* 14.1333). However, Enda Duffy has argued that the "good fight" (*U* 14.1313) of "the brave woman" (*U* 14.1312) "occurs offstage" and the text's "sidestepping of the actual birth" instead foregrounds "the banter of drunkards" rather than "the birth of a baby" (Duffy 1999, 212).[6] Indeed, the "hard birth unneth to bear" (*U* 14.114–15) is only repre-sented by an occasional "upfloor cry on high" (*U* 14.170) noticed by the atten-tive Bloom, who "still had pity of the terrorcausing shrieking of shrill women in their labour" (*U* 14.264–65).

Significant fractions of the drunken debate among Lenehan, Dr. Dixon, Bloom, Stephen, and the medical students Lynch, Madden, Costello, the Scot-tish Crothers, and Mulligan, who joins them in the course of the episode, fo-cus, to all appearances, on the "gravest problems of obstetrics and forensic medicine" (*U* 14.977–78):

> Every phase of the situation was successively eviscerated: the prenatal repugnance of uterine brothers, the Caesarean section, posthumity with respect to the father and, that rarer form, with respect to the mother, the fratricidal case known as the Childs Murder and rendered memorable by the impassioned plea of Mr Advocate Bushe which secured the acquittal of the wrongfully accused, the rights of primogeniture and king's bounty touching twins and triplets, miscarriages and infanticides, simulated or dissimulated, the acardiac *foetus in foetu* and aprosopia due to a conges-tion, the agnathia of certain chinless Chinamen (cited by Mr Candidate Mulligan) in consequence of defective reunion of the maxillary knobs along the medial line so that (as he said) one ear could hear what the other spoke, the benefits of anesthesia or twilight sleep, the prolongation of labour pains in advanced gravidancy by reason of pressure on the vein, the premature relentment of the amniotic fluid (as exemplified in the ac-tual case) with consequent peril of sepsis to the matrix, artificial insemi-nation by means of syringes, involution of the womb consequent upon the menopause, the problem of the perpetration of the species in the case of females impregnated by delinquent rape, that distressing man-ner of delivery called by the Brandenburghers *Sturzgeburt*, the recorded instances of multiseminal, twikindled and monstrous births conceived during the catamenic period or of consanguineous parents—in a word

all the cases of human nativity which Aristotle has classified in his masterpiece with chromolithographic illustrations. (*U* 14.955–77)

No doubt, a number of the scenarios in this passage from "Oxen" are cases
lifted out of contemporary medical debates. The reference to anesthesia and
its use in midwifery cases is the most obvious example.[7] Nevertheless, some of
the students' concerns regarding "the most popular beliefs on the stage of pregnancy such as the forbidding to a gravid woman to step over a countrystile" (*U*
14.978–80) and the "explanation of those swineheaded (the case of Madame
Grissel Steevens was not forgotten) or doghaired infants occasionally born"
(*U* 14.986–88),[8] have a more folkloristic orientation. Indeed, the passages cited
above provide a striking example of how contemporary medical debates about
sepsis are infiltrated by more populist and superstitious belief systems.[9] Hence
Andrew Gibson's claim that "the students' modernity is most evident in the
various discussions of modern medical issues" is very puzzling (Gibson 2002,
168). Their assumed unfaltering scientific outlook is clouded by repeated references to popular medical lore. The medical discussion in the National Maternity Hospital is clearly a concoction of ancient and current medical wisdom.
Scientific expertise and superstitiousness are equally well represented in the
students' discussion that forms a curious blend of conflicting medical philosophies.

However, medicine's scientific, progressive, and modern self-image is, in
this passage from "Oxen," most effectively subverted by the students' allusion
to *Aristotle's Master-Piece*, the "best-selling guide to pregnancy and childbirth
in the eighteenth century" (Fissell 2003, 43). Roy Porter has written compre-
hensively on the publishing and reception history of this popular pronuptual-
ist and pronatalist advice manual. Although it first appeared in 1684, Porter
identifies at least four different versions with distinctively divergent contents,
published between the end of the seventeenth century and the middle of the
nineteenth century (Porter 1987, 2). But while these editions differed slightly
in content, they all made biological reproduction and its potential obstacles
their primary concern, "tackling hindrances to conception and overcoming
the spectre of sterility" while elaborating on "the most terrifying outcomes of
reproduction" such as "Siamese twins" or "black, hairy, or Simian infants" (7,
10, 11). The *Master-Piece's* instructive remarks were accompanied by dramatic
illustrations of the kinds of "monstrous births" mentioned in "Oxen."[10]

Of course, the *Master-Piece* makes several noteworthy appearances in *Ulysses*, first in the "Wandering Rocks" episode, where Leopold Bloom "turned
over idly pages of *The Awful Disclosures of Maria Monk*, then of Aristotle's

Masterpiece" (*U* 10.584–85). Molly, too, reflects on this particular manual and its "rotten pictures children with two heads and no legs" (*U* 18.1241) and rechristens its author "Aristocrat" (*U* 18.1240) instead of "Aristotle." In both cases, a reference to "Oxen" is added to the consideration of the *Master-Piece*. Bloom instantly thinks of Mrs. Purefoy (*U* 10.590) when flicking through its pages and Molly amusingly transports some of the advice manual's sexual lore into her remark: "when I wouldnt let him lick me in Holles street one night" (*U* 18.1245). Although the *Master-Piece* certainly does not contain advice on how to perform cunnilingus, Molly associates the medical advice book with the National Maternity Hospital and thinks of the Blooms' sexual practices during their residency in Holles Street. These textual crossings suggest that the *Master-Piece*'s import for Joyce's novel becomes most apparent with its strangely anachronistic appearance in "Oxen."

At this point in the text the allusion to *Aristotle's Master-Piece* might well signal Joyce's attempt to correlate literary style with historical context. After all, the episode's section that mentions the *Master-Piece* parodies the literary style of the eighteenth-century philosophical historian Edward Gibbon. A reference to an eighteenth-century medical manual is therefore very appropriate. Nevertheless, Joyce's decision to introduce this specific eighteenth-century pseudomedical text remains an oddity, especially because Udo Benzenhöfer has identified Giulio Valenti's 1893 *Lezioni Elementari di Embriologia applicata alle Scienze Mediche*, particularly its passages on the history of embryology, as the most likely source for some of the obstetrical monstrosities and curiosities paraded in "Oxen" (Benzenhöfer 1989, 608–11). Consequently, Joyce, by using the *Master-Piece* as the students' medical reference text, openly questions their professional agenda. As Stephen E. Soud concisely suggests, by "undermining the discourse of the medical students, whom we presume to be among the most educated of Dublin . . . with the callous talk of monstrous births and the bygone trivia of medical history, Joyce evinces a profound skepticism about the possibilities of medical science" (Soud 1995, 198).

Additionally, the puzzling reference to *Aristotle's Master-Piece* in "Oxen" provides interesting insights into medicine's crucial cooperation in delivering the episode's intertextual practices and interplays. Although the *Master-Piece* was certainly outdated in the spring of 1920 when Joyce was writing the "Oxen" episode, this specific text makes a conspicuous appearance in a particular eighteenth-century literary text: Laurence Sterne's *The Life and Opinions of Tristram Shandy, Gentleman*, written at the time when this pseudomedical manual enjoyed great popularity. It is therefore Joyce's salient assimilation of

Aristotle's Master-Piece that first hints at the intertextual relationship between
"Oxen" and *Tristram Shandy*.

On closer scrutiny the similarities between "Oxen" and *Tristram Shandy*
are probably very obvious. The first three volumes of Sterne's book relate, like
"Oxen," the event of a complicated birth. And, as in "Oxen," this important
incident occurs "off-stage" and is represented only by Mrs. Shandy's occasional groans and, as Tristram suggests, sporadic "trampling over head near my
mother's bed side" (Sterne 1998, 133). In analogy to Joyce's "Oxen," the digres-
sive narrative of *Tristram Shandy* focuses, among many other things, on the
debate surrounding the "[i]mprovements . . . made of late years in all branches
of obstetrical knowledge, but particularly in that one single point of the safe
and expeditious extraction of the *foetus*" (115), which takes place among Walter
Shandy, Uncle Toby, and Dr. Slop, the male accoucheur. The beneficial effect of
the Caesarean section on the fetus's sensorium is discussed, the podalic version
considered—the child being "extracted by the feet" (120)—until Dr. Slop seizes
the moment and demonstrates the workings of "his new-invented *forceps*" on
Uncle Toby's hand, tearing "every bit of the skin" and crushing the "knuckles
into the bargain with them, to a jelly" (147–48). This instrument that Dr. Slop
maintains "to be the safest instrument of deliverance" (122) eventually delivers
Tristram and brings Mrs. Shandy's labor to an end.

"Oxen" replicates many aspects of its *Shandean* precursor.[11] Bloom, for instance, contemplates "Punch" Costello, who "seemed to him a cropeared creature of a misshapen gibbosity, born out of wedlock and thrust like a crookback
toothed and feet first into the world, which the dint of the surgeon's pliers in his
skull lent indeed a colour to" (*U* 14.854–57). Without doubt, Bloom's confused
understanding of childbirth—the podalic version would, of course, make the
intervention of the "surgeon's pliers" redundant—reinforces the episode's suggested intertextual relationship to Sterne's novel. Before the eponymous hero is
clumsily extracted with the help of Dr. Slop's forceps, an event which also leaves
conspicuous traces on Tristram's face, his father, a fanatical believer in the "topsy-turvy" version (Sterne 1998, 120), encourages Dr. Slop to "begin that way"
(148). Unfortunately for Tristram, Dr. Slop's attempt to perform the podalic
version comes too late. "Tristram's head is too large for the opening" and he
"*must* be delivered by the forceps or by the *tire tête*," a commonly used and for
the fetus lethal device, which destroys the child's head during the delivery process.[12] In "Lestrygonians" Leopold Bloom suspects that similar circumstances
complicate Mina Purefoy's labor and, in analogy to the *Shandean* original, suggests that the use of the forceps might be useful: "Three days imagine groaning

on a bed with a vinegared handkerchief round her forehead, her belly swollen out. Phew! Dreadful simply! Child's head too big: forceps" (*U* 8.373–74).

But the two texts' connection is best illustrated by the respective references to *Aristotle's Master-Piece*. In *Tristram Shandy* the conspicuous allusion occurs shortly before Dr. Slop enters Shandy Hall: "It is said in *Aristotle's Master-Piece*, 'That when a man doth think of any thing which is past,—he looketh down upon the ground;—but when he thinketh of something which is to come, he looketh up towards the heavens'" (Sterne 1998, 82). Interestingly, the passage does not mention obstetrical practices at all, and is, moreover, a misquotation, the borrowed words coming not from *Aristotle's Master-Piece* but from a book called *Aristotle's Book of Problems*, another popular eighteenth-century reference guide.[13] The *Master-Piece*'s value as obstetrical advice manual is therefore, once more, as in Joyce's "Oxen," undermined. Additionally, Sterne's readers receive a first warning about the potential inaccuracy or infidelity of the *Shandean* narrator's referencing—we will come back to this aspect of the Sternean text.

More important, in *Tristram Shandy* the textual proximity of the *Master-Piece* and Dr. Slop's first entrance suggests the medical manual's relevance to the novel's developing debate on midwifery. That *Tristram Shandy* represents a contentious eighteenth-century debate on obstetrical professionalism has been well-documented (Landry and Maclean 1990, 522–43). Whereas midwifery had essentially been a female vocation, the sixteenth-century invention of the forceps by William Chamberlen produced, in the eighteenth century, the man-midwife or accoucheur, invading the professional space of the traditional female midwife, who built her reputation less on scientific expertise than on experience and ancient wisdom, represented by reference manuals such as *Aristotle's Master-Piece*. In *Tristram Shandy* the short allusion to the *Master-Piece* suggests the midwife's presence shortly before Dr. Slop and his forceps invade the text to take over the task of delivering the infant.[14] And the apparent proximity of the *Master-Piece* allusion and Dr. Slop's entrance shows that even the textual space of Sterne's novel has become a heavily contested site where two competing medical practices compete for dominance. Hence Sterne, in representing the current sociotechnological and gendered debate about obstetric activity, the professional rivalry between the traditional midwife, represented by the *Master-Piece*, and the accoucheur, aims, like Joyce's "Oxen," to provide readers with contextual information and a concise review of much-debated contemporary obstetrical affairs.

Moreover, as much as Joyce hinted at the medical students' potential medical lapses, in *Tristram Shandy* Sterne also indicates, in the characterization of Dr. Slop, his reservations about the upcoming male accoucheur's alleged scientific agenda. As Arthur H. Cash has noted, Sterne's absurd and pompous Dr. Slop is a satirical depiction of the eminent York man-midwife Dr. John Burton, the author of several books on midwifery such as the 1751 *Essay towards a Complete New System of Midwifery* and the 1753 *A Letter to William Smellie*. In his *Essay* Burton "recommends a new forceps of his own devising" (Cash 1968, 136). The York man-midwife is therefore a very likely prototype for Sterne's portentous Dr. Slop.

In view of all this, the similarities between Sterne's *Tristram Shandy* and Joyce's "Oxen" are, in terms of content, suggestive enough. Even the notable differences between the two texts, paradoxically, consolidate this comfortable intertextual handholding. Whereas the complications in the Purefoy birth finally result, in the episode's Dickensian passage, in "a happy *accouchement*" (*U* 14.1311), and the "touching scene" (*U* 14.1315) that sees Mina Purefoy reclining "there with the motherlight in her eyes, that longing hunger for baby fingers (a pretty sight it is to see)" (*U* 14.1316–17), Tristram's delivery is by no means as favorable. The "child of wrath! child of decrepitude! interruption! mistake! and discontent!" (Sterne 1998, 236) is "black in the face" and "in a fit" (229), hastily baptized, christened Tristram, and therefore given the name of which his father "had the lowest and most contemptible opinion" (46). The haphazardness and contingency that governs the narrator's birth in *Tristram Shandy* is not imitated by Joyce in "Oxen," where the last "pledge" of the Purefoy "union" (*U* 14.1332–33), "[y]oung hopeful will be christened Mortimer Edward after the influential third cousin of Mr Purefoy in the Treasury Remembrancer's office, Dublin Castle" (*U* 14.1333–36)—a name, unlike Tristram's, confidently indicating the offspring's promising future. Furthermore, if Mortimer Edward Purefoy is indeed partly modeled on Sterne's hero, then he differs in one very significant aspect from his literary forerunner. Whereas Joyce's newborn is adorned with a more than satisfying olfactory organ, "the true Purefoy nose" (*U* 14.1333), fate has, once more, ill-treated poor Tristram. Inelegantly delivered by Dr. Slop's forceps, the "safest instrument of deliverance," Tristram's nose is, as Tristram laments, "squeez'd as flat to my face, as if the destinies had actually spun me without one" (Sterne 1998, 36).

Yet in spite of such apparent differences, Joyce's episode unreservedly reproduces textual details from Sterne's original. In addition Joyce also imitates some of Sterne's stylistic and formal innovations. Most notable is his attempt to copy a specifically Sternean device: aposiopesis, the narrative's sudden breaking off at crucial and, for the reader, titillating moments. Unsurprisingly, the Sternean passage in "Oxen," which culminates in the recollection of the erotic babble between Lynch and Kitty about the most effective use of contraceptives, is vigorously interrupted: "But at this point a bell tinkling in the hall cut short a discourse which promised so bravely for the enrichment of our store of knowledge" (*U* 14.797–98). Generally this Joycean attempt to imitate Sterne's elliptic and interruptive prose is traced back to the most erotically charged passages, "The Temptation. Paris" and "The Conquest," in Sterne's *A Sentimental Journey* (Gifford 1989, 427) where Yorick and his conquest, the fair *fille de chambre*, first engage in a mutual cloth alteration contest before Yorick's interventions "unavoidably threw the fair *fille de chambre* off her centre" (Sterne 1994, 79). The textual ellipsis then leaves it up to the reader to imagine the rest of the scene.

Although the correspondence between "Oxen" and this passage from *A Sentimental Journey* is evident in terms of the amorous content, a particular passage from *Tristram Shandy* seems a much more likely source for Joyce's aposiopetic experiment. The particular passage, which announces the arrival of the destructive Dr. Slop only lines after Sterne's text references *Aritstotle's Master-Piece*, catastrophically interrupts Walter Shandy's exquisite explanation of female anatomy developed for the benefit of Uncle Toby, who had previously admitted to his "total ignorance of the sex" (Sterne 1998, 82): "Here a Devil of a rap at the door snapp'd my father's definition (like his tobacco-pipe) in two,— and, at the same time, crushed the head of as notable and curious a dissertation as ever was engendered in the womb of speculation;—it was some months before my father could get an opportunity to be safely deliver'd of it" (Sterne 1998, 83). As in "Oxen," the discussion of the particulars of female physiology is rudely interrupted. Not by a bell but rather "a rap at the door." Also, like Joyce's "Oxen," a chapter replete with phrases such as "a pregnant word" (*U* 14.259) and "[i]n woman's womb word is made flesh" (*U* 14.292), the above-quoted passage uses obstetrical imagery to describe the process of intellectual or creative production or, in this case, sterility, since Walter's dissertation remains "undelivered."

Indeed, this metaphorical exploitation of obstetrical vocabulary is central to the analysis of the two texts' intertextual correspondences. Both texts, Sterne's *Tristram Shandy* and Joyce's "Oxen," correlate concepts of physiological growth with authorial self-creation. Whereas Tristram fails to recap the precise events of his biological birth in his autobiography's first two volumes, the conditions of his thwarted delivery produce the text's volcanic discursiveness and establish the narrator's literary persona. "Oxen" shares its textual precursor's interest in genesis and origins, both in a biological sense and in terms of intellectual self-begetting. In surveying and imitating his literary ancestors' works Joyce gives birth to himself as an author. However, being a text, which so unequivocally accentuates its imitational practices, "Oxen" seems to differ substantially from the *Shandean* original with regard to its understanding of innovation and creativity. "Oxen" openly and unapologetically reproduces. Mark Osteen has suggested that "Joyce wants us to recognize his sources (he named them to his friends)" (Osteen 1995, 230). In a conversation with Eugene Jolas, describing the composition technique of *Finnegans Wake*, Joyce, for example, voluntarily acknowledged Sterne's influence on his work: "I might easily have written this story in a traditional manner. . . . But I, after all, am trying to tell the story of this Chapelizod family in a new way. . . . There is nothing paradoxical about this. . . . Only I am trying to build many planes of narrative with a single esthetic purpose. . . . Did you ever read Laurence Sterne. . . . ?" (Jolas 1948, 11–12).[15] Although he never deliberately identified *Tristram Shandy* as textual blueprint for "Oxen," Joyce openly acknowledged his intellectual debts to Sterne, hinting at the fact that his literary originality was partly based on reproductive principles. In "Oxen" imitation is, paradoxically, Joyce's way to ascertain literary maturity.

Laurence Sterne, by contrast, was never so cooperative and forthcoming when it came to revealing his textual sources. But intriguingly, if Joyce cribbed liberally from Sterne's *Tristram Shandy*, he is in fact only repeating Sterne's specific strategy of intertextual composition. Sterne, whose "*Tristram Shandy* had made itself synonymous with modernity and fashion" and therefore by extension with novelty and originality (Keymer 2000, 1), was, of course, a notorious plagiarist, borrowing freely from such different sources and writers as Robert Burton's 1621 *Anatomy of Melancholy*, John Locke's 1690 *Essay Concerning Human Understanding*, François Rabelais, and Jonathan Swift,[16] a fact that, in 1823, induced Walter Scott to ironically remark that Sterne is "one of the greatest plagiarists, and one of the most original geniuses, whom England has produced" (Howes 1974, 374). Technically, therefore, Sterne's claim to literary originality and authorial self-invention, trumpeted vigorously by *Tristram Shandy*, appears fundamentally flawed. Worse even, the text contains an outspoken condemnation of literary piracy.

Hypocrisy might thus be added to the list of Sterne's literary felonies: "Tell me, ye learned, shall we for ever be adding so much to the *bulk*—so little to the *stock*? Shall we for ever make new books, as apothecaries make new mixtures, by pouring only out of one vessel into another? Are we for ever to be twisting, and untwisting the same rope? for ever in the same track—for ever at the same pace?" (Sterne 1998, 275). Ironically, though, Sterne copied this ferocious attack on plagiarism from another textual source, Robert Burton's *Anatomy of Melancholy*, "once the favoured of the learned and the witty and a source of surreptitious learning" (Ferriar 1798, 56): "As apothecaries, we make new mixtures every day, pour out of one vessel into another; . . . We weave the same web still, twist the same rope again and again" (Burton 1977, 23–24). In stealing this passage from Burton, Sterne lets semantics wrestle with form. The text's forthright attack on literary plagiarism, which is packaged into a passage lifted from another literary text, is effectively challenged by Sterne's own intertextual practices. Moreover, it is worth remembering at this point that Burton's *Anatomy of Melancholy* is itself an assembly of quotations and citations. By verbally usurping another copyist Sterne fundamentally challenges the insistence on authorial self-creation vehemently advocated by his own text. Therefore, what *Tristram Shandy* really seems to satirize and criticize is not literary bootlegging but a philistine insistence on an artistic self-conception, which is unblemished by self-conscious intertextual strategies commonly used in pastiche, sophisticated satire, and light-hearted parody—the literary genres and techniques that were most appealing to Sterne.

Naturally, this Sternean satire on moralistic ideas of authorial self-formation should be read in the context of changing eighteenth-century attitudes toward imitative literary composition practices. Although an epistemological break cannot be associated with one particular event or a specific year, the first English copyright legislation act, the 1710 Statute of Anne, which established unequivocal author-text relationships to combat the problems of literary piracy, and the gradual emergence of a marketplace for mass-produced, printed books are important signposts marking the altered eighteenth-century understanding of plagiarism and originality. Unsurprisingly, notions of literary ownership and property changed drastically when writing and publishing became an economically valuable occupation.[17]

Hand in hand with such economic concerns went a shift in the cultural understanding of hitherto more or less unproblematic conceptions of literary copying, imitation, and plagiarism. The early eighteenth-century neoclassical tradition of learned wit revered the Ancient masters and advocated an artistic theory that tolerated literary craftsmanship based on imitative techniques. Simultaneously, because "the things of the world are simply too few, so it was maintained, for it not to be inevitable that literary works will furnish essentially the same ideas, images and observations" (Baines 2003, 188), the Augustans

associated literary borrowings with other mimetic literary practices that translated phenomenological experiences into referential prose.

By the end of the eighteenth century the situation had changed substantially.
Whereas the Augustans seemed to favor literary "authority rather than originality" (Groom 2003, 78) and accepted plagiarism as an undesirable albeit unavoidable literary practice, the value of imitative art had, by mid century, started to be rigorously questioned. Critical treatises on plagiarism such as Joseph
Wharton's 1756 *Essay on the Writings and Genius of Pope* and Edward Young's
1759 *Conjectures on Original Composition* tried to establish rules concerning
acceptable and deplorable literary borrowings. Naturally, the formation of such
cultural binaries, positioning originality and creativity in opposition to imitation and plagiarism, fundamentally affected both the literary profile and the
critical reception of many eighteenth-century writers such as Alexander Pope
or Jonathan Swift.[18] Swift, for instance, tackled this predicament face-on by
inserting the lines: "To steal a hint was never known, / But what he writ was all
his own" into his 1731 "Verses on the Death of Dr Swift, D.S.P.D" (Swift 1993,
161)—lines borrowed from John Denham's 1667 elegy "On Abraham Cowley
his Death and Burial amongst the Ancient Poets" ("To him no Author was
unknown, / Yet what he wrote was all his own;") (quoted in Terry 2005, 593).
Henceforth, as Richard Terry has argued, "plagiarism, once used to name a
reproachable sub-category of imitation, shifts over to refer to what is reproachable about imitation in general" (Terry 2003, 196). And so, copying, pastiche,
and imitation, established and accepted early eighteenth-century composition
techniques, were heavily contested and stigmatized as plagiaristic by the time
Sterne was writing *Tristram Shandy*.

Understandably, given the changed cultural climate, the revelation that
Sterne's innovative, witty, and above all idiosyncratic novel was, in fact, a mosaic of plagiarized textual sources could only create a critical furor. The following extract from the *Gentleman's Magazine* illustrates some of the spite and
disdain that the late eighteenth century and the Romantics reserved for an
author, whose compositional techniques had been identified as plagiaristic:
"How are the mighty fallen! The works whose fancied originality, in spite of
their lewdness and libertinism, procured them 'an envied place' in the pocket
of every young lady who was able to read them, and in the library of the col-
legiate, are debased to the level of the lowest of all literary larcenies; they are
found to shine with reflected light, to strut in borrowed plumes" (Howes 1974,
313–14). Yet, as the earlier-cited remarks by Walter Scott demonstrate, in spite
of the fact that he had cribbed freely from literary precursors, Sterne's original-

ity and his inimitability of style could hardly be questioned. Paradoxically, he is "one of the greatest plagiarists, and one of the most original geniuses, whom England has produced."

Evidently, concepts of originality and literary innovation are historically conditioned. Sterne's disobedient composition techniques might well have been regarded as detestable criminal acts by his contemporaries and the early critical reception. But by positing *Tristram Shandy* in its resemblance to Joyce's *Ulysses* alternatively as a modernist or even postmodernist text *avant la lettre*, twentieth-century interpretations prefer to understand Sterne's nonconformist writing style as evidence of *Tristram Shandy*'s nature as an unruly and unconventional literary text. Also, as Jonathan Lamb argues, in *Tristram Shandy*, events are frequently textually mediated: "The Shandy family are chiefly concerned to convert literature into action" (Lamb 2002, 146). Mimesis, imitation, and simulation are thus essential aspects of Sterne's development of hyperbolic and self-conscious characters. And while Tristram, Toby, and Walter Shandy are busily copying and reenacting textual scenarios, Sterne's palimpsestic prose participates in this imitative performance, "collating, collecting and compiling,—begging, borrowing, and stealing," like Slawkenbergius, held up by Sterne's text as "a prototype for all writers," "all that had been wrote or wrangled thereupon in the schools and porticos of the learned" (Sterne 1998, 185).

Joyce, who in "Oxen" voluntarily embraces the literary practices condemned by Sterne's late eighteenth-century readers, was certainly familiar with his precursor's notoriety and his reputation as a plagiarist. And, if the early Sterne reception censored literary borrowings and imitation, T. S. Eliot's famous 1920 claim that "[i]mmature poets imitate; mature poets steal; bad poets deface what they take, and good poets make it into something better, or at least something different" (Eliot 1976, 206), illustrates the modernist rediscovery of Augustan writing techniques. In fact, Joyce, in order to consolidate the specific cross-historical connection between the eighteenth and the twentieth centuries, seemed to have drawn on two particularly distinctive Augustan tropes widely used to describe literary lineage and writers' pedigrees. Richard Terry indicates that the English Augustan era extensively used "paternity" and "metempsychosis" as metaphors for describing the "image of biological generation" for writers' succession (Terry 2001, 156–58). As Joyce critics will know very well, both "paternity" and "metempsychosis" are portentous and loaded concepts in *Ulysses*. While Stephen, who is on a mission to find a spiritual father, is, from "Proteus" onward, obsessed with paternity imagery (*U* 3.45–50), Bloom is similarly haunted by the metempsychosis theory all day (*U* 4.339, *U* 13.1118, *U* 14.897, *U* 14.1100, *U* 15.1226, *U* 17.686). In conceptually using these generic eighteenth-century images for literary lineage Joyce's text, once more, feeds on a particularly Sternean context.

Given the palimpsestic nature of the Sternean text, it is not surprising that obstetrical manuals were among the many sources Sterne plundered while writing *Tristram Shandy*. Most notably Sterne exploited the 1753 *Letter to William Smellie, M.D. Containing Critical and Practical Remarks upon his Treatise on the Theory and Practice of Midwifery*, written by Dr. Slop's real life model, the York accoucheur Dr. John Burton. As its title implies, Burton's publication minutely analyzed and, rather unprofessionally, criticized William Smellie's 1752 well-received textbook *A Theory and Practice of Midwifery* (Hawley 1993, 94–97). In *Tristram Shandy*, many passages from Burton's *Letter* reappear. For instance, Walter Shandy, who has "dipp'd into all kinds of books" on midwifery, learns:

> That the lax and pliable state of a child's head in parturition, the bones of the cranium having no sutures at that time, was such,—that by force of the woman's efforts, which, in strong labour-pains, was equal, upon an average, to a weight of 470 pounds avoirdupois acting perpendicularly upon it;—it so happened that, in 49 instances out of 50, the said head was compressed and moulded into the shape of an oblong conical piece of dough, such as a pastry-cook generally rolls up in order to make a pye of.——Good God! cried my father, what havock and destruction must this make in the infinitely fine and tender texture of the cerebellum! . . .
>
> But how great was his apprehension, when he further understood, that this force, acting upon the very vertex of the head, not only injured the brain itself or cerebrum,——but that it necessarily squeez'd and propell'd the cerebrum towards the cerebellum, which was the immediate seat of the understanding. (Sterne 1998, 119–20)

A similar passage can be found in John Burton's 1753 *Letter to William Smellie*:

> When the head is squeezed along with great Force, we find it pressed into a very oblong Form, the longest Axis of which extends from the Face to the Vertex. . . . All these Things shew that the Head is, at this Time, capable of being moulded and pressed into different Shapes. And whoever understands the true Fabric of the Cranium, will find the Os Frontis, and each Os Bregmatis will yield more than the other Bones. For Nature

has made the Occiput the strongest Parts, and consequently it yields the least, by which Contrivance the Cerebellum is guarded from being too much compressed. . . . When, therefore, the Child's Head is so large as not to enter the Pelvis without the greatest Difficulty . . . let the Force of the Mother's Effort, that propells the Child, be ever so strong or weak, the Cerebellum will, in such Proportion, become pressed; because Action and Re-action are, in this Case, equal; whence it follows, that the more the Head is squeezed, or resisted by the Bones of the Pelvis, the more the Brain is forced towards the Cerebellum, and consequently, the Mischiefs abovementioned will ensue. (Burton 1753, 122–23)

Although Sterne heavily embellished Burton's clinical prose the similarities are easily recognizable.

At this point it is vital to recall that the *Shandean* text constantly associates childbirth and obstetrical practice with textual production and especially with articulacy. Whereas, in *Tristram Shandy*, metaphors of creativity and obstetrics persistently intersect, Sterne's imitative composition draws heavily upon scientific debates surrounding biological reproduction while simultaneously probing established notions of originality, imitability, and artistic reproduction. Walter Shandy's undelivered dissertation about female anatomy, for instance, was, as we have seen, "engendered in the womb of speculation." Sterne himself often employed the same metaphors when talking about his efforts of bringing his brainchild into the world: "I am going to ly in of another child of the Shandaick procreation, in town; I hope you wish me a safe delivery"; "I miscarried of my tenth Volume by the violence of a fever . . . I am all this week in Labour pains; & if to Day's Advertiser is to be depended upon shall be safely deliver'd by tuesday" (Curtis 1935, 290 and 294).[19] In light of all this, Sterne's textual appropriations from obstetrical manuals are particularly significant. Suddenly, the well-established metaphorical relationship between obstetrical imagery and literary creativity can be understood in a very literal sense: obstetric manuals effectively assist in giving birth to Sterne's text.

Reminiscent of Sterne, medical imagery in "Oxen," for which Joyce also "dipp'd into all kinds of books" on midwifery, also has an apparent parturient function, bringing forth playful speculations on authorship, artistic originality, and creative indebtedness. Drawing explicitly on and stealing from Sterne's all-inclusive, all-consuming textual model in "Oxen," Joyce seems to suggest that artistic ontology is not defined by authenticity and intellectual independence but by imitation, fakery, and fraudulence.[20] In Joyce, the forging of an artistic identity is based on textual forgeries and verbal reproductions. It is hardly surprising, therefore, that the Linati schema identifies "fraud" as the symbol for "Oxen" and the Gilbert-Gorman plan lists "frauds" as its "crime."

This suggests that Joyce, who consciously built on his literary precursor's intertextual edifice in "Oxen," was well aware that he was adorning himself with borrowed plumes.[21] Occasional references in his texts illustrate that he was, indeed, very alert to potential plagiarism charges. In "Circe," for instance, Bloom is accused of being a plagiarist by both Mr. Philip Beaufoy and Lenehan (*U* 15.822 and 15.1734)[22] and the *Wake* openly alludes to forgery: "what do you think Vulgariano did but study with stolen fruit how cutely to copy all their various styles of signature so as one day to utter an epical forged cheque on the public for his own private profit" (*FW* 181.14–17). Additionally, Shem's un-orthodox writing style, which uses his excrement and body for ink and paper respectively, produces "forged palimpsests" (*FW* 182.2) with "his pelagiarist pen" (*FW* 182.3) and establishes an explicit connection between the creative act and recycling—in this case with the recycling of discarded bodily products. "Oxen," in addition to the episode's obvious pollination by other literary texts, also refers to a particular instance of literary plagiarism. The content of Stephen's telegram, "—*The sentimentalist is he who would enjoy without incurring the immense debtorship for a thing done.* Signed: Dedalus" (*U* 9.550–51), sent to Buck Mulligan and quoted in "Scylla and Charybdis," is, as "Oxen" suggests, "[c]ribbed out of Meredith" (*U* 14.1486). That Mulligan explicitly refers to Stephen's signature when reading out the telegram further highlights Stephen's verbal borrowing. The signature here functions like a misapplied copyright notice, given the fact that the note deliberately appropriates somebody else's words.

In addition to such textual borrowings, one other, very distinctive, imitative strategy is probed in "Oxen." In describing his intertextual composition techniques to Frank Budgen, Joyce indicates that the episode's "procession is also linked back at each part subtly with some foregoing episode of the day" (*LI* 140). Not only do textual borrowings in "Oxen" come from other writers, but Joyce also quotes freely from earlier parts of his own novel. Phillip Herring identifies the episode's "recapitulation of previous episodes" as "nothing more than a leitmotiv technique" (Herring 1972, 33). Nevertheless, since they add a further layer of citationality, the reoccurrence of textual fragments from earlier chapters of *Ulysses* appears much more significant. Since the intratextual interpolations will be familiar to readers of earlier episodes, they become identifiable as conspicuously Joycean. When Haines's vacant expression "it seems, history is to blame" reappears in "Oxen" (*U* 1.649; *U* 14.1016) to infiltrate the episode's Walpole section, it has more than a purely parodistic purpose.

In inseminating his precursor's writing style with his own prose, Joyce, in a chapter based on literary borrowings and imitation, establishes his own distinctive literary voice by quoting himself. At times, this can lead to confusing and complex scenarios. When "Oxen" reproduces the content of Stephen's telegram, "[c]ribbed out of Meredith," readers unfamiliar with the original will, of course, attribute the saying to Stephen (or Joyce). Because Stephen or Joyce are identified as having produced this particular passage earlier, the Joycean copy in "Oxen" (copy in many ways now) makes, all of a sudden, claims to literary authenticity. The repetition of an earlier *Ulysses* fragment, plagiarized from another writer, appropriates Meredith's right to literary ownership, and effectively confuses unambiguous notions of textual origins and artistic genuineness. Whose progeny is it? Joyce, it seems, truly turns things "topsy-turvy." The result, "Oxen," is a script reminiscent of the "monstrous births . . . which Aristotle has classified in his masterpiece" (*U* 14.974–76). Whereas eighteenth-century medical folklore advised parents on reproduction technique so as to avoid generating grotesque biological offspring, "Oxen," Joyce's formalistic curiosity, which is based on reproductive art, presents itself like a textual version of those dreaded monster children.

Moreover, in dismantling an artistic theory based on personal integrity and authenticity, "Oxen" recycles numerous expressions familiar to readers of "Scylla and Charybdis": *"that life ran very high in those days"* / "for life ran very high in those days" (*U* 9.733, *U* 14.359–60), "lecturer on French letters" / "professor of French letters" (*U* 9.1101, *U* 14.363), "his Secondbest Bed" / "the secondbest bed" (*U* 9.698–99, *U* 14.366), Mulligan's "chinless Chinamen" (*U* 9.1129, *U* 14.963) and, of course, the already mentioned content of Stephen's telegram (*U* 14.1030–31). And given the fact that it actually shows Stephen Dedalus, Joyce's artist figure, at work, "Scylla and Charybdis" is extremely significant for discussing Joyce's understanding of artistic formation—especially because Stephen, in trying to be "original" in order to sell his Shakespeare theory to Eglinton for "a guinea" (*U* 9.1085), copies, imitates, and recycles and therefore confirms the Joycean insistence on artistic phoniness.[23] Unsurprisingly, John Eglinton calls Stephen "a delusion" (*U* 9.1064) and Stephen, when asked if he believes his own theory, answers in the negative. But if Stephen's theory is a fake, it is meant to be one. Sterne, as we have seen, playfully undermined his text's condemnation of literary imitation by copying a specific passage out of Burton. Joyce, in analogy to Sterne, juxtaposes the Shakespeare theory's formal and semantic import. At first glance, Stephen's account of Shakespeare's creative labor suggests a biographical reading of his plays: "the player is Shakespeare who has studied *Hamlet* all the years of his life which were not vanity in order to play the part of the spectre" (*U* 9.166–68). Intriguingly though, Stephen produces his own verbal creation, the Shakespeare theory, by excessively quoting from Shakespeare's plays and other textual sources. The straightforward author-based analysis of Shakespeare is therefore instantly undermined by the fact that Stephen's own artistic creation is based on textual reproduction.[24] And so, while Stephen advocates a contextual approach to Shakespeare, "[l]ocal colour. Work in all you know" (*U* 9.158), his own words, an assembly of literary borrowings, contradict the theory's new-historicist tenor. If this example suggests that for Joyce literary texts are not exclusively historically conditioned, as Stephen would have us believe in "Scylla and Charybdis," it is precisely their dependence on and reproduction of other, earlier verbal sources that interrupts readings resolutely rooting them in a particular contextual setting.

"Oxen," in a bold imitation of Stephen's plagiaristic Shakespeare theory, suggests similar approaches to textual genesis. In self-consciously reproducing the works of his precursors, Joyce's episode stages the double-bind of artistic originality. Etymologically "origin" and "originality" go back to the Latin *origin-, origo*, meaning ancestry, coming into being, beginning, that from which something is derived, source (OED). Interestingly, as Ian Watt notes, it is in the eighteenth century that the meaning of the term "original" changed fundamentally. Whereas "original" "in the Middle Ages had meant 'having existed from the first,'" it now "came to mean 'underived, independent, first-hand'" (Watt 1974, 14). And, as Nick Groom pointedly argues, plagiarism "[i]s the perversion of theories of origin: it is a narrative of discovery that seeks to disguise its origins and present itself without precedent. In a sense, plagiarism is an absolute veneration of the point of origin . . . But in its attentions seeks to obliterate its origins entirely by moving them forward to the here and now" (Groom 2002, 25). By making imitation a characteristic literary practice, Sterne and Joyce both emphasize, but also confuse, the relationship between the two interrelated concepts, "origin" and "originality." This is especially evident in Laurence Sterne's case, who, in spite of self-consciously commenting on his plagiaristic tendencies, kept his readers in the dark about his many textual sources.

Joyce, one could argue, made his intertextual borrowings extremely recognizable by identifying them for Frank Budgen. Because he willingly identifies his sources, his case is therefore very different from Sterne's. In openly leaning on his literary precursors and allowing them to pollinate the textual space of his novel, Joyce demonstrates a surprising and very atypical deference. However, this deference is only superficial. In "Oxen" the stylistic achievements of Joyce's predecessors are used to underscore Joyce's own, albeit unorthodox, literary triumph: in turning imitation into his artistic paradigm, Joyce produces "Oxen," a stylistic rebel, inimitable precisely because it refuses to believe in the idea of original sources and textual beginnings that could be used as models for counterfeiting and copying. Imitation itself has been transformed into artistic inventiveness. In "Oxen" originality, authenticity, and reproduction cease to be distinctive paradigms.

As an immediate consequence, "Oxen" even more than Sterne's *Tristram Shandy*, fogs unequivocal understandings of literary reproduction and artistic ingenuity. Although the episode employs the image of embryonic development, mimics the evolution of English literature, and seems to emphasize sequence, growth, and progression, the intertextual borrowings, linked to biological reproduction processes, crucially challenge straight-lined conceptions of artistic formation, creative genesis, and literary lineage. Whereas a chronological model of English literary history would insist on unequivocal understandings of linguistic and literary sources and starting points, Joyce's imitative writing practice, modeled directly on Sterne's, undercuts theories that aim to identify precise verbal and textual origins. And medicine, in providing the obstetrical imagery necessary for reading the episode's intertextual practices, assists in bringing forth Joyce's playful assault on clear-cut notions of authorship and its twisted relationship to stylistic innovation and verbal imitation. In "Oxen" medicine delivers the metaphors for Joyce's reproductive art.

5

"Nerves Overstrung"

Neuroscience and Ergography in "Eumaeus"

If Joyce relied heavily on medical symbolism in the colossally intricate "Oxen of the Sun" chapter, the relatively unpretentious-looking "Eumaeus" episode— written "fairly quickly during the several months needed for the typing of 'Circe'" (Groden 1977, 53) and completed in the early months of 1921 (*LIII* 38)—shows that Joyce's *Ulysses* continues to rely on medical debates, contexts, and metaphors. This time, however, it seems as if Joyce's interest in medicine was driven by decidedly personal circumstances. While "Eumaeus" is interested in everything concerning the brain and the human nervous system, Joyce's correspondence is interspersed with references to his "exasperated state of . . . nerves" and his "frightful attacks of neuralgia" (*LI* 159, 162). As the following extract from a letter to Harriet Shaw Weaver illustrates, writing *Ulysses*, fighting battles with his publishers, and coping with his never-ceasing financial difficulties definitely put a strain on Joyce's nerves: "Dear Miss Weaver: Kindly excuse me for my delay in answering your letter. I have been ill lately. I have had three or four collapses which I feared were due to syncope but the doctor says I am not a cardiac subject and that the collapse is due to nervous breakdown. Today I feel better" (*LI* 97).[1] "Eumaeus," with its references to contemporary neuroscientific and neurological debates, reads therefore almost like Joyce's own medical case story. Yet, it is vital to remember that the exhaustive attention that Joyce paid to his nervous state was more than a personal obsession.

At the turn of the century, the relatively young discipline of neurophysiology had revolutionized the perception of physiological and psychological ailments. Like its equally groundbreaking sister discipline, radiology, neuroscience, relying on a new silver-chromate staining technique developed by Camillo Golgi in 1873, literally turned the subject inside out and made the individual's innermost and intimate physiological mechanisms the object of medical scrutiny. How revolutionary Golgi's new silver-chrome staining technique was can be seen in the following description provided by the Spanish neuroscientist Santiago Ramón y Cajal, who comments ecstatically on the Golgi technique, which makes the detailed organization of nerves visible under the microscope: "What an unexpected sight! Sparse, smooth and thin black filaments, or thorny, thick, triangular, stellate, or fusiform black cells could be seen against a perfectly translucent yellow background. One might almost liken the images to Chinese ink drawings on transparent Japanese paper" (Ramón y Cajal 1995, 1: 26). Advanced microscopic techniques further provided precise and detailed images of the nervous system, which eventually helped to emphasize the mechanistic elements in human physiology and psychology: "the varying electrical conditions of nerves seem at first sight to justify the popular illustration, which likens the brain to a galvanic battery and the nerves to telegraph wires" (Gasquet 1880, 373).[2]

With this new scientific and mechanistic understanding of the human individual came the widespread fear that the organism might easily break down. For not only did the images of the microscopically revealed nervous system with its neurons, axons (single fibers conducting impulses away from the cell body), and dendrites (multiple fibers on a cell body receiving information from axons of other neurons) underline the complexity of its organization, they also suggested its vulnerability (figure 2). Neuroscientific research demonstrated that things could easily go wrong; that nerve impulses could be misdirected and cause havoc in the human organism. And that this was by no means a small concern can be seen by the variety of references to neuroscientific debates in the nineteenth-century print media. Articles about neurophysiology and the brain could be read regularly in journals and newspapers varying from Charles Dickens's *Household Words* to the London-based magazine *Belgravia*. These informative pieces kept the readership updated about the most recent neurophysiological discoveries and potential health implications.[3]

Concurrently, patent medicine companies took advantage of the newly developed mechanistic understanding of the human nervous system and advertized gadgets such as electrophatic girdles and electric belts as promising remedies for pathological nervous conditions (figure 3). Understanding and thinking of the nervous system figuratively as a worn-out battery in need of recharging, these advertisements advocated electricity as a cure for damaged nerves. The omnipresence of such advertisements, insisting that the turn-of-the-century readership must look after the state of its nerves, suggests that Joyce, in spite of his hypochondriac tendencies, was no exception in paying minute attention to the complexities of his health and his nervous system in particular.

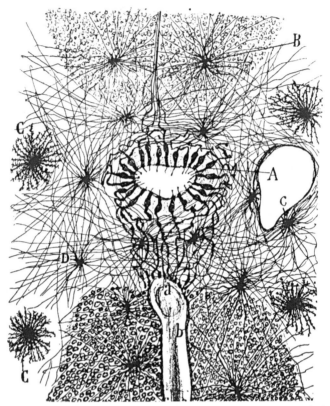

FIG. 107. Glial cells in the central gray and neighboring parts of the white matter; spinal cord of an 8-day-old human infant. Golgi method.

A, ependymal cells; *B*, glial cells of the white matter; *C*, glial cells with short processes; *b*, terminal swellings of glial fibers.

Figure 2. "Spinal Cord of an 8-Day-Old Infant." An image from Santiago Ramón y Cajal. 1995. *Histology of the Nervous System of Man and Vertebrates.* Trans. Neely Swanson and Larry W. Swanson, 1: 250. 2 vols. New York: Oxford University Press. By permission of Oxford University Press, Inc.

Although it was hailed by such critics as T. S. Eliot as an experimental epic masterpiece, many of Joyce's contemporaries might have associated the density of his *Ulysses* with that of the microscopically exposed nervous system. Indeed, it could be argued that Joyce's literary experimentation and neurophysiology as an academic science are equally significant manifestations of modernity. With the allocated organ "nerves" (in the Linati schema), the "Eumaeus" episode develops this associative relationship between Joyce's *Ulysses* and contemporary neuroscience by reproducing vocabulary relating to thought processes, brain activity, and neuroscientific manifestations: "Stephen thought to think of

Figure 3. "Advert for Pulvermacher Electric Belt." An image from *Pearson's Weekly*. 1905. Special Nelson Centenary Edition. 118: 20 (October): n.p.

Ibsen" (*U* 16.52); "[h]e began to remember" (*U* 16.106–7); "picking your brains" (*U* 16.298–99); "the intelligence, the brainpower as such" (*U* 16.749); "it has been explained by competent men as the convolutions of the grey matter" (*U* 16.751–52).[4]

In the schema for *Ulysses* that Stuart Gilbert published in his *James Joyce's Ulysses*, Joyce also seemed to have allocated "navigation" as the episode's "art" (Gilbert 1955, 30), suggesting therefore that the episode, while corresponding to the nervous system, also replicates the processes taking place in nerve circuits. After the raucous interlude in Bella Cohen's brothel, Bloom and Stephen indeed navigate their way, as Joyce would later call it in *Finnegans Wake*, through "Dublire, per Neuropaths" (*FW* 488.26) from Dublin's red-light district, "Monto," to the cabman's shelter near the Custom House by the river Liffey. Additionally, the "Eumaeus" episode investigates the importance of "connections" in every possible sense: domestic, interpersonal, and genealogical, but also nautical and logistic. The "redbearded sailor" (*U* 16.367) in the cabman's shelter has "circumnavigated a bit" (*U* 16.458–59), claiming to have been in the Red Sea, China, North, and South America. John Corley, whom Stephen and Bloom meet on their way, is "connected through the mother in some way" (*U* 16.151–52) to the "lords Talbots de Malahide" (*U* 16.136–37). And, as John Gordon further notes: "Of the eight occurrences of 'connection' in *Ulysses*, four are in 'Eumaeus': Bloom re-acts to one of sailor Murphy's stories by wondering 'what possible connection' (*U* 16.386) it could have to something else, assures himself that there could be 'no possible connection' (*U* 16.1272) between one letter in the newspaper and another, considers an adulterous wife's promise to 'sever the connection' (*U* 16.1539), and advises Stephen to 'sever his connection' with Mulligan (*U* 16.1868–69)" (Gordon 2004, 218–19). However, these "Eumaean" connections are very often interrupted, problematic, or insufficiently developed.

Like the scene at the "Great Northern railway station, the starting point for Belfast, where of course all traffic was suspended at that late hour" (*U* 16.46–47), "Eumaeus" demonstrates what effects a tired and exhausted brain can have on communication and on connecting intellectually with the environment. It seems as if brain functions are in disorder in "Eumaeus" and the episode presents the logical consequences; misdirected dialogue, misunderstandings, and the breakdown of verbal communication:

> —Sounds are impostures, Stephen said after a pause of some little time, like names. Cicero, Podmore. Napoleon, Mr Goodbody. Jesus, Mr Doyle. Shakespeares were as common as Murphies. What's in a name?
> —Yes, to be sure, Mr Bloom unaffectedly concurred. Of course. Our name was changed too, he added, pushing the socalled roll across. (*U* 16.362–66)

The more intellectual of the two, Stephen, is, as always, interested in a theoretical problem. Bloom, on the other hand, cannot follow Stephen's abstract analysis. Yet as the repeated references to his father's name change in *Ulysses* illustrate, Leopold Bloom is well aware of the overpowering influence of a foreign-sounding name.[5] Bloom and Stephen talk at cross-purposes. As John Gordon notes, in "Eumaeus" we hear "of all kinds of mistakings, misfirings, and missed connections, of people missing one another's point or not seeing eye to eye or failing to see the connection or being out of their depth" (Gordon 2004, 215). Whereas Bloom is practically sober, Stephen is tired and his thoughts are fogged up with alcohol: "Needless to say the fumes of his recent orgy spoke then with some asperity in a curious bitter way foreign to his sober state" (*U* 16.1175–77); "Stephen had to make a superhuman effort of memory to try and concentrate" (*U* 16.754–55) not to sink into the "arms of Morpheus" (*U* 16.947–48). Intellectually, Bloom and Stephen clink together. Their conversation is dragging on. It is jerky and misses its target.

A similar observation can be made for the episode's language. Whereas Stephen in "Scylla and Charybdis" aims to use precise and clear-cut expressions, his "dagger definitions" (U 9.84), the Eumaean prose is "unsteady."[6] Indeed, "Eumaeus" is commonly seen as the "stylistic black sheep of *Ulysses*" (Lamos 1999, 242). It is an episode where "clichés encircle each other in uneasy mutual orbits" (Osteen 1995, 359). As Fritz Senn notes, "[n]owhere else are there so many rumours, pretenses, distortions, questionable origins and dubious identifications. The syntax takes part in all of these efforts; they often take the form of belletristic ambitions. High aspirations result in rhetorical fumbles" (Senn 1995, 177). Joyce himself called the prose "relaxed" (Ellmann 1984, 151). The Eumaean-style embarrassments, in imitating the disrupted functions of defective neurotransmission, could therefore simply be the result of mental fatigue.

This reading of the tired-out Eumaean prose is, in many ways, very convincing. "Eumaeus" is indeed anticlimatic and has a sobering and tiring effect on the reader. After the stylistically extravagant "Circe," the language in "Eumaeus" reverts to a conventionally looking narrative: "Preparatory to anything else Mr Bloom brushed off the greater bulk of the shavings and handed Stephen the hat and ashplant and bucked him up generally in orthodox Samaritan fashion which he very badly needed" (*U* 16.1–3). No doubt, the recourse to such a disenchanted and prosaic narrative style in "Eumaeus" thwarts readers' expectations. After all, it is in "Eumaeus" that Stephen and Bloom have their first proper "*tête-à-tête*" (*U* 16.354)—a moment long anticipated by the reader who might expect that the episode's prose should reflect the distinctiveness of the moment. Presenting the meeting between Bloom and Stephen in worn-out, cliché-ridden language, the episode instead questions the significance of the long-expected encounter between the novel's two protagonists.

Critics such as John Gordon and Karen Lawrence have defended the episode's anticlimatic effect by commenting on its mimetic attempts. Karen Lawrence argues that "the language of 'Eumaeus' is enervated . . . not merely to reflect the fatigue of the characters or a narrator but to reveal that language is tired and 'old,' used and reused so many times that it runs in grooves" (Lawrence 1981, 168), whereas John Gordon proposes that "the principals are tired, their brains fagged out, and the prose reflects it by repeatedly reenacting the process of unfocused or misfired movement" (Gordon 2004, 215).[7] Both critics suggest that the prose mimics the mental state of its protagonists whose nervous systems received excessive stimulation in "Circe," the brothel episode, and who are now worn out and tired. Joyce himself humorously acknowledged this, stating that "[t]he nerves of my head are in such a bad way that I think Circe must be revenging herself for the unpleasant things I have written about her legend" (*LI* 150).

Persuasive as it sounds, I would like to complicate this straightforward referential reading of "Eumaeus." Instead of solely emphasizing the episode's mimetic elements, I want to use its medical allusions and its reliance on neuroscientific intertexts in order to foreground the modernist stylistic extravagances in "Eumaeus." At this point it is worth remembering that our understanding of the word "nervous" is a relatively recent and modern one. We have seen that the above-mentioned turn-of-the-century patent medicine advertisements firmly connected "nervous" mental disorders with weakened nerves and recommended the recharging of the nervous system with electricity. But the etymological derivation of the word "nerves" and "nervous" suggests a much more multifaceted understanding of the mental ailment—nervousness—that excessively occupied the turn-of-the-century public. While in classical Latin the term *nervus*, according to the OED, stands for "nerve, sinew, tendon, penis, plant fibre, animal tendon or bowstring," it also signifies strength, vigor, or energy. The word "nervous," too, indicates, again in classical Latin, a person who is sinewy, has tough fibres or is vigorous. Furthermore, as the OED states, *nervosus* also refers to a literary style that is decidedly energetic.

I would like to believe that Joyce knew about the multiple meanings of the words "nerve" and "nervous" and thought about them when writing "Eumaeus." Although Stephen experiences Bloom's arm as "sinewless and wobbly and all that" (*U* 16.1724), this chapter will show that the allegedly "fagged out" (*U* 16.189) Eumaean prose is not necessarily sinewless and lacking in vigor or energy. Instead "Eumaeus" can also be seen as a script full of nervous energy. We should remember here that it is only Stephen and maybe the redbearded sailor, who are tired and feel worn-out ("—I'm tired of all them rocks in the sea, he said, and boats and ships. Salt junk all the time. Tired seemingly, he ceased" [*U* 16.622–24]). Bloom, by contrast, is, as the texts suggests, alert and very perceptive: "[a]ll kinds of Utopian plans were flashing through his (B's) busy brain" (*U* 16.1652). Consequently, we can equally well suggest that the Eumaean prose is as awake and alert as Leopold Bloom—distinguished by a literary style as energetic as the classical root of the word "nervous" indicates.

The following double-reading of "Eumaeus" takes both possible and conflicting readings of the episode as referential or self-consciously modernist into consideration. Although tiredness is certainly an important topic in "Eumaeus," it is not the exclusive aim of Joyce's episode to replicate Stephen's mental exhaustion by ways of its referential prose. Instead "Eumaeus" continues the Circean study of nervous overexcitation. And while the two receptors, tired Stephen and busy Bloom, clash and collide, Joyce, in writing this seemingly dull and unexciting episode, furtively tests the text's interaction with another principal interlocutor: the Eumaean reader.

So while Joyce's own nerves might have been in a sad or frightful state when he was writing "Eumaeus," this episode underscores, once again, the importance of medical metaphors in *Ulysses*. And once again, the "Eumaean" case illustrates that Joyce's stance toward medicine is, in *Ulysses*, less critical than in *Dubliners* or *A Portrait*. The topic of nervous energy was clearly one very close to Joyce's heart (or nerves). This might be one reason why medical symbolism is more willingly assimilated in "Eumaeus" than in Joyce's earlier works, where the pathologization of "drunken" or "sexually degenerate" individuals is critically interrogated. But it is worth remembering that neuroscience, as a new empirical science, also offered Joyce and his contemporaries a more tangible alternative to reading the human mind than the psychological doctoring of "a certain Doctor Jung," "the Swiss Tweedle-dum" or "the Viennese Tweedledee, Dr Freud" (*LI* 166). Critics are only just beginning to realize the full extent to which modernist writers were indebted to neuroscientific theories about the human mind and the nervous system.[8] However, as the example of Joyce's "Eumaeus" will show, alongside such already well-documented modernist narratives as Freudian psychoanalysis, Bergsonian philosophy, or Einsteinian relativity theory, neuroscience—this important twentieth-century medical debate—had equally strong resonances in the modernist literary canon.

.

As we have seen, through the occasional references to the brain and the nervous system, "Eumaeus" suggests a connection to turn-of-the-century neuroscientific debates. But what exactly are the physiological processes that the episode replicates? Microscopic evidence had clearly suggested that the nervous system was a highly complicated and complexly organized arrangement of nerve cells, of pathways and passages, that suggested an equally complex system of interneuronal communication. By the time Joyce was writing the "Eumaeus" section, neuroscience had unraveled many of the complexities of the nervous system so that a 1922 article in *The Times* could confidently argue that "the nervous system [is] the integrator of the scattered organs of the body, the seat of the mechanism which turns a colony or an assemblage of cells and organs into a unit individual" (Anonymous 1922, 9).

However, until the neuron doctrine was introduced in 1888, the question of how exactly nerve impulses were transmitted in the nervous system remained a very pressing one. A promising start had been made when the neuroscientist David Ferrier in his 1876 work on "reflex action" had effectively separated sensory and motor functions in the cerebral cortex, distinguishing between nerves that "carry impressions from the periphery to the cord and brain, and are therefore called *afferent* nerves," and another set which "carry impulses from the brain and cord to the periphery, and are therefore called *efferent* nerves" (Ferrier 1876, 2). An article from the *Dublin Review*, written for a general readership, shows how widely the concept of nerve impulse conduction had, by 1885, taken root in the understanding of neuroscientific processes, especially in regard to the workings of the central and the peripheral nervous system: "There is wanted first a centre (consisting of cells, of course) in which impressions from all the nerves should be received and grouped ready for transmission to the 'reflecting' organ; then there must be a centre—another mass of cells—for the purpose of receiving and subjecting to the process of reflection, in its double sense, these impressions; and finally another centre to receive the single impulse of the will and transmit it with order and precision to the muscles suited to carry out its command" (Sibbald 1885, 382).[9]

A central problem remained unanswered though, one that could for a long time not be solved satisfactorily and one that concerned the interneuronal impulse conduction on a cellular level. Scientists asked questions such as the following: "How did nerve impulses flow from one neuron to the next?" and "How were nerve cells connected?" These were subjects widely discussed in academic circles. Whereas one school favored the reticular theory, "a sort of cellular hand-holding" (Rapport 2005, 29), arguing that "cells were connected by a network of fibres conducting impulses from cell to cell" (Porter 1999, 535), another school challenged this assumption by stating that nerve cells were independent units. Improved microscopic equipment and especially better staining techniques proved to be vital in solving these neurophysiological puzzles.

Above all, it was the work of two scientists that became instrumental in revealing and explaining the microscopic processes of nerve impulse transmission: Charles Scott Sherrington and Santiago Ramón y Cajal.[10] Although Sherrington, professor of physiology at Oxford, coined the neurophysiological term "synapse" as a nexus between neuron and neuron as early as 1897, it was

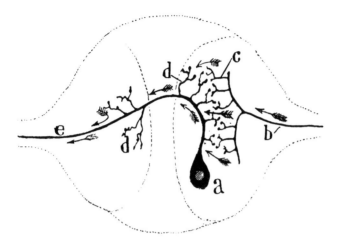

Fɪɢ. 31. Diagram of synapses between a sensory and motor neuron in an earthworm *(Lumbricus agricola)* ganglion.

a, crossed motor neuron; *b,* bifurcating afferent sensory fiber; *c,* collaterals arising from *b; d,* initial processes of the motor axon that function as dendrites, or receptive elements; *e,* crossed motor axon.

Figure 4. "Diagram of Synapses between a Sensory and Motor Neuron." An image from Santiago Ramón y Cajal. 1995. *Histology of the Nervous System of Man and Vertebrates.* Trans. Neely Swanson and Larry W. Swanson, 1: 108. 2 vols. New York: Oxford University Press. By permission of Oxford University Press, Inc.

only in his comprehensive 1906 textbook, *The Integrative Action of the Nervous System,* that the term is discussed explicitly:

If the conductive element of the neurone be fluid, and if at the nexus between neurone and neurone there does not exist actual confluence of the conductive part of one cell with the conductive part of the other, e.g. if there is not actual continuity of physical phase between them, there must be a surface of separation. Even should a membrane visible to the microscope not appear, the mere fact of non-confluence of the one with the other implies the existence of a surface of separation. Such a surface might restrain diffusion, bank up osmotic pressure, restrict the movement of ions, accumulate electric changes, support a double electric layer, alter in shape and surface-tension with changes in difference of potential, alter in difference of potential with changes in surface-tension or in shape, or intervene as a membrane between dilute solutions of electrolytes of different concentration or colloidal suspensions with different signs of charge. (Sherrington 1947, 16)

Sherrington's theory on the nexus between neuron and neuron proved to be correct. But whereas his understanding of the "surface of separation" remained vague and he stated in general terms that "histology on the whole furnishes evidence that a surface of separation does exist between neurone and neurone" (Sherrington 1947, 17), it was the microscopic evidence, provided since 1888 by Santiago Ramón y Cajal, the 1906 Nobel Prize winner, that decisively established the neuron doctrine, the concept of independent, freely branching nerve cells.[11] Based on his extensive experiments with stained nerve tissue, Ramón y Cajal demonstrated that the "terminal ramifications of axons, axon collaterals, and dendrites always end freely" (Ramón y Cajal 1995, 1: 27). He could, therefore, convincingly argue that there "is no continuity between processes, only simple contiguity" (1: 59). What Sherrington had conceived of as a membrane, turned out to be an interneuronal gap (figure 4).

The theory of neuronal independence had far-reaching consequences for the understanding of interneuronal impulse transmission. On the one hand the perplexing fact that information could flow continuously through the nervous system, in spite of innumerable gaps between nerve cells, gave rise to the image of the synapse that conducted impulses "in much the same way that electric current crosses a splice between two wires" (Ramón y Cajal 1995, 1: 78). On the other hand, Ramón y Cajal's research went a step further and demonstrated that the synapse, the "protoplasmatic kiss" as he humorously coined it (1: xxvii), was functionally polarized. That impulses travel "along the axonal ramifications of a neuron, and are only propagated to another cell or cells where the ramifications contact the cell body and/or dendrites of another neuron" (1: 78–79). As Ramón y Cajal suggested, nerve impulses had a specific direction.

The image of the polarized synapse helped considerably to systematize the chaos of the interwoven nerve strands and their functions. Ramón y Cajal suggested that dendrites "receive incoming information and propel the nervous impulse down a single departing axon to stimulate the next cell" (Rapport 2005, 104). The complexity and variability of neuronal communication could now be explained by the need of the dendritic trees to "synapse with a larger number (and richer variety) of axon terminals" (Ramón y Cajal 1995, 1: 83). From now on, synapses were regarded as the gateways of interneuronal communication. They turned the individual nerve cell into a microcosm capable of interacting on countless and complex levels with its environment. The nervous system consists of a network of such infinitesimal, interactive neurons: "If we did not fear to abuse a comparison, we could uphold our conception by saying that the cerebral cortex is similar to a garden filled with trees, the pyramidal cells, which, thanks to an intelligent culture, can multiply their branches, sending their roots deeper and producing more and more varied flowers and fruit" (Ramón y Cajal 1988, 87). But as neuroscientific research implied, the normal and healthy functions of the nervous system could easily be upset with the onset of illnesses such as neurasthenia. One of the most disconcerting influences on nerve cell conduction, however, proved to be fatigue.

As John Gordon has recently demonstrated, the study of fatigue had become, independent of neuroscience, a popular field of inquiry in the second half of the nineteenth century, a time when degeneration theory's pessimistic prognoses suggested cultural and social regression (Gordon 2004, 216 and 293). Weariness and exhaustion were pedantically analyzed and meticulously classified until different analytical categories such as "conscious fatigue, unconscious fatigue, fatigue of sense organs, fatigue of nerves, fatigue of muscles, chemical fatigue, neurasthenic fatigue" could be distinguished (Cason 1935, 338). Coincidentally, the year chosen by Joyce as the one in which the events of *Ulysses* supposedly take place, 1904, had also seen the coining of the term *ergography* as the official designation for the developing science of fatigue (Rabinbach 1992, 138). Explicit in the new term was the reference to the *ergograph*, a machine invented in 1884 as a recorder of fatigue curves by the Turin physiologist Angelo Mosso, who also published the gospel of fatigue studies, the 1891 *La Fatica*. And since his *Scribbledehobble* notebook contains a reference to Angelo Mosso's ergograph, Joyce must have know something about ergography, the scientific study of fatigue (Connolly 1961, 161).

On the cellular level, fatigue became relevant in the analysis of reflex arc conduction. Charles Sherrington had observed in 1906 that normally "nervous integration has the feature of relatively high *speed*" (Sherrington 1947, 3). Effectively, the impulses, transmitted in the vertebrate's nervous system, were associated with velocity and thus with the modern world and its enthralling manifestations. Three years later, in 1909, Filippo Tommaso Marinetti's "Manifesto of Futurism" would explicitly celebrate the speed of airplanes and automobiles as manifestations of "modern life as a dynamically unfolding forcefield of bodies in motion, technologies, and urban space" (Miller 2006, 169). Neurophysiology, in paying specific attention to the velocity with which nerve impulses were conducted, also situated itself on the threshold of modernity. But Sherrington also noticed that reflex arc transmission slowed down when neurons were overstimulated and tired: "a spinal reflex under continuous excitation or frequent repetition becomes weaker, and may cease altogether" (Sherrington 1947, 215). Sherrington proposed the term "refractory phase" for this integrative condition, which allowed conflicting nerve impulses to alternate in the human nervous system. Naturally, it did not take long for turn-of-the-century ergography to make the connection between the neurophysiological processes and the human organism at large; the individual nerve cell turned into a synecdoche for the individual. Whereas the overexcitation of a nerve cell trunk resulted in the decline of intercellular impulse conduction, exhaustion after overstimulation of the nervous system showed noticeable manifestations of fatigue in the human being—a condition traded on determinedly by turn-of-the-century patent medicine campaigners.

Consequently, whereas fatigue was regarded as a positive and essential component in the organization of the nervous system because it regulated the tension between intercurrent reflexes in a nerve path, physical and psychological exhaustion in the human organism was a condition that fatigue experts such as Mosso hoped to cure and abolish. Ironically, fatigue-related illnesses such as neurasthenia were seen both as the product and the rejection of a modern lifestyle (Rabinbach 1992, 153–60). Mental and physical exhaustion were understood as the body's resistance to productivity and labor, the cardinal points of the modern social order. As the French ergonomist Jules Amar succinctly argues in 1920: "Fatigue can be defined as the effect which limits the duration of work" (Amar 1920, 206). While turn-of-the-century culture "subordinated all social activities to production, raising the human project of labor to a universal attribute of nature" (Rabinbach 1992, 4), the human organism took revenge by breaking up. It was, therefore, essential to meticulously study exhaustion and provide precise formulas to guarantee that fatigue could be overcome with the help of modern science.

Unfortunately, science's efforts remained, for the most part, fruitless in Joyce's own medical case. Although he subjected himself voluntarily to the inspections of numerous doctors, his repeated attacks of neuralgia and his nervous breakdowns demonstrated exactly the kind of individual defiance to the impact of modernity that was to be studied and cured by ergographic endeavors. A similar observation can be made for Stephen Dedalus in *Ulysses*. Ergography provides another theoretical framework that can help to explain Stephen's social paralysis. His passive resistance to the contemporary Irish social order takes the form of social fatigue in an ergrahic sense—Stephen refuses to participate in the production of valuable labor. His efforts as a teacher in Mr. Deasy's school are half-hearted at best and, as noted in the previous chapter, the outcome of Stephen's most apparent mental labor, the Shakespeare theory, turns out to be nothing but a "French triangle" (*U* 9.1065). Although Stephen tries to sell it to John Eglinton for "a guinea" (*U* 9.1085), he admits that he does not believe it himself. Therefore he instantly wrecks the potential market value of his labor. Yet, nowhere can we see Stephen's exhaustion better than in the "Eumaeus" episode. Here physical and mental weariness are added to his pathological social fatigue. He is "trying his dead best to yawn if he could, suffering from lassitude generally" (*U* 16.348–49).

Again, the neurophysiological context is worth considering at this point. If we metaphorically adapt the neuron doctrine to the situation of the "Eumaeus" episode and read the individual nerve cell as a synecdoche for the human being as turn-of-the-century ergography suggested, Stephen appears like a single neuron, tired and unresponsive to the stimulation of environmental impulses. Ramón y Cajal had vehemently emphasized the independence of the individual neuron, and "Eumaeus" supports this presumption in presenting Stephen and Bloom as intellectual antipodes. But Stephen also seems to be highly sensitive about his subject boundaries; even the physical contact with Bloom's arm is unpleasant: "—Yes, Stephen said uncertainly because he thought he felt a strange kind of flesh of a different man approach him" (*U* 16.1723–24). Like the free-ending dendrites of nerve cells Stephen allows only physical contiguity, not immediate physical contact.

While Stephen's behavior takes on distinctively pathological tendencies in "Eumaeus," Bloom makes various attempts to render Stephen once more receptive to environmental stimulation. Most important, he sensibly suggests that Stephen "ought to sample something in the shape of solid food, say, a roll of some description" (*U* 16.332–33), parroting thereby the ergographic conception of fatigue and its relationship to productivity and labor: "I'm a stickler for solid food" (*U* 16.811), the "reason being not gormandising in the least but regular meals as the *sine qua non* for any kind of proper work, mental or manual" (*U* 16.812–13). When his well-meant attempts fail, Bloom voices the suspicion that Stephen's companions mischievously tried to poison him: "But it wouldn't occasion me the least surprise to learn that a pinch of tobacco or some narcotic was put in your drink for some ulterior object" (*U* 16.284–86). Bloom might just fire a guess here, but his misgiving introduces "the much vexed question of stimulants" (*U* 16.89–90), a prominent neuropathological debate that analyzed the effects of specific aliments on fatigue-curves and the nervous system.

Joyce's episode is indeed littered with references to so-called stimulants and narcotics. It lists allusions to coffee, "good burgundy" (*U* 16.92), "chaw" (*U* 16.443), "pulpy quid" (*U* 16.468), "coca" (*U* 16.479), "Dr Tibble's Vi-Cocoa" (*U*

16.805–6), and "a cup of Epps's cocoa" (*U* 16.1621). All of these substances were familiar markers in the ergographic topography that categorized coffee, tea, cocoa, alcohol, and tobacco as so-called "nervine aliments" (Amar 1920, 147). Although these substances were thought to have little calorific value for the human organism, nervine aliments could have, when correctly dosed, extremely beneficial effects on the nervous system. Jules Amar, in taking on a Eurocentric, scientific perspective, suggests this when commenting on the tea-consumption habits of foreign populations: "Numerous populations (Russians, Moroccans) make a continual use of strongly sugared tea. According to our own observations, the Moroccan of average condition absorbs, per day, 15 to 20 cups of tea, representing nearly 12 grammes of dried tea and 400 grammes of sugar. His strength and resistance to fatigue are remarkable. Afghans use a substitute for tea called 'catha edullis,' which enables them to make long night marches and increases their muscular strength" (Amar 1920, 218–19).

Whereas stimulants such as tea, coffee, and cocoa were "defined as that which ministers to healthy activities, supporting the processes of life in health and restoring them in disease," a narcotic, on the other hand, was understood to be "a substance which by poisoning the nervous system produces a gradual paralysis of vital actions" such as "intelligence, volition, reason, consciousness, even life itself" (Fox 1885, 924). A very vivid illustration of narcotics' poisonous effect for the human organism can be found in Wilkie Collins's 1868 novel *The Moonstone*, a text that capitalizes on nineteenth-century anxieties about narcotics when one of its protagonists, Franklin Blake, unwillingly steals a precious jewel from his cousin's bedroom while he is under the influence of laudanum.[12]

In ergographic theory alcohol and tobacco, in large quantities, were regarded as having an equally narcotic effect on the organism as laudanum. Although nineteenth-century physiology regarded them per se as stimulating for the nervous system, large doses were believed to have a distinctively toxic effect. A similar case was made for tea. Contrary to Amar's suggestion, the unrestrained consumption of too much tea was believed to poison the human organism. An article published in 1895 in the *Irish Homestead*, for instance, identifies "headache, vertigo, insomnia, palpitation of the heart, mental confusion, nightmares, nausea, hallucinations, morbid depression of spirits, and sometimes . . . suicidal impulses" as some of the symptoms commonly found in "Tea Drunkards" (Anonymous 1895, 174). Like its nosological antagonist "low disease" (Fox 1885, 924)—the insufficient stimulation of the nervous system— the overexcitation of the nerves had to be avoided by all means. It was essential to get the balance right. The human organism required an appropriate amount of intellectual and nervous stimulation. Informing this intricate notion was the firm belief in maintaining a state of mental and nervous equilibrium. In the view of nineteenth-century neurophysiology and neuropathology only an individual who carefully and soberly economized his or her exposure to environmental stimulation deserved to be labeled normal or healthy. Leopold Bloom faithfully reiterates this belief in "Eumaeus": "Intellectual stimulation, as such, was, he felt, from time to time a firstrate tonic for the mind" (*U* 16.1221–22). Unsurprisingly, Bloom is "in complete possession of his faculties" (*U* 16.61–62) and, as the episode's narrator suggests, "disgustingly sober" (*U* 16.62). Stephen, however, has carelessly gambled with the reserves of his nervous system. It has been subjected to too many "chemical insults" (Ramón y Cajal 1995, 1: 183). The amount of alcohol consumed in the Maternity Hospital and the nervous excitation triggered by the visit in Bella Cohen's brothel have effectively poisoned his powers of life and thrown him, neuropathologically speaking, off balance. His "[n]erves" are "overstrung" (*U* 11.699). The result is mental fatigue, exhaustion, and intellectual anesthesia that coincide with a pathological resistance to social interaction. In Stephen's case the emphasis on physical borders becomes decidedly morbid.

Ramón y Cajal, in spite of his passionate argument for the autonomy of the neuron, had indicated that nerve cells are in constant contact and communication with their immediate environment—that there exists a form of interneuronal interdependence. "Eumaeus" represents the collapse of this intercellular exchange. We can therefore think of Stephen and Bloom as independent neurons whose reciprocal impulse conduction is flawed. In accordance with contemporary neurophysiological research "Eumaeus" further suggests that, because of Stephen's pathological exhaustion, the transmission of nervous signals is interrupted at some neurophysiological site between Stephen and Bloom. And it is not surprising to note that in early twentieth-century neurophysiology this site was thought to be the synapse.

Defined by Sherrington as the most distinctive feature of the central nervous system, the synapse provides the many "junctions which belong characteristically to 'gray matter'" (Sherrington 1947, 312). In relation to the decline of reflex arc transmission, Sherrington also suggested that the "seat of fatigue is intraspinal and central more than peripheral and cutaneous; and that it affects the afferent part of the arc inside the spinal cord, probably at the first synapse" (Sherrington 1947, 219). Sherrington was not alone in making the claim that the synapse's working was crucially upset by fatigue. His hypothesis was eagerly supported by the Polish-born Josefa Ioteyko, director of the Institute de Physiologie de Bruxelles (Amar 1920, 210). An article in the *American Journal of Psychology* further shows that this suggestion had become widely accepted in 1935: "It is generally thought that the synapse is more susceptible to fatigue, to anesthetics, and to nicotine than other parts of the nervous system" (Cason 1935, 340–41).

Ramón y Cajal developed Sherrington's insights further and claimed that not just fatigue but all forms of neurological ailments and pathologies could be traced back to synaptic malfunctioning: "One might also imagine that amnesia, a paucity of thought associations, retardation, and dementia could result when synapses between neurons are weakened as a result of more or less pathological conditions, that is when processes atrophy and no longer form contacts, when cortical mnemonics or association areas suffer partial disorganization" (Ramón y Cajal 1995, 2: 726). The synapse, the junction or the nexus that transmits nerve impulses from one neuron to the next, was thus understood as the crucial locus fundamentally affected by fatigue, mental overstimulation, and intoxicants such as alcohol and nicotine. We see all these at work in "Eumaeus." Stephen is tired and drunk whereas Bloom's nervous system seems to have received a substantial amount of stimulation.

In the Eumaean context it is therefore useful to think, neurophysiologically, of defective synaptic functions when considering the relationship between the two receptors, Stephen and Bloom. Their communication is disruptive and dysfunctional as much as nerve impulse conduction is inhibited in a nervous system affected by synaptic malfunctioning. And if the flow of communication between its protagonists is thus interrupted, it is only natural to suggest that the "Eumaeus" episode replicates this breakdown of communication on a textual level. Again the image of the malfunctioning synapse can be helpful here. While the Eumaean linguistic misfirings imitate the mental state of the episode's protagonists, the linguistic parameters clash and collide like nerve impulses gone astray in an overstimulated or worn-out nervous system. If this is the case Joyce's text not only incorporates contemporary neurophysiological debates, but also formally mimics some of the neuroscientific processes described by Ramón y Cajal and Sherrington. The Eumaean text then works like a pathological nervous system with all its defects and deficiencies. However, considering the scientific image of the synapse in this way would mean to underline only the mimetic qualities of the Eumaean prose. If such a reading is pursued, Joyce's episode would simply imitate its protagonists' nervous states. But interestingly, whereas the conduction of nerve impulses between Joyce's protagonists might well be fundamentally inhibited, the "Eumaeus" episode itself establishes new paths of communications with its implied reader.

As I noted above, many Joyce critics have commented on the fact that the Eumaean style appears embarrassingly flawed. On the one hand this could be understood as Joyce's attempt to emphasize that the structural components of syntax and style begin to disintegrate when communication collapses between Stephen and Bloom. On the other hand, however, if the Eumaean style imitates the breakdown of an overstimulated or worn-out nervous system, the prose clearly overshoots the mark so that the reader becomes uncomfortably aware of its many stylistic flaws. It is precisely because of its clichés, the knotted prose, and other formal shortcomings that the writing draws attention to itself. Because the prose is so terribly out of tune, readers cannot help noticing the stylistic artificialities of the text. Ironically, whereas "Eumaeus" formally imitates Stephen's and Bloom's mental condition through its linguistic ineptness, it is precisely this stylistic incompetence that creates a self-conscious script, which, in turn, establishes new synaptic connections between the text and the reader.

Additionally, the Eumaean narrator underlines this surfacing connection to the implied reader by parenthetically clarifying issues. This can be seen in the following passage, which has Bloom contemplate the criminal offences of Skin-the-Goat, who was implicated with the Phoenix Park Murders that took place in Dublin in 1882, the year of Joyce's (and Stephen's) birth. No doubt, this excerpt also provides a remarkable illustration of the convoluted and long-winded prose that we find exclusively in the "Eumaeus" episode:

And as for the lessee or keeper, who probably wasn't the other person at all, he (B.) couldn't help feeling and most properly it was better to give people like that the goby unless you were a blithering idiot altogether and refuse to have anything to do with them as a golden rule in private life and their felonsetting, there always being the offchance of a Dannyman coming forward and turning queen's evidence or king's now like Denis or Peter Carey, an idea he utterly repudiated. Quite apart from that he disliked those careers of wrongdoing and crime on principle. Yet, though such criminal propensities had never been an inmate of his bosom in any shape or form, he certainly did feel and no denying it (while inwardly remaining what he was) a certain kind of admiration for a man who had actually brandished a knife, cold steel, with the courage of his political convictions (though, personally, he would never be a party to any such thing), off the same bat as those love vendettas of the south, have her or swing for her, when the husband frequently, after some words passed between the two concerning her relations with the other lucky mortal (he having had the pair watched), inflicted fatal injuries on his adored one as a result of an alternative postnuptial *liaison* by plunging his knife into her, until it just struck him that Fitz, nicknamed Skin-the, merely drove the car for the actual perpetrators of the outrage and so was not, if he was reliably informed, actually party to the ambush which, in point of fact, was the plea some legal luminary saved his skin on. (*U* 16.1048–69)

In terms of content Bloom's monologue leads to a disastrous dead end and the painfully twisted Eumaean prose mimics his circuitous statements. Stripped of its many subordinate conjunctions the main clause of the last sentence would probably read: "Yet he certainly did feel a certain kind of admiration for a man who had actually brandished a knife with the courage of his political conviction until it just struck him that Fitz merely drove the car for the actual perpetrators of the outrage and so was not actually party to the ambush." However, with its many syntactic extravaganzas the prose, resembling the misfired impulses in a complexly organized nervous system, goes haywire.

As Derek Attridge suggests in comparing "Eumaeus" to "Sirens," "instead of an intense concentration of meaning in a confined linguistic space we have sense spread thinly across a seemingly endless flow of words" (Attridge 1988, 172). However, while readers lose sight of Bloom's argument, they cannot help noticing the failing style that inadequately packages the substance of his speech. In this short representative passage, style completely overwhelms semantics. And more than anything else it is the bracketed information that grabs readers' attention. The passage, it seems, is the product of a narrator anxiously insisting to be noticed, a narrator who constantly signals his or her presence to the reader and his or her independence from the episode's content. And it is precisely with such a self-conscious relater that Joyce's text establishes a set of new nerve circuits that, neurophysiologically speaking, regard the conventional barrier between the reader and the text instead as a synapse and thus as a vital path of communication. While synaptic functions between Stephen and Bloom might very well be sapped by tiredness, exhaustion, or overstimulation, the conduction of nerve impulses between the "Eumaeus" episode and its reader is wired and active.

A close reading of the short Eumaean passage also shows how effectively Joyce's episode brings together linguistic fields and how it creates a mosaic of lexical dissonances. In general the Eumaean prose style is identified as Joyce's attempt to mock newspaper journalism's style idiosyncrasies. Stanislaus Joyce applaudes his brother's success in recreating a "flabby Dublin journalese, with its weak effort to be witty" (*LIII* 58). With phrases such as "queen's evidence" (*U* 16.1053),[13] "criminal propensities" (*U* 16.1056), "inflicted fatal injuries" (*U* 16.1064), and "perpetrators" (*U* 16.1067), which are all taken from the parlance of criminal justice, the editorial piece, which is mimicked in the above-cited passage, also references the language of jurisprudence. However, the legal terminology is awkwardly paired with vernacular expressions such as "blithering idiot" (*U* 16.1050) and "have her or swing for her" (*U* 16.1061); with eccentric figurative phrases such as "inmate of his bosom" (*U* 16.1056); with recourses to foreign tags such as "*liaison*" (*U* 16.1065); and with almost comical idiomatic jargon: "a man who had actually brandished a knife" (*U* 16.1058–59). This means that the episode's attempted verbalism and its efforts at stylistic supremacy are counterbalanced by impulses to resort back to a more comfortable and less academic idiom. Likewise, the already mentioned brackets obviously speak to readers physically looking at the book's printed page. They are joined by expressions such as "who probably wasn't the other person at all" (*U* 16.1048) and "couldn't help feeling" (*U* 16.1049), clearly belonging into the medium of spoken language. This unabashed mix of orality and writing further accentuates the episode's desire to create a complex linguistic composite.

With expressions such as "private life" (*U* 16.1051) and "personally" (*U* 16.1060), the passage also confusingly mixes elements of the private and public to intensify the text's cognitive and verbal indecision and irresolution. Naturally, the case of Skin-the-Goat, the Invincibles, and the Phoenix Park Murders, which is the subject of Bloom's discourse here, belongs into the sphere of turn-of-the-century Irish public life. Intriguingly though, "Eumaeus" has Bloom compare the politically motivated murder with the complexities of his own domestic situation; a situation that might well make him think of "love vendettas" (*U* 16.1061) and of "plunging his knife into her" (*U* 16.1065), but that is hardly relevant to the point about "political convictions" (*U* 16.1059) he is trying to make. By first establishing and then undercutting the significance of this ill-fitted simile between a public and private event, the text therefore distracts, evades, and circumnavigates epistemological clarity and precision.

The episode's hybrid style thus creates interpretative ambiguity, discomfort, and uneasiness for the reader who is unable to decide what exactly the

Eumaean prose is or wants to be. This is particular noteworthy because the above-quoted passage relies so heavily on legal language and aims, with an almost forensic intensity, to uncover the exact nature of Skin-the-Goat's criminal complicity. But if the legal language is here reminiscent of court proceedings, supposed to establish factual clarity and get to the bottom of things, "Eumaeus" and its blend of lexical fields instantly undermines this mission to create cognitive certainty and clarity. Christine O'Neill coins the fitting term "doubtful reassurance" for this Eumaean tendency to oscillate between efforts to establish epistemic precision and simultaneously distract from these attempts by ways of elaborate syntactic and lexical detours (O'Neill 1996, 46–47). She particularly notes the episode's passion for insistence and obstinacy: "so many emphatic words in succession suggest that the language is at pains to distract" (1996, 46). The quoted passage illustrates this compulsion to accentuate and to emphasize issues by listing a number of adverbs, functioning as linguistic intensifiers: "he utterly repudiated" (*U* 16.1054) and "he certainly did feel" (*U* 16.1057).

Unfortunately though, in spite of the narrator's insistence and the passage's employment of linguistic intensifiers, the example of Skin-the-Goat not only fails to illustrate Bloom's sentiments, but also draws a lot of attention to his logical lapse. As if to cover up this semantic embarrassment, the Eumaean narrator flourishes it with syntactic and verbal digressions and diversions. Although this tactic creates additional confusion, it gives the Eumaean arranger the possibility to create a script full of linguistic clashes and odd verbal resonances—a script in which different literary styles assertively compete for prominence.

All this shows that information is processed in an unorthodox manner in "Eumaeus." Although it is not always fruitful to apply pathological labels to a text, it might be useful here to refer back to the often-repeated ergographic reading of the Eumaean prose in order to illustrate the episode's textual practices. The analysis of one of the episode's passages has shown that, on a textual level, nerve impulses indeed go astray. If, however, "Eumaeus" represents the misfiring of neuronal impulses, it is not because the corresponding nervous system is necessarily tired out and exhausted. In "Eumaeus" linguistic registers irritatingly collide but synaptic passages continue to transmit nervous impulses—and they do this with extreme intensity and velocity, bundling together the most unlikely verbal fragments. Only an extremely alert or an overstimulated nervous system could produce such a colorful linguistic canvas. I would therefore like to suggest that the prose is far from being tired and sapped out. It is nervous and active, making different linguistic registers collide and synapse.

Moreover, "Eumaeus" also calls for an extremely alert and perceptive reader. As Derek Attridge notes, the "inefficient, self-referring, self-propagating language requires the reader to process it with extreme alertness in order to avoid misinterpretation or confusion" (Attridge 1988, 175). Only an attentive reader is able to unscramble the semantic components from the excess of inadequately evoked stylistic registers. The rhetorically heavy-handed narration therefore refuses an exclusively referential reading of its allegedly "fagged out" prose. If a mimetic reading of "Eumaeus" is feasible, so is the understanding of the episode as self-consciously modernist.

Not surprisingly, a number of Joyce critics such as Hugh Kenner, Fritz Senn, and Derek Attridge have suggested that the "Eumaeus" episode reminds of "the textual operations of *Finnegans Wake*" (Kenner 1978, 37; Senn 1984, 110–11; Attridge 1988, 183).[14] The analysis of the neuroscientific intertext in "Eumaeus" has shown that what we as readers perceive, at first glance, as the text's mimetic practice—representing fatigue and exhaustion on the level of its allegedly exhausted prose—can also be read as a script that is vibrant and alert—a text that is not tired but full of nervous energy, making different linguistic registers clash and compete with each other. On the textual surface Joyce's complex episode therefore negotiates conflicting interpretations of its prose as either tired and exhausted or alert and active.

Both readings are possible. Like the stress produced in a pathologically stimulated nervous system they compete for interpretative prominence. Likewise, "Eumaeus" mediates referential interpretations with alternative modernist readings of its prose. Ultimately, this juxtaposition of diverse and contrasting interpretations illustrates how the stylistic clashes that we can find in "Eumaeus" generate a productive analytical tension. Only an extremely animated and energetic script, full of incompatible stylistic registers, can produce a textual scenario that allows its reader to oscillate comfortably between such different or contradictory readings.

In "Eumaeus" neuroscience, neurology, and literary language surprisingly synapse. Joyce thus creates an animated dialogue between disciplines that are generally not associated with each other. In the case of "Eumaeus," the groundbreaking results of the research, undertaken in neuroscientific and ergographic laboratories, provided Joyce with the metaphors and the associative framework that produced his avant-garde writing. As we have seen, the consideration of the Eumaean medical background enables us to read Joyce's allegedly dull and monotonous prose in all its complexity. With its stylistic clashes, its self-referential narrator, and above all its awareness of the text-reader nexus, "Eumaeus" takes its well-deserved place in the catalogue of Joyce's ongoing experimentation with literary style. The neurological processes that Joyce creatively appropriated in this episode assisted in launching a revolution in writing as innovative as the scientific discourses implicated.

6

"On the Hands Down"

Eugen Sandow and Physical Culture in "Ithaca"

Joyce was by no means concerned only about the state of his nerves. Lately, critics have developed a special interest in the "rheumatic fever episode of 1907," suspecting syphilitic-related disorders as the source of Joyce's many complaints.[1] And rheumatism certainly did trouble Joyce. Writing to his sister in Dublin on December 8, 1908, he announced: "I feel a little better of the rheumatism and am now more like a capital S than a capital Z" (*LII* 226). Like Leopold Bloom, who in "Circe" diagnoses "sciatica in [his] left gluteal muscle" (*U* 15.2782–83), Joyce repeatedly suffered from "Hexenschuss" and arthritis (Ellmann 1983, 308, 536),[2] tracing his ailments back to a pub crawl in 1910 and to the resulting early morning hours that he spent on the ground (535). That Joyce's excessive drinking habits were really indirectly responsible for his arthritis was never confirmed, but, nevertheless, Richard Ellmann states knowingly that this night out "had started arthritic pains in [Joyce's] right shoulder and left the deltoid muscle in his right arm atrophied" (535).[3] Doctors recommended a strict diet and frequent exercise to alleviate Joyce's suffering, asking him to "walk eight or ten kilometers a day" (570). This was a remedy that Joyce did not approve of, complaining in a letter to Harriet Shaw Weaver: "I have been training for a Marathon race by walking 12 or 14 kilometres every day and looking carefully in the Seine to see if there is any place where I could throw Bloom in with a 50 lb weight tied to his feet" (*LI* 171).

Obviously, Leopold Bloom does not drown in *Ulysses*. However, Joyce still insisted on strapping Bloom to a dumbbell—at least metaphorically. Notably, Bloom's thoughts on June 16, 1904, are interspersed with references to physical culture and Eugen Sandow, the turn-of-the-century's most famous strongman and performer.[4] As R. Brandon Kershner insightfully notes (Kershner 1993, 682), Sandow's exercise regime appears as a promising remedy whenever Bloom faces self-doubt or failure during the day: "Got up wrong side of the bed. Must begin again those Sandow's exercises. On the hands down" (*U* 4.233–34).[5] Just as Joyce's own lifestyle was reorganized and subjected to a therapeutic fitness routine, he turned physical culture into one of Bloom's many obsessions in *Ulysses*.

Eugen Sandow makes a particularly prominent appearance in the "Ithaca" episode where readers are told that his 1897 publication, *Strength and How to Obtain It*, adorns Bloom's bookshelf.[6] That "Ithaca" spotlights both Sandow and his most popular publication is hardly surprising though. "Ithaca" is Joyce's most engaging reflection on contemporary science. Astronomy, eugenics, and experimental psychology are just a few examples of the great number of exact or empirical sciences that inform the content of *Ulysses*'s most inquisitive section. The episode, with its formal reliance on the catechism, also adopts the style of a scientific discourse, presenting a good deal of loose textual material as though it were factual and precise observations of social reality. Indeed, while this particular form of inquisitive discourse can be associated with ecclesiastical practices, the episode's probing and questioning manner, demanding precise answers based on information and facts, also evokes a specifically scientific or diagnostic rhetoric—a matter of fact, rational discourse interested, above all, in a clinical and detached observation and representation of Bloom's social reality.

At first glance "Ithaca" is, therefore, astonishingly lifeless and dispassionate. Consider, for example, the following passage that observes Stephen and Bloom in the attempt to gain access to Bloom's house on Eccles Street:

What act did Bloom make on their arrival at their destination?
At the housesteps of the 4th of the equidifferent uneven numbers, number 7 Eccles street, he inserted his hand mechanically into the back pocket of his trousers to obtain his latchkey.

Was it there?
It was in the corresponding pocket of the trousers which he had worn on the day but one preceding.

Why was he doubly irritated?

Because he had forgotten and because he remembered that he had reminded himself twice not to forget.

What were then the alternatives before the, premeditatedly (respectively) and inadvertently, keyless couple?
To enter or not to enter. To knock or not to knock. (*U* 17.70–82)

No doubt, the inclination toward diagnosis and scientific precision of the Ithacan narrator is very well-illustrated in this passage. Note, for example, that the door of number 7 Eccles Street is not just the fourth on one side of the road. No, it is in front of the fourth of the *equidifferent* ("arithmetically proportional," OED) uneven house numbers that Stephen and Bloom come to a standstill. It is also not sufficient to state that Bloom is frustrated by having left his latchkey behind. No, "Ithaca" insists on getting to the bottom of things by asking "why was Bloom *doubly* irritated" [my emphasis]. Stripped of many of the rhetorical flourishes and stylistic embellishments that we can find in other sections of Joyce's text, the language in many sections of the "Ithaca" episode seems inexpressive and emotionless.

At first glance, Bloom, in "Ithaca," appears to be equally detached and cut off from the incidents that have, in all likelihood, very strong emotional resonances for him. It is, of course, on his return to 7 Eccles Street, that he is confronted with concerns that he has successfully managed to suppress throughout the day. Thoughts about Molly's adultery, his social alienation, and racial "Otherness" all await him there. On coming home, Bloom, quite literally, has his nose rubbed into the reality of Molly's adulterous affair when hitting his head on the rearranged furniture in the front room—a definite sign that the marital coordinates of his domicile have been fundamentally altered:

> What suddenly arrested his ingress?
> The right temporal lobe of the hollow sphere of his cranium came into contact with a solid timber angle where, an infinitesimal but sensible fraction of a second later, a painful sensation was located in consequence of antecedent sensations transmitted and registered. (*U* 17.1274–78)

At this, no doubt, very emotional moment for Bloom, pain is registered exclusively as a physical sensation. Moreover, the experience of this physical sensation is couched into a hyperbolic scientific register that makes it difficult to understand that Bloom, in fact, has hit his head on a sideboard. Emotional pain is, in this passage, translated twice: first into a purely physical sensation and then into an almost surgical language that scientifically scrutinizes this physical sensation. The emotional experience is displaced and the episode's scientific perspective actively assists in this complex process of emotional deferral.

Bloom has, of course, used exactly this strategy to cope with unpleasant emotional experiences in "Sirens." This episode that takes place in the Ormond Hotel at exactly the hour of Molly's scheduled appointment with Boylan, con-

fronts Bloom, not just with Blazes himself, but also with a number of sentimental songs and soppy ballads, sung and performed by Dedalus senior, Ben
Dollard, and Father Cowley. But instead of giving in to the sentimental mood
by pondering gloomily about Molly's imminent adultery, Bloom occupies himself with a scientific analysis of music and tonality: "Numbers it is. All music
when you come to think. Two multiplied by two divided by half is twice one.
Vibrations: chords those are. One plus two plus six is seven. Do anything you
like with figures juggling. Always find out this equal to that. Symmetry under
a cemetery wall . . . Musemathematics. And you think you're listening to the
etherial. But suppose you said it like: Martha, seven times nine minus x is thirtyfive thousand. Fall quite flat. It's on account of the sounds it is" (*U* 11.830–37).
Bloom's mathematical scrutiny of music foregrounds its mechanistic elements
and downplays its sentimental effects to sidestep an uncomfortable confrontation with emotional experiences. Given Bloom's personal situation, it would
have been only too understandable if the encounter with music had generated
melancholic thoughts about his domestic circumstances. But instead of focusing on his own emotional response to music, Bloom turns his energy toward its
analytical study as a means to distract himself from his upsetting thoughts. For
Bloom, scientific analyses therefore have the function to displace sentimental
traps. This is why his scientific musings appear, at times, very hyperbolic: for
instance when the aria "Martha" is, in Bloom's interior monologue, picked into
mathematical pieces: "seven times nine minus x is thirtyfive thousand." In terms
of his turn to science, Bloom overinvests when he feels emotionally vulnerable.
In "Ithaca," when Bloom, on coming home, is likely to feel most vulnerable, it is
no longer his interior monologue that is infused with scientific references. Instead, the episode's arranger firmly adopts Bloom's strategy. "Ithaca" therefore
transposes a Bloomian device to cope with unpleasant emotional experiences
into its narrative principle. When Joyce's protagonist is likely to feel the lowest, scientific rhetoric, with its surgical quality and all its hyperbolic moments,
becomes the defining feature of the narrative.

However, in "Ithaca" science is also used for another purpose. While the episode appropriates a clinico-analytical perspective to copy a Bloomian defense
mechanism, it also shows that the imagery provided by a particular pseudoscientific discourse, physical culture, has a stimulating and invigorating effect
on Bloom's imagination. While "Ithaca" shows that the unexpected encounter
with Stephen Dedalus has had a remarkably uplifting effect on Bloom—left
alone, he conjures up "Bloom of Flowerville" (*U* 17.1581), a confident, lionized
alter ego—the ideas and concepts associated with Eugen Sandow's popular fitness cult provide the impetus for Bloom to imagine idealistic and idealizing

social prospects and personal scenarios. Bloom's reveries after Stephen's departure thereby repeat a central assumption of Sandow's fitness manuals: a firm belief in dormant potential. Like the mystical figure of the glorious strongman, Bloom of Flowerville is the product of self-improvement stretched to the utmost. And whereas Bloom's transformation obviously remains an idealizing fantasy, it is significant to remember that Sandow's physical culture empire firmly relied on advertising fantasies of perfection and on promoting psychological determination as a requirement for physical empowerment.

Turn-of-the-century physical culture is also related to other themes that form an integral part of the "Ithaca" episode. In *Ulysses* the glamorous Sandow evolves into a complementary figure to Leopold Bloom. Like Bloom, who is stigmatized on grounds of his racial identity in "Cyclops," Sandow's Germanic background made him the target for verbal assaults from contemporaries. The topic of race is further linked to physical culture by its growing significance in the Zionist context, which in turn is a principal motif in "Ithaca," the chapter of homecoming. This chapter will examine the impact of this popular pseudo-medical discourse on Joyce's *Ulysses* and the "Ithaca" episode in particular, demonstrating how crucially Bloom's perceptions of his masculinity and racial identity are tied to Sandow's fashionable fitness system. Moreover, Joyce's episode is also formally dependent on physical culture vocabulary. Physical culture, the narrative of inflated chests and flexed biceps, literally gives shape to "Ithaca." As we will see, a medical intertext once again provides Joyce with the metaphors to develop his aesthetic practices in *Ulysses*.

.

Physical culture, which had its heyday in the years between 1850 and 1918, became, at the turn of the century, practically synonymous with the name Eugen Sandow, whose publication *Strength and How to Obtain It* marked the zenith of a fitness craze relying on new media such as advertising and photography, growing degeneration paranoia, and resurfacing concepts of Hellenistic body aesthetics as a means for its effective dissemination. In fact, the muscular gentleman Eugen Sandow was regarded as the representative male body in turn-of-the-century England. Doctors eagerly categorized him as "the most perfect male specimen alive" (Budd 1997, 44). Arthur Conan Doyle and W. T. Stead were both ecstatic supporters of the strongman, and, in 1901, a Sandow body cast was commissioned for the Natural History Museum in London.

Sandow's origins were decidedly more humble though. He grew up as Friedrich Wilhelm Müller in Königsberg in East Prussia.[7] Here, Sandow had, from early childhood, witnessed the growing interest in physical fitness in his home country. By 1870, the time of Sandow's birth, no fewer than 1,500 gymnasiums had been established in the German States (Chapman 1994, 6). After the Prussian army experienced a humiliating defeat by the Napoleonic armed force in 1812, physical education became a key concern of patriots such as Friedrich Ludwig Jahn (*Turnvater Jahn*), who established the famous Turn-vereine, athletic unions with a distinctive nationalist agenda. Sandow himself claimed that his fascination with bodybuilding started in his tenth year while he was on a trip to Italy with his father. Visiting the art galleries in Rome and Florence, the young Sandow "was struck with admiration for the finely developed forms of the sculptured figures of the athletes of old" (Sandow 1897, 85). More impressive still was his father's remark. Müller senior told his son that: "[T]hese were the figures of men who lived when might was right, when men's own arms were their weapons, and often their lives depended upon their physical strength. Moreover, they knew nothing of the modern luxuries of civilization, and, besides their training and exercise, their muscles, in the ordinary course of daily life, were always being brought prominently into play" (85).

At this point, Sandow's narration obviously taps into contemporary debates about the damaging effects of a modern lifestyle. This pathologizing of modern-day living standards correlated with aesthetic arguments that ecstatically glorified classical beauty ideals. The recovery of Hellenistic corporality was regarded as a remedy for deteriorating turn-of-the-century muscles and bodies, and Sandow, on his return from Italy, started to train excessively in order to participate in the general attempt to retrieve the virility smothered by the onset of modernity.[8] Interestingly, his claim that his efforts remained fruitless until he started to study anatomy at the age of eighteen (Sandow 1897, 86), thereby emphasizes the distinctive scientific agenda of Sandow's fitness tutorials. For not only did Sandow lift dumbbells, but also he developed an exercise system that, based on a thorough knowledge of human physiology and anatomy, methodically optimized the body's muscular potential. The "Anatomical Chart" accompanying Sandow's *Strength and How to Obtain It*, and especially the impressive images of the flayed bodies with muscles flexed, demonstrate that its author used his alleged medical expertise and comprehensive understanding of the workings of the human body very effectively as a selling point for this publication (figure 5).

With this therapeutic and scientific agenda in mind, Sandow set out to reform turn-of-the-century male bodies. And because the development of the new fitness cult that he witnessed in his home country was by no means re-

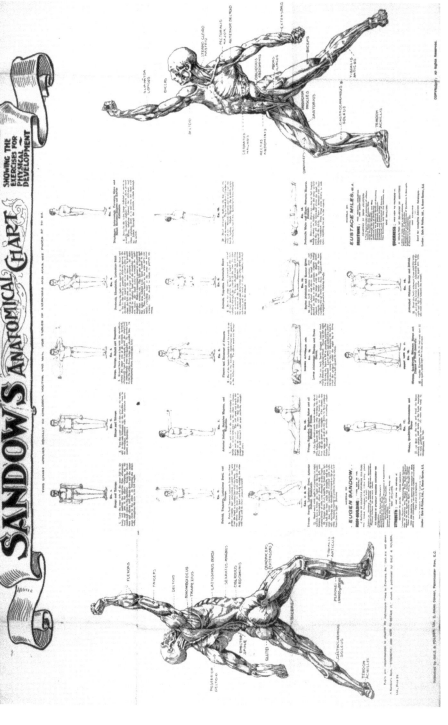

Figure 5. "Sandow's Anatomical Chart." An image from Eugen Sandow. 1905. *Strength and How to Obtain It*. London: Gale and Polden. © British Library Board. All Rights Reserved. Shelfmark 7912137.

stricted to Germany alone, he could not have chosen a better moment for this endeavor. Throughout nineteenth-century Europe, as industrialization, deteriorating working and living conditions, and poor diet threatened to crush working-class male bodies and spirits in vast numbers, the idealized muscular body of the male strength performer was hailed as the symbol of social and national progress (Budd 1997, 7). Moreover, the suggestion that the strength of an unruly male body could be modeled, organized, and its vigor and strength controlled by a rigid system of physical exercises was widely applauded by Sandow's contemporaries. Although Chartist agitations were no longer a political reality in turn-of-the-century Britain, and although the revolutionary tides that had threatened to overthrow the political status quo on the Continent in 1848 had not erupted for a while, these midcentury revolts were still very much present in the minds of many people.

Sandow's fitness regime promised to curb and restrain male (working-class) energy and strength that could, if mismanaged, break out into physical violence and riots. As Sandow argues, "[t]he man who means to make his body as nearly perfect as possible must perforce cultivate habits of self-control and of temperance. . . . The man who has cultivated his body has also cultivated self-respect" (Sandow 1897, 6). The firm, fit, and healthy body of the muscular gentleman and above all his self-possessed nature thus allegorized the stability of the body politic at the turn of the century. All this, combined with the fear of national degeneration and a craving for self-improvement that captivated European citizens in the second half of the nineteenth century, amply explains the fanatic turn-of-the-century promotion of fitness, strength, and health. By the time the first Modern Olympiad was held in 1896, this obsessive belief that the body could be shaped, formed, cultivated, and improved with the help of scientifically approved training systems such as Sandow's had been firmly established.

Joyce's *Ulysses* shows a remarkable indebtedness to different aspects of this fascination with athleticism. The "Nymph" in "Circe" gives "[u]nsolicited testimonials for Professor Waldmann's wonderful chest exuber" (*U* 15.3257–58). The sailor in "Eumaeus" has a distinctively "manly chest" (*U* 16.690), and Bloom and Molly both contemplate Boylan's muscularity. While Molly reflects on his "big hipbones," his heaviness, and his "hairy chest" (*U* 18.415–16), Bloom rejects "[d]uel by combat" (*U* 17.2201–2) as a potential retribution with the thought of the "muscularity of the male" (*U* 17.2216). Young Patrick Dignam is fascinated by a prize fight in "Wandering Rocks" (*U* 10.1130–49), and this boxing match between an Irish and an English champion is further examined in "Cyclops," the episode that also discusses the "revival of ancient Gaelic sports and the importance of physical culture, as understood in ancient Greece and ancient Rome and ancient Ireland, for the development of the race" (*U* 12.899–901). Gerty MacDowell fantasizes about her future husband's virility: she wants a "manly man" with "sheltering arms" (*U* 13.210–12). And Bloom, when reflecting on Father Coffey in "Hades," calls him a "Muscular christian" (*U* 6.596), referring thus to Charles Kingsley's "Muscular Christianity" movement, which had, since the 1850s, widely advocated the strong and healthy body as contributing to improved moral and religious standards (*mens sana in corpore sano*).[9]

For Leopold Bloom, who admits in "Circe" that he feels "exhausted, abandoned, no more young" (*U* 15.2778), health and physical fitness are particularly significant. This is why the image of the strongman Sandow repeatedly pops up in Bloom's thoughts, serving as inspiration and idealized role model. Both physically and commercially Sandow has achieved what Leopold Bloom can only dream of: physical superiority and professional success in advertising. For not only was Sandow hailed as "the perfect man," he was also known as a prosperous entrepreneur and promoter. Indeed, as Maurizia Boscagli suggests, Sandow "managed to turn his body into a walking advertisement for himself, his shows, and his clubs" (Boscagli 1996, 115). Some of his noteworthy marketing successes included the famous "Grip Dumbells," introduced around 1899; the "Sandow cigar," manufactured by S. Cantrovitz and Sons in Chicago between 1896 and 1898; and various publications, especially his magazine *Sandow's Magazine of Physical Culture* (1898–1907).

Noteworthy is also an early incident in Sandow's career that demonstrates how well "the most perfect male specimen alive" had mastered the art of successful self-advertising. As R. Brandon Kershner notes, Sandow, when staying in Amsterdam and failing to secure an engagement as a strongman, repeatedly "wandered the city at night, wrecking all the available strength-test machines" (Kershner 1993, 668). After a reward was offered, Sandow gave himself up to the police, demonstrating in a public trial that his colossal strength was responsible for vandalizing the machines. Having achieved public renown as a strong man, Sandow was instantly employed by a theater as a strongman. From Amsterdam Sandow then went straight to his next engagement in the Crystal Palace in London (Chapman 1994, 12–14). Contrary to Sandow's dazzling professional successes, however, Bloom's most cherished advertising project for Hely's, the "illuminated showcart, drawn by a beast of burden, in which two smartly dressed girls were to be seated engaged in writing" (*U* 17.608–10), remains unfulfilled while his corporeal measurements "after 2 months' consecutive use of Sandow-Whiteley's pulley exerciser" (*U* 17.1816–17) continue to be, if one believes the narrator in "Ithaca," grotesquely undersized for a man of Bloom's height.[10]

In spite of this apparent dissimilarity between the strongman and Bloom, they still share a similar fate regarding the precarious issue of racial difference. Undoubtedly, because racism was such a charged topic at the time Sandow was publishing his manuals, his physical culture movement constantly emphasized its universal and democratic nature. Sandow thus opens his fitness gospel, the 1897 *Strength and How to Obtain It*, with the following words: "You can all be strong, all enjoy the heritage which was intended for you" (Sandow 1897, n.p.). The second part of the book—the "Incidents of My Professional Career," which begins with Sandow confessing his delicacy as a child—contains the notable statement: "It is not necessary, as some may think, to be born strong in order to become strong. Unlike the poet, who, we are told, has to be born a poet, the strong man can make himself" (85). The physical culture movement and Sandow as its primary campaigner therefore advocated a radically different agenda to that of another pseudoscientific discourse widely in use at the turn of the twentieth century and one that Joyce regarded skeptically throughout his life: eugenics.[11] Whereas turn-of-the-century eugenicists preached biological determinism and racial elitism, Sandow and his followers underlined the egalitarian nature of their programs and the utopian promise of bodily empowerment for all. Although Sandow allegedly chose the Christian name "Eugen" out of admiration for Francis Galton's new science eugenics (Budd 1997, 147), his physical culture movement relied on psychological determination rather than biological determinism, thereby serving as an important historical counternarrative to eugenics' rhetoric of exclusivity.

Nevertheless, although Sandow continuously advertised his egalitarian philosophy, physical culture pamphlets, published in Great Britain, became an opportune location for the distribution of the eugenic movement's racial sermons. And although Sandow had renounced his German citizenship, married an Englishwoman in 1894, and put his educational system into the service of the English crown, his Prussian background became a prime target for the scorn of some British strongmen. One particularly violent onslaught came from William Bankier, a Scottish strongman, who used the stage name "Apollo." In his 1900 *Ideal Physical Culture and the Truth about the Strong Man*, Bankier intertwined the promotion of his professional philosophy with a ferocious attack on Sandow that denigrated the world-famous performer for one thing in particular: his Germanic descent. While stating that he is "no believer in patent 'exercises'" and boldly claiming that "a strong man is *naturally* so, and has been strong even from boyhood, and not, as one tells us, that he was a weak child up to seventeen, and only then began to exercise and develop strength" (Bankier 1900, 24–25; emphasis Bankier's), Apollo's argument is visibly indebted to the rhetoric of eugenics: "Can any sensible man imagine that by pulling at a rubber, or doing any other violent exercise, he will become a strong man, unless he comes from a perfectly sound stock and has a perfectly strong physique to start with?" (24–25). The specific racial aspect of Apollo's argument is further accentuated when the Scotsman declares that "no nation in the world can excel in bone and muscle our own countrymen," that "there are better athletes in Britain than ever came from Germany," and that Sandow "has three very grave faults—viz., the sloping shoulders, small calves and flat feet, common to all the German athletes" (1, 3, 40).

Ironically, then, while Sandow was busying himself with the patriotic task of outlining programs for raising the physical fitness of the British nation, his adversaries were using his racial "Otherness" as a welcome opportunity for the expression of professional dispute and the slander of Sandow's reputation. In this, Sandow resembles Joyce's Leopold Bloom, who, in spite of his emphatic answer to the Citizen's question: "—What is your nation if I may ask? says the citizen.—Ireland, says Bloom. I was born here. Ireland" (*U* 12.1430–31), his active interest in Arthur Griffith's Irish Home Rule politics (*U* 12.1574, *U* 18.383–86), and his adopted anglicized name nevertheless becomes, not unlike Sandow, the target for racial prejudices and hostilities in "Cyclops."

The nature-nurture dispute that informed the physical culture rhetoric at the turn of the century is also relevant to Bloom's Jewish background in yet another sense. It is not only in the "Cyclops" episode that Bloom is assaulted on grounds of his racial difference. With Stephen's offensive recital of the legend of "Little Harry Hughes" (*U* 17.802–28), "Ithaca" also introduces racism as a subtext. That Bloom is uncomfortably aware of his complex Semitic background during his nocturnal get-together with Stephen is illustrated by his equally convoluted meditations on whether or not he has been identified as a Jew: "He thought that he thought that he was a jew whereas he knew that he knew that he knew that he was not" (*U* 17.530–31). And while "Ithaca" is the chapter of homecoming, it is interesting to note that physical culture plays a very significant role in a specific Jewish context: the Zionist movement that responded to recurring pogroms in Russia (1881 and 1882) and the French Dreyfus affair (1894–1906) with insistent demands for an independent Jewish state.

Of course, Zionism also plays a salient role in *Ulysses*. Joyce developed a curious fascination with topics such as Judaism and racial anti-Semitism.

Through Theodor Herzl's book *Der Judenstaat* (1896), which he owned in Trieste, Joyce also became familiar with the political agenda of Zionism. His Triestine and Zurich friends Ettore Schmitz (Italo Svevo) and Ottocaro Weiss further fostered his sustained and intrigued interest in the question of a Jewish national state. And although Joyce ridiculed Zionism at times,[12] his novel frequently emphasizes the political parallels between the Jewish and the Irish people as dispossessed nations.[13] In the pork butcher Dlugacz, Bloom encounters a Zionist "[e]nthusiast" (*U* 4.493), and the picked-up newspaper advertisement for a Zionist colony "Agendath Netaim" (*U* 4.191–92) repeatedly engages his thoughts (*U* 8.635–36, *U* 8.1184, *U* 13.1284, *U* 14.1086–87). Yet Bloom's attitude toward the movement that advocated a Jewish free state is ambiguous: "Nothing doing. Still an idea behind it" (*U* 4.200).

Significantly, Bloom identifies the Zionist movement as a utopian project characterized not by forceful action and aggressive realpolitik but by its prophetic philosophy, its "idea."[14] And while he burns the Agendath Netaim prospectus in "Ithaca" (*U* 17.1321–29), his thoughts on the new Zion as a "barren land, bare waste" (*U* 4.219) mirror exactly this kind of skepticism about the movement's political triumph:

> Vulcanic lake, the dead sea: no fish, weedless, sunk deep in the earth. No wind could lift those waves, grey metal, poisonous foggy waters. Brimstone they called it raining down: the cities of the plain: Sodom, Gomorrah, Edom. All dead names. A dead sea in a dead land, grey and old. Old now. It bore the oldest, the first race. A bent hag crossed from Cassidy's, clutching a naggin bottle by the neck. The oldest people. Wandered far away over all the earth, captivity to captivity, multiplying, dying, being born everywhere. It lay there now. Now it could bear no more. Dead: an old woman's: the grey sunken cunt of the world. (*U* 4.219–28)

In this passage commonplaces such as the reference to the Jewish people as a wandering and persecuted race are complemented by an interesting reference to the "Old Gummy Granny" (a "bent hag crossed from Cassidy's"), a Kathleen ni Houlihan figure representing Ireland, who also overshadows Stephen's thoughts in "Telemachus": "Old shrunken paps. She poured again a measureful and a tilly. Old and secret she had entered from a morning world, maybe a messenger" (*U* 1.398–400).[15] In fusing the Irish nationalist icon with Bloom's review of the Promised Land's forlornness and barrenness, this rather pessimistic passage already draws attention to the many similarities between the Irish and the Jewish political status at the beginning of the twentieth century. But the theme is developed most effectively in the "Aeolus" episode when J. J. O'Molloy impersonates John F. Taylor's patriotic speech. Delivered to rouse political resistance to British colonial politics in Ireland, Taylor's address establishes, like the passage from "Calypso" quoted above, a simile yoking the Irish and the Jewish people in comparing the *"youth of Ireland"* (*U* 7.829) in contemporary colonial Ireland to the *"youthful Moses"* (*U* 7.833) in Ancient Egypt, who forcefully resisted the assimilation of the Jewish nation by the Egyptian host.

While Joyce busied himself with writing the Zionist topic into his novel, Zionist leaders such as Theodor Herzl and Max Nordau openly lobbied the possibility of a Jewish state.[16] And with this political perspective in mind, the question of the Jewish physique and the fitness of the Jewish male body became of utmost importance. The genesis of racial anti-Semitism and pseudoscientific debates of Jewish "Otherness" forced Zionist advocates to challenge the prevalent image of the crippled and degenerate Semitic male body, classified by degeneration theories as social and medical deviation from the Aryan norm. A text passage from Leopold von Sacher-Masoch's *Neue Judengeschichten (New Jewish Stories)*—allegedly one of Joyce's favorite writers in Trieste—can serve as an illustrative example of how much this racial dichotomy, which aggressively contrasted the Jew and the Aryan, inspired the popular imagination at the fin de siècle: "Ruben rose but he did not really consider defending himself, he, the narrow-chested, pale, weak house-mouse facing the country child bursting with strength, whose beautiful face had been colored by the sun with a savage Indian brown and whose blue eyes glittered threateningly" (Sacher-Masoch 1881, 117).[17] Unsurprisingly, such depictions of Jewish racial inferiority were fiercely debated in Zionist contexts, and exercise and muscular development were hailed as a remedy for the repudiation of such hostile associations and as a welcome method for creating an improved Jewish self-image. Sandow's physical culture tutorials, it seems, could be the answer.

Correspondingly, the first issue of Sandow's *Physical Culture* magazine, launched in 1898, contains an article entitled "Physical Culture Among the Jews," which suggested the centrality of exercise and bodybuilding to the Zionist movement. It argues that "the physical culture movement among the Jews may fairly be described as a communal one," one that "is followed with the closest possible attention by its leaders" (Dettass 1898, 128). And the correspondent in Sandow's magazine is right. Zionist activists willingly adopted the democratic claim of Sandow's physical culture rhetoric. In his 1902 article "Was bedeutet das Turnen für uns Juden?" ("What is the Meaning of Exercise for us Jews?"),

Max Nordau thus argues that: "Our muscles have an outstanding potential for development. One can say without exaggeration: no one has to be satisfied with his muscles. On the contrary, everybody can have the muscles he himself wishes. Methodical and persistent exercise is all that is required. Every Jew who considers himself weak or is weak indeed has the capacity to build up an athlete's muscular system" (Nordau 1909b, 385).[18]

As we can see, Nordau aimed to refute the antagonistic idea of an inborn Semitic "Otherness." Instead, he stressed that environmental factors determined a particular Jewish body type. A similar argument can be found in one of Joyce's sources, used to flesh out the Jewish facets in *Ulysses*: Maurice Fishberg's 1911 *The Jews: A Study of Race and Environment*. In his study Fishberg explicitly foregrounds the social milieu's importance in the development of Jewish physiques:

> In countries in which the Jews are generally poor, of sedentary habits, employed at indoor occupations, deprived of the invigorating and growth-accelerating influence of outdoor life and only rarely or never engaged in agricultural pursuits, they are shorter of stature than in places where they are on a higher economical level. This is best shown by the rich Jews of the West End of London, who are as tall as the average Englishman, reaching 171.4 cm. in height, while their poorer co-religionists in the East End only average 164.1 cm. in height. (Fishberg 1911, 32–33).

Fishberg's rhetoric echoes Nordau's, who also accentuated nurture over nature in his argument about Jewish masculinity and physicality.

Although the question of Jewish muscularity did not take center stage in Herzl's *Der Judenstaat*,[19] Nordau repeatedly underlined the educational benefit of exercise and physical instruction for his race. In fact, how much he valued the instructive and therapeutic nature of fitness cults such as Sandow's can be seen in a text that made the question of "Muskeljudentum" ("Muscular Jews") (Nordau 1909a, 379–81) its central topic. Moreover, a 1901 text establishes a synecdochical relationship between physical culture and the Zionist movement. Nordau here asks: "[w]ho is better constituted than the Zionist movement to organize the helpless, chaotic Jewish masses in the East?" (Nordau 1901, 24).[20] In his eyes, sculpturing the individual Jewish body meant working toward the management and shaping of the Jewish population at large. Whereas Bloom reproaches Zionism for inefficiency and passivity, its leaders challenged this commonplace allegation by the attempt to steel male Jewish bodies in anticipation of the new Zion.

In *Ulysses* physical culture provides the suggested Irish-Jewish analogy with further material. While Zionist leaders prescribed exercise for their citizens to be, the Gaelic Athletic Association, founded in 1884, simultaneously promoted new muscular Irish manhood and distinctively Irish Games. But given the historical setting that blends physical culture, idealized masculinity, the question of Jewish muscularity, and Zionism, the suggestion that Sandow's body cult and his fitness vocabulary come to the fore predominantly in "Ithaca," *Ulysses*'s chapter of homecoming, can hardly be a surprise. In "Ithaca" Bloom, in accordance with the Zionist leaders' designs for a Jewish Palestine, ambitiously imagines the scene of Bloom of Flowerville: "planting aligned young firtrees, syringing, pruning, staking, sowing hayseed, trundling a weedladen wheelbarrow without excessive fatigue at sunset amid the scent of newmown hay, ameliorating the soil, multiplying wisdom, achieving longevity" (*U* 17.1583–87)—in other words, Bloom imagines an improved and idealized version of his present social and economic situation.

This image of Bloom of Flowerville also leads to a more metaphorical interpretation of the fitness intertext in relation to Joyce's episode, for "Ithaca" adopts one central aspect of the physical culture movement: the emphasis on latent potential. Defining the term "physical culture" Sandow explicitly stressed the importance of developing dormant physical aptitude: "To constantly and persistently cultivate the whole of the body so that at last it shall be capable of anything that sound organs and perfectly developed muscles can accomplish— that is physical culture" (Sandow 1897, 4).

"Ithaca" is an episode obsessed with latent potential, possibilities, and revisionist settings. And it is Leopold Bloom's unexpected encounter with Stephen Dedalus that triggers his reflections on alternative scenarios. Simply put, while Stephen's presence has a distinctively rejuvenating effect on Bloom, it makes alternatives more conceivable. Joyce himself baptized *Ulysses*'s penultimate episode "a mathematico-astronomico-physico-mechanico-geometrico-chemico sublimation of Bloom and Stephen" (*LI* 164), and, as Andrew Gibson recalls, "sublimation" in scientific language means a "transmutation into a higher or purer substance" (Gibson 1996, 7)—in other words a transformation or growth into an improved state. This is why "Ithaca" excessively catalogues images of horticulture (*U* 17.1553, *U* 17.1568, *U* 17.1701), lists among Bloom's "civic functions" (*U* 17.1606) "that of gardener, groundsman, cultivator, breeder" (*U* 17.1608–9), and finally presents Bloom in "loose allwool garments with Harris tweed cap, price 8/6, and useful garden boots with elastic gussets and wateringcan" (*U* 17.1582–83); this is the prototypical image of the passionate gardener and cultivator of both muscles and plants. In this context it is also important to remember that "Agendath Netaim," the name of the Zionist organization whose leaflet Bloom picks up in "Calypso," means "planters' company" (*U* 4.192)—a name that foregrounds the importance of an agrarian and agricultural reorganization of the new Zion. All this suggests that in spite of his conflicting notions about Zionist designs, Bloom, in "Ithaca," participates mentally in the prospective land cultivation that Jewish settlers were supposed to undertake in Palestine. Zionism becomes an important utopian context cultivated in "Ithaca."[21]

But there are, of course, other Bloomian designs listed in this episode; mainly these are designs for urban improvement that Bloom had contemplated at various moments throughout the day and that are now collected and expanded. The cattle trains Bloom first envisions in "Hades" (*U* 6.400) reappear in "Ithaca" in an extended version under the heading of the appropriate question "Were there schemes of wider scope?" (*U* 17.1709). Other projects include a "scheme to enclose the peninsular delta of the North Bull at Dollymount" (*U* 17.1714–15) for the development of an amusement esplanade and a "scheme for the development of Irish tourist traffic" (*U* 17.1720). And although Bloom's schemes are mainly of a logistical nature, they are reminiscent of Eugen Sandow, another social reformer, who never tired of advocating his quest for national physical education, and who suggested that the British army adopt his patent exercise regime (Chapman 1994, 127–28).

In "Ithaca" it is primarily Molly's education that is at stake. Whereas Bloom reasons that Stephen's prolonged visit at 7 Eccles Street could have assisted her in the "acquisition of correct Italian pronunciation" (*U* 17.939), Bloom's habit of "assuming in her, when alluding explanatorily, latent knowledge" (*U* 17.695–96) demonstrates both his intention to firmly believe in Molly's intellectual potential and the episode's passion for dormant abilities and potential growth. That growth, potential, and alternatives are indeed thematic concerns in "Ithaca" is further illustrated by Joyce himself, who, in writing to Harriet Shaw Weaver, famously called the episode "the ugly duckling of the book and therefore, I suppose, my favourite" (Ellmann 1983, 500). Critics have read Joyce's comment as a remark on the alleged monotony of the chapter. After the phantasmagoric "Circe," the two following episodes may strike the reader as dull; especially "Ithaca," in which the reader will "know everything and know it in the baldest coldest way" (*LI* 159–60), is probably, contrary to Joyce's own preference, the least favorite chapter of many Joyceans. But the story of the ugly duckling is, as the best example of a narrative dealing with imminent transformation and latent potential, indeed a very adequate marker for the "Ithaca" episode.

Additionally, growth, expansion, and proportions are relevant to the structure and style of "Ithaca." Given the episode's stylistic reliance on the catechism, it seems that no other chapter is as occupied with the question of form and shape. Hence, it is interesting to note that "Ithaca" comprises astonishingly many expressions that can be linked, in one way or another, to the rhetoric of physical culture. Independent of Sandow's book title (*U* 17.513–14, *U* 17.1397), the word "strength" is mentioned four times (*U* 17.38, *U* 17.217, *U* 17.520, *U* 17.1196). The word "proportion" appears five times in *Ulysses*, only in "Ithaca" (*U* 17.450, *U* 17.452, *U* 17.2145, *U* 17.2148, *U* 17.2165). "Expansion" is referenced twice in "Ithaca" (*U* 17.1433, *U* 17.1644), "growth" three times (*U* 17.14, *U* 17.44, *U* 17.1005), and "inflated" once (*U* 17.494). "Ithaca," it could therefore be argued, displays, more than any other episode in *Ulysses*, an above-average linguistic dependence on the vocabulary of Sandow's physical culture movement.

Then again, it should not be forgotten that "Ithaca," although its language appears reduced and stripped to the bone,[22] "swelled to become the second largest chapter in the book" (Senn 1996, 53). Information is crammed into the pages, often more than the reader requires. The best example is the disproportionate relationship between the short question, "Did it flow?" (*U* 17.163), and the long answers. On the one hand, the strict, disciplining, and restricting form of the catechism underlines the latent potential of the answers. It seems as if the language constantly tries to break out of the shaping form of the episode, emphasizing that there are always more answers and in turn more questions to be asked. The language in "Ithaca" thus simulates exuberant narrative expansion, growth, and potential. On the other hand, it can be noted that the restrictive nature of the catechism is tantamount to the emphasis placed on discipline in the physical culture movement. While social and economic paradigms were threatening to spin out of control during the nineteenth century, the composed yet muscular body of the strongman suggested ideologies of continuous, well-managed growth and development. Likewise, "Ithaca" carefully and skillfully negotiates this correlation between discipline and growth, between narrative restriction and narrative expansion.

The playful reliance on Sandow's physical culture movement thus provided Joyce with a metaphorical backdrop for the most scientific of his episodes. Both in terms of form and content "Ithaca" shows a significant indebtedness to Sandow's popular fitness cult and relates its aesthetic and political concerns to Joyce's reflection on contemporary pseudomedicine and pseudoscience.

Leopold Bloom is in part modeled on Sandow, the famous strongman, whose racial "Otherness" made him the target for professional and personal slander. In addition, the theme and structure of the episode owe a lot to Sandow's example. "Ithaca" thematically adopts physical culture's emphasis on latent talent and potential, and its narrative structure, while relying on the mutual interaction of enormous expansion and closely-monitored control, imitates the essential characteristics of the strongman as the remarkable creation of Sandow's fitness tutorials.

Zionism is the intertext that connects all aspects that inform the "Ithaca" episode. Physical culture, xenophobia, expansion, growth, and the firm adherence to and belief into a utopian concept mark both the Jewish political vision and Bloom's troubled conception of his masculinity and cultural identity. Although Bloom's homecoming is indeed a distressed one, the meditations facilitated by the physical culture intertext trigger thoughts on optimistic alternatives. A question that has occupied Joyceans since the publication of *Ulysses* is whether or not Molly will indeed get up the next morning and serve Bloom "breakfast in bed" (*U* 18.2). Joyce's text does not answer this pressing query. But Molly's surprise and puzzlement over what she interprets as Bloom's unexpected request, illustrate the revisionist atmosphere with which "Ithaca" ends and "Penelope" opens. Options, choices, and opportunities become feasible. And as I have shown, a pseudomedical discourse becomes one of the foundations for the creation of such liberating and optimistic visions in "Ithaca."

Most important, therefore, the imagery and concepts associated with Sandow's popular fitness cult allow us to tie the episode's firm reliance on scientific principles to the working of the creative imagination. Pseudomedical designs and metaphors stimulate Bloom's daydreams and reveries and lead away from the prosaic and pessimistic representation of Bloom's reality that the Ithacan narrator seems to insist on developing. It is with the help of Sandow and his optimistic "empowerment for all philosophy" that we can most effortlessly bring the two temperaments of Joyce's protagonists—"The scientific. The artistic" (*U* 17.560)—into a productive dialogue in "Ithaca."

The following chapter on "Penelope" continues the examination of Joyce's use of modern medicine in *Ulysses*. But while "Penelope," once again, illustrates Joyce's interest in medical discourses, we will also see that the last chapter of *Ulysses*, through the representation of Molly Bloom and her rebellious soliloquy, resumes the political dispute with medicine that had characterized Joyce's earlier works. In "Penelope" it is medicine's interventions into women's lives that are critically examined. For not only did pseudomedical discourses, such as the physical culture movement, develop standards of idealized masculinity at the time Joyce was writing *Ulysses*, but medical practitioners also made the "science of woman" a particular topic on their agenda. With the last chapter of his novel and the confident voice of Molly Bloom, Joyce, once again, contests modern medicine's assertive cultural prescriptions.

7

Jack the Ripper and *The Family Physician*

Gynecology and Domestic Medicine in "Penelope"

When Carl Gustav Jung read *Ulysses* he admitted that the "book as a whole has given me no end of trouble and I was brooding over it for about three years." The "Penelope" episode in particular seemed to have grabbed the attention of his analytically trained mind: "The 40 pages of non stop run in the end is a string of veritable psychological peaches. I suppose the devil's grandmother knows so much about the real psychology of a woman. I didn't" (*LIII* 253). Joyce did not approve of Jung's psychoanalytical reading, suggesting that the Swiss doctor "seems to have read *Ulysses* from first to last without one smile. The only thing to do in such a case is to change one's drink" (*LIII* 262). But whether Joyce liked it or not, Jung's professional evaluation of Molly Bloom marked the starting point for subsequent medical readings of this final episode of *Ulysses*. Often, however, and especially in early Joyce criticism, these medical readings focus on Molly's "pathological" character traits. A very aggressive interpretation of Molly and Joyce's representation of femininity comes from J. B. Lyons, who regrets that "within that marvellous passage, like a canker in the rose, there lies the soiled sexuality of an immature and inadequate woman" (Lyons 1973, 173).

It seems a little more than unfortunate that "Penelope," with Molly's open and uncensored references to sexuality and bodily functions, should invite such negative readings of its protagonist. Joyce's aim in writing the last episode of *Ulysses* was to bring an intricate representation of femininity and womanhood before his readers. And in this attempt to realize such a representation, he explicitly drew on an equally complex set of turn-of-the-century discourses that focused on so-called female pathologies and that were instigated by contemporary gynecological research. Through this interest in gynecology, "Penelope" thus works, in many ways, as a counterpart to the "Oxen of the Sun" episode, in which Joyce's *Ulysses* also expresses an interest in medical theories of womanhood and female physiology.

Interestingly, though, Joyce's own curiosity about gynecological matters reaches back much further. More than fifteen years before the completion of "Oxen" in 1921, when the signs of Nora's first pregnancy in Trieste in 1904 could no longer be ignored, Joyce wrote to Stanislaus with an unusual request, asking him and Vincent Cosgrave to read books on midwifery and embryology and to send him "the results" (*LII* 73). Astoundingly, although she might have been able to give much better advice, Aunt Josephine, Joyce's usual source of information, was not addressed with this particular concern. Instead, Joyce seemed to have preferred textbook guidance on how to handle a pregnant woman. This anecdote signals that, at the turn of the century, the subject of women's diseases was rigidly controlled by a congregation of medical experts. By the time Nora became pregnant in Trieste, obstetrics and gynecology had emerged as new medical specialties, and their spokesmen argued authoritatively on the topic of female pathologies. Unsurprisingly, then, Joyce's ongoing interest in the "science of woman" resurfaces in "Penelope." Here, explicit references to contemporary gynecological research launch the episode's debate with medicine's political resonances.

However, important to note in this context is that the gynecological theories developed in Joyce's time remained crucially connected to the aim of maintaining established gender dynamics. At the end of the nineteenth century, medical men, instead of substantiating their organized intervention into modern social politics with references to theological or philosophical arguments, referred to scientific objectivity as the sanction for perpetuating the argument about women's social and professional limitations. Irrefutable biological evidence was quoted as the motive for establishing a detailed theory of female deficiency. Accordingly, women were equated with their biological functions, and the newly established medical science, gynecology, suggested that they were "by definition, disease or disorder, a deviation from the standard of health represented by the male" (Moscucci 1993, 102).

Nineteenth-century preoccupations with adolescent masturbation and Sandow's physical culture movement aside, no corresponding medical science of masculinity escorted the "science of woman" into the Victorian age. Women's bodies, however, became the object of medical scrutiny, and specialists created an extensive range of female ailments. Yet this burgeoning interest in women's organs did not emerge accidentally in the second half of the nineteenth century. On the contrary, medical science responded to a particular cultural phenomenon that threatened to capsize the conditions of the current social order: the woman question, advocated most energetically by the suffragette movement. It is no coincidence that at the time when women took up the battle for intellectual and social emancipation and demanded the right to study medicine, reactionary medical practitioners created a biological argument that cited medical evidence as a means to reinforce the social status quo.

In "Penelope" Joyce uses this controversial debate on women's so-called diseases as a provocative intertext for the representation of Molly Bloom's sexuality. Her recollection of a gynecological visit, which took place in 1888, responds explicitly to the complex turn-of-the-century discourse that related womanhood, pathology, and social politics. Further, it recalls fin-de-siècle fears about medical abuse that were most sensationally captured in the image of Jack the Ripper. While doctors multiplied the number of surgical operations performed on women's anesthetized bodies, feminists and antivivisectionists ferociously condemned both the ideological foundation for and the consequences of the mutilations resulting from doctors' surgical interventions.

Surprisingly, though, as "Penelope" reveals, the argument about women's social inferiority that the biological model had established received support by another, much more subtle medical interventionism. Patent medicine forms an equally central medical subtext in "Penelope." Molly's references to her *Family Physician* and to advertisements for patent medicine unmistakably disclose her awareness that domestic medicine propagated the image of domesticated womanhood. In the last episode of *Ulysses*, Joyce thus shows that both gynecological theory and domestic medicine actively participated in reinforcing women's conventional social roles. Consequently, in commenting overtly on turn-of-the-century gender politics, it is the last episode of *Ulysses* that packages one of Joyce's most versatile critiques of modern medicine's impact on the social and cultural landscape of modernity.

·

As her remarks about Bloom's "mad crazy letters" (*U* 18.1176) underline, Molly's encounter with the gynecologist Dr. Collins took place in 1888, the year of Bloom's courtship. By that time gynecology was firmly established as a respectable medical specialty, and the "access of the male physician to the female patient finally received full legitimation" (McLaren 1994, 275). Accordingly, the gynecological surgeon James Murphy could celebrate its most controversial operation, ovariotomy, in front of the first conference of the British Gynaeco-logical Society in 1891: "It has opened up the wide field of abdominal surgery, so that many men who started as gynaecologists are now our most brilliant surgeons, successfully attacking the uterus, the kidneys, the spleen, the liver, and all the organs contained in the abdomen" (Murphy 1891, 404). Murphy's almost aggressive emphasis on surgery must seem puzzling. However, the successful execution of various gynecological operations had effectively en-nobled the gynecological profession, so that the practitioners of a formerly stigmatized medical specialty now had as much social status as the highbrow surgeons. Surgery provided gynecological practice with the desired label of an established medical science, and the question of the practitioner's social status was in no way inconsequential. As we have seen in this study's introduction, following the British Medical Act of 1858, the medical profession had launched a sustained battle against its unappealing public image by elevating the physi-cian to the rank of upper-crust gentleman. Yet both obstetrics and gynecol-ogy were medical specialties that proved to be very resistant to this universal refashioning of the medical profession. Indeed, their practice remained so branded that until 1886 students could pass an official medical examination without obstetrical training (Porter 1999, 382).

The gynecologist's problematic reputation had much to do with the subject matter of his studies. The alleged indecency of his daily practice remained in-compatible with the image of the gentleman doctor, and childbirth continued to be perceived as an unpleasant medical incident with which the high-society practitioner did not want to be associated. Besides, throughout the nineteenth century, obstetrics and gynecology remained controversial because they were medical professions that traditionally had been practiced by women. In Tu-dor and Stuart England, it was the responsibility of the midwife, the "wise women" or "sages femmes" (Ackerknecht and Fischer-Homberger 1977, 264), to attend to gynecological and obstetric cases. Academic medical assistance was a luxury and was called for only in emergencies. However, even then the arrival of the medical professional was delayed as much as possible because his intervention often resulted in craniotomy and the subsequent loss of the child. The situation changed dramatically with the introduction of surgical tools such as the forceps. The emergence of this device around 1730 effectively supported the establishment of so-called men-midwives or accoucheurs and was therefore instrumental in polarizing the public image of the midwife.[1] By 1800 male-midwives had successfully charted a public image of "rational, scientific expertise" for themselves that conspicuously opposed traditional and "incompetent" female midwifery (Moscucci 1993, 50). At the beginning of the nineteenth century, surgeon-apothecaries habitually delivered infants as part of their daily practice.

In spite of this general public acceptance of the man-midwife's intervention in obstetrical and gynecological cases, the medical corporations in Victorian England were for a long time reluctant to welcome the accoucheur into the ranks of medical specialists. Although the College of Physicians had introduced a license in obstetrics in 1783, the evolving conflation of midwifery and general practice persuaded the corporation in 1804 to withdraw its institutional support of the male midwife. Obstetrics had become an integral part of mixed practice, and the general practitioner therefore threatened to undermine the medical corporation's hierarchical structure, which was jealously guarded by the physicians and surgeons. For a long time, the medical colleges resisted the "academicisation" of the obstetrician, although men-midwives increasingly lobbied their common interests for institutional representation. Things changed in 1852 when a midwifery license was introduced by the College of Surgeons. The year 1859 finally saw the foundation of the Obstetrical Society of London. Yet the real acceptance of the obstetrician's and the gynecologist's practice within the medical profession was delayed until gynecological surgery modernized and sanitized their professional status. By the time Molly walks into Dr. Collins's waiting room in 1888, the medical profession had finally accepted its illegitimate offspring.

Ironically, it was exactly at this moment that gynecological surgery came under fire from another side: feminists and antivivisectionists. Frances Power Cobbe, feminist and founder of the Society for the Protection of Animals Liable to Vivisection, established in 1875, comments disapprovingly on the increasing influence of medical authority in the scientifically oriented nineteenth century: "There is no denying the power of the great Medical Order in these days. It occupies, with strangely close analogy, the position of the priesthood of former times, assumes the same air of authority, claims its victims for torture . . . and enters every family with a latch-key of private information, only comparable to that obtained by the Confessional" (Cobbe 1878, 292). Frances Power Cobbe observed this growing "power of the great Medical Order" in practitioners' ruthless animal experiments and in the equally cruel surgical operations performed by gynecologists. Interestingly, the tortured animal and the mutilated woman became rhetorically linked in campaigns for animal welfare and women's rights. Women identified strongly with the cruelly treated creatures that doctors strapped to their dissection tables. Gynecological examinations, after all, required similar practices: "the woman would have been strapped to a frame which raised her pelvis while her feet were held in stirrups or footrests" (Lansbury 1985, 416). Elizabeth Blackwell, the first woman who took up medical studies in the United States, was understandably appalled by the common practices that dominated gynecological examinations. In 1847 she commented: "Dr Webster sent for me to examine a case of a poor woman at his rooms. 'Twas a horrible exposure; indecent for any poor woman to be subjected to such a torture; she seemed to feel it, poor and ignorant as she was. I felt more than ever the necessity of my mission" (Blackwell 1914, 58). And if a "poor and ignorant" working-class woman was able to sense the indecency of her medical examination, what about her better educated and more "delicate" sisters? Frances Power Cobbe amply illustrates the anguish that Victorian women experienced during gynecological examinations: "A girl who would willingly go to a man-doctor and consult him freely about one of the many ills to which female flesh is heir, would be an odious young woman. Violence must be done to her natural instincts, either by the pressure of the mother's persuasion (who has undergone the same *peine forte et dure* before her), or else by unendurable anguish, before she will have recourse to aid which she thinks worse than disease, or even death" (Cobbe 1878, 295). Especially for unmarried women, the doctor's gynecological examination represented an attack on the patient's moral and mental virginity.

This concern about "dulling of the edge of virgin modesty, and the degradation of the pure minds of the daughters of England" (Hall 1850, 661 quoted in Moscucci 1993, 115) received additional attention with the reintroduction of the speculum in gynecological consultations. It was the French physician Joseph Récamier who rediscovered the utility of an instrument that had been employed in antiquity but that had fallen into oblivion during the Middle Ages and the Renaissance. With its reinstitution in 1801, a fierce controversy over its use broke out, even among physicians. Doctors who decided to employ the speculum in their gynecological practice were accused of instrumental rape. Unsurprisingly, its use after the introduction of the Contagious Diseases Acts of 1864, 1866, and 1869, which provided a legal justification for the compulsory medical examination of prostitutes, was greeted with even more ferocious opposition. Feminists were outraged by the double moral standard aiming to make "vice" safe for men, while women could be imprisoned if they failed to comply with the enforced gynecological examination. Even the otherwise liberally minded Leopold Bloom, seeing a black straw hat belonging to the "face of a streetwalker" (*U* 16.704) in "Eumaeus," aggressively reiterates the institutional rhetoric that aimed to assert control over the difficult issue of prostitutes' sexual health:

> —It beats me, Mr Bloom confided to Stephen, medically I am speaking, how a wretched creature like that from the Lock hospital reeking with disease can be barefaced enough to solicit or how any man in his sober senses, if he values his health in the least. . . . The elder man, though not by any manner of means an old maid or a prude, said it was nothing short of a crying scandal that ought to be put a stop to *instanter* to say that women of that stamp (quite apart from any oldmaidish squeamishness on the subject), a necessary evil, were not licensed and medically inspected by the proper authorities. (*U* 16.728–43)

Of course, Bloom might have his own reasons for avoiding and for demanding the institutionalization of this particular "lady of easy virtue." But even if Bloom appears to be unusually harsh in this instance, his remarks demonstrate how widely known the debate about prostitutes' forced medical examination was at the turn of the century.

Given this particular historical context, we might appreciate Molly's unease about her confrontation with a gynecologist. Indeed, in letting her remember the encounter so vividly over a distance of sixteen years, Joyce crucially illustrates Molly's discomfort. He underlines Molly's awkwardness further by making her recall the rhetorical difficulties that characterized the patient-doctor conversation. It is indeed very interesting to take a closer look at the nature of Dr. Collins's interview since it shows a striking resemblance to a theological confession. But as Molly's medical manual, *The Family Physician*, illustrates, this was, after all, the predominant form of medical interrogation in the scientifically reformed nineteenth century:

> The modern physician occupies a very different position to that of the old-fashioned family medical attendant, and assumes much more the role of the scientific adviser. He is not satisfied with a mere recital of aches and pains, but tries to find out by patient investigation *why* it is that the system of the sufferer has gone wrong. . . . He feels that he has not properly performed his duty until he has got to the bottom of it. . . . He demands implicit confidence and will take no denial, every detail of the patient's life must be laid bare, and no fact, however trivial, escapes his investigation. (Anonymous 1894, xxvii)

Molly is subjected to exactly this type of interrogation. However, the doctor's medical jargon causes confusion: "your vagina he called it" (*U* 18.1154). "Vagina" is certainly not a word Molly Bloom would use. It seems almost as if in using anatomical terminology Dr. Collins alienates Molly's body from its rightful owner. His medical questions and Molly's dismissive comments—"asking me if what I did had an offensive odour what did he want me to do but the one thing gold maybe what a question" (*U* 18.1160–61); "could you pass it easily pass what I thought he was talking about the rock of Gibraltar" (*U* 18.1163–64); "asking me had I frequent omissions where do those old fellows get all the words they have omissions" (*U* 18.1169–70)—exemplify the contrasting views that doctor and patient hold in regard to Molly's body. Molly's organic and intuitive understanding of her body is confronted by the doctor's attempt to theorize her sexual parts. Their points of view are incompatible, and this incompatibility results in Molly's perplexed and rebellious remarks, which assign absurdity and incompetence not to her own but instead to the doctor's idiom.

Both the gynecologist's scientific jargon and his examination practices are further parodied in "Circe" when Bloom, in a comic mirroring of Molly's experience, endures first a sex change and then a gynecological exam that is undertaken by Dr. Mulligan, Dr. Madden, Dr. Crotthers, Dr. Punch Costello, and Dr. Dixon and that also involves, like in Molly's case, a question about "the patient's urine" (*U* 15.1793). As a result of this disconcerting physiological inspection Bloom is diagnosed to be "bisexually abnormal" (*U* 15.1775–76), "*virgo intacta*" (*U* 15.1785–86), and "a finished example of the new womanly man" (*U* 15.1798–99) who is "about to have a baby" (*U* 15.1810). Even more grotesquely, Bloom is then violated by Bello, who "*bares his arm and plunges it elbowdeep into Bloom's vulva*" (*U* 15.3089) and "*shoves his arm in a bidder's face*" (*U* 15.3090–91)—an act with obvious allusions to the brutal nature of gynecological examination practices.

Molly's unease about Dr. Collins might also be the reason why the gynecologist, unlike Father Corrigan—the other male authority figure Molly recalls in her soliloquy—is not turned into the object of her erotic fantasies. In fact Molly hardly regards the doctor as a man at all. Conversely, she assures herself that Dr. Collins is a "dry old stick" (*U* 18.1153) when he has his "shortsighted eyes" (*U* 18.1171) on her. Here it appears as if Molly is trying to follow the customary advice given to women in the last decades of the nineteenth century: look on the doctor with his unpleasant questions and surgical tools as an old woman (Cobbe 1878, 294), or at least as an old man. In reading age and impotence into Dr. Collins's image, Molly desexualizes the encounter that is overdetermined by the gynecologist's tainted reputation.

In "Penelope" Joyce is thus distinctly alluding to the problematic relation-ship among gynecologists, their female patients, and sexuality. He might even have had one specific case in mind. In the early 1860s, Sir William Wilde, father of Oscar Wilde, was accused of rape by one of his patients, Mary Travers. She repeatedly reported that he had sexually violated her while she was under the influence of chloroform (Ellmann 1988, 13–15).[2] Although her case was never a strong one, rumors spread in Dublin and even in England so that *The Lancet* found it necessary to defend Sir William publicly (14). His guilt was never as-certained, but the case nevertheless helped to propagate tales of sexual abuse by male doctors in Ireland.

It is no surprise, therefore, that Molly emphasizes her mistrust of Dr. Col-lins by announcing, "I wouldnt trust him too far to give me chloroform or God knows what else" (*U* 18.1171–72). Since the beginning of its career as a narcotic in the 1830s, and independent of Sir William's case, chloroform and its medical administration had been controversial (Poovey 1989, 24). However, in spite of criticism and widespread disapproval, the use of chloroform became com-mon practice in gynecological operations. Indeed, the development of narcotic anesthetics was one reason for the explosive rise of surgery in the second half of the nineteenth century. Naturally, the anesthetized patient facilitated surgi-cal treatment. Instead of operating on a screaming and squirming creature in excruciating pain, doctors now performed surgical procedures on sedated bodies that had more resemblance to corpses on the dissection table than to individuals. Nevertheless, the image of a chloroformed woman subjected to the gynecologist's surgical knife reinforced the established connection between gynecological surgery and vivisection. Especially after specific operations had become the accepted treatment of pathologies that dominated nineteenth-century medical theories of femininity.

One such operation, performed in the 1860s as a radical therapy for so-called female diseases such as masturbation, nymphomania, and mental disor-ders was clitoridectomy, the surgical removal of the clitoris. And as we can see, the female pathologies that, in the eyes of nineteenth-century medical theory, made this extreme form of corrective intervention necessary are illnesses con-nected to sexual activities that defy the approved image of conventional female sexuality. Clitoridectomy, as Gayatri Chakravorty Spivak has argued, literally deprives women of their status as a "sexed subject" since the clitoris "escapes the reproductive framing that dominates the metaphorical or symbolic clito-ridectomy of women in the name of motherhood and 'normal womanhood'" (Spivak 1988, 151). In the 1860s clitoridectomy was medical reality. Notorious among the numerous doctors who performed this operation was Dr. Isaac Baker Brown. His flourishing practice was eventually closed when the Obstetrical Society of London expelled him for malpractice in 1867. According to the court proceedings, Brown had failed to inform his patients and their husbands about the operation's resulting mutilation.[3]

Interestingly, though, the administration of chloroform receives particular attention in the description of Brown's day-by-day practice: "The patient is put under the influence of chloroform. The inducement has, of course, been enlarged upon. The operation is so very trifling; it is a mere nothing: perhaps the excision of a pile, or the division of a nerve; at all events, nothing of importance. Then the husband is taken down stairs, and the patient is taken up; and, having been placed under the influence of chloroform, her clitoris is cut out" (Anonymous 1867, 431). Both the administration of chloroform and the absence of the protecting husband are equally disastrous to the woman who is placed under Baker Brown's surgical knife. Again, the court description portrays the female patient as the victim of the medically abusive gynecologist who has used his patient's ignorance in medical and anatomical terminology to enforce the controversial treatment.

Although clitoridectomy had lost its appeal for medical practitioners when Molly Bloom seeks medical advice in 1888, it had been replaced by another operation: ovariotomy. This medical procedure advocated the removal of healthy ovaries as a cure for the above-mentioned female pathologies. After its first employment as a remedy for ovarian cancer and cysts in 1809 by the American surgeon Ephraim McDowell, the number of ovariotomies carried out in Britain rose steadily during the nineteenth century. Apparently, it had been performed over 130 times by 1851 (Moscucci 1993, 137). But whereas it had originally been introduced as a cure for physiological illnesses, ovariotomy was soon applied as a corrective treatment for psychological diseases. Hysteria and nymphomania were female maladies that doctors expected to treat with the removal of healthy ovaries. Yet despite its celebration as scientific progress in gynecological surgery, the operation was, in the 1880s, greeted with fervent opposition from both medical practitioners and the public. First of all, the mortality rate was high. This, however, was not the main reason for the operation's condemnation. In attacking the patient's reproductive organs with the surgical knife, ovariotomy literally "castrated" the woman. In an age obsessed with national regeneration, this operation was regarded as a much more fundamental surgical intervention than its equally controversial counterpart, clitoridectomy. Whereas the one operation mutilated only one individual, the other, in preventing reproduction, was damaging to the nation at large.

In the decade that witnessed the controversy about ovariotomies, a specific event crucially highlighted the woman's role as victim of the surgeon's knife. In 1888, curiously the same year that Joyce chose for Molly's gynecological consultation, Jack the Ripper dissected his victims in Whitechapel. The mutilated bodies of the discovered prostitutes had been cut open, and allegedly certain female organs such as the uterus and ovaries were found to be conspicuously absent. Naturally, theories of the Ripper's identity mushroomed. At times a Jewish anarchist was believed to be the culprit (Gilman 1993, 263–84), but it was also "popularly believed that Jack the Ripper was an abortionist" or a "vivisecting surgeon of London University who had extended his research from animals to women" (Lansbury 1985, 431; McLaren 1994, 273). This identification of the Ripper with a medical practitioner has become a compelling part of popular nineteenth-century mythology. As Judith Walkowitz and Elaine Showalter have shown, the Whitechapel cases evoked and helped to disseminate themes of "medical violence against women that pervaded fin de siècle literature—of opening up, dissecting, or mutilating women" (Showalter 1991, 127–43; Walkowitz 2000, 1999). The Ripper's image is thus turned into a popular cultural metaphor for medical abuse. Women appeared in these discussions as helpless victims of the doctor's or the Ripper's knife.

In "Circe" Joyce uses the many speculations that circulated around the Whitechapel mystery to create Bloom's criminal profile: accused of sending obscene letters and postcards to Mrs. Yelverton Barry, Mrs. Bellingham, and the Honourable Mrs. Mervyn Talboys, he is charged with being both "Jack the Ripper" (*U* 15.1153) and an "[a]narchist" (*U* 15.1156) until Mrs Bellingham vindictively suggests to "[v]ivisect him" (*U* 15.1105). Given his suspicious connection to the Ripper, Bloom's culinary preferences—"Mr Leopold Bloom ate with relish the inner organs of beasts and fowls" (*U* 4.1–2)—appear in a very different light indeed. If the Ripper cases were primarily about disembowelment, then Bloom's interest in "thick giblet soup, nutty gizzards, a stuffed roast heart, liverslices fried with crustcrumbs, fried hencods' roes" (*U* 4.2–3) and above all "grilled mutton kidneys" (*U* 4.4) could be a comic reference to the alleged Jewish anarchist who roamed the streets of Whitechapel. The sensationalist Ripper cases indisputably belonged to the cultural matrix of the turn-of-the-century society that Joyce consciously explored in *Ulysses*. Moreover, Joyce's interest in the Whitechapel murderer is also apparent in *Finnegans Wake*. The theme is here incorporated in Shaun's sermon to the girls of St. Bride's. Once again, the notorious Whitechapel slasher is associated with male authority and sexual violence: "Rip ripper rippest and jac jac jac. Dwell on that, my hero and lander! That's the side that appeals to em, the wring wrong way to wright woman. Shuck her! Let him! What he's good for. Shuck her more! Let him again! All she wants!" (*FW* 466.13–17).

As we have seen, Molly is aware of the cultural discourses that associated the gynecologist with the image of a vivisector of women. In her particular case, it is also vital to remember that the operations performed by Victorian gynecologists were factual punishments for female sexual transgression. Doctors performed clitoridectomies and ovariotomies to cure female diseases that were, in the first place, a form of sexual rebellion (nymphomania or masturbation).[4] Yet even in simple cases of menstrual irregularities, medical practice suggested a cure that advocated the application of leeches to the pelvis, the labia, and the uterus; if this did not cause the wished-for results, then it recommended the use of a lancet to secure the extraction of blood (Shuttleworth 1990, 62). With regard to these potential threats, it is not surprising that Molly is at pains to hide her masturbation over Bloom's "mad crazy letters" (*U* 18.1176) from the gynecologist, although she herself is certain that it is the reason for her illness. It is understandable too, that she recalls the encounter with Dr.Collins on the night of Bloomsday. In committing adultery Molly has, according to turn-of-the-century medical theory and social conventions, distinguished herself as a sexually disobedient woman. And although she is admittedly blasé about her social "crime," the vivid recollection of the doctor's unpleasant examination and especially her fearful reference to chloroform show that Molly's guilty conscience imagines punishment in the form of gynecological practices.

Independent of Molly's case, though, women's anxiety and uneasiness, prompted by the image of gynecological consultations, made the cry for medical women in the second half of the nineteenth century understandable. Women started to seek admission to medical studies in order to create more humane medical conditions for themselves and other women, thereby attacking the strict patriarchal orientation of the medical profession. However, as Elizabeth Blackwell argues, that women should be allowed to practice medicine was a groundbreaking suggestion in the middle of the nineteenth century. One of her numerous requests for university enrollment generated the following remark: "You cannot expect us to furnish you with a stick to break our heads with." Blackwell comments, "the attempt of a woman to leave a subordinate position and seek to obtain a complete medical education" was regarded as "revolutionary" (Blackwell 1914, 49). Indeed, women's attempt to gain access to medical practice was a slow and tiring procedure. Despite first successes in the United States and in continental Europe, the first women doctors were not allowed to practice legally in England until 1876 when the Russell Gurney Act granted women the right to sit for medical examinations. In the same year the General Medical Council agreed to enlist women doctors in the national register, thus effectively sanctioning women's right to practice medicine. Finally, in 1877, Sophia Jex-Blake became the first female doctor in England (Jex-Blake 1886, 96).[5] The year 1874 had also seen the opening of the London School of Medicine for Women. By 1886 fifty medical women had been registered.

Expectedly, women's march into the medical profession was greeted with sustained opposition by their male counterparts. Especially gynecologists and obstetricians feared competition from women doctors. Naturally, the argument that women were better qualified to handle the controversial gynecological examinations deprived male practitioners of their legitimate professional authority. No wonder, then, that one of their representatives, the gynecologist Robert Barnes, commented in 1876: "Why is it that women have selected medicine as the special point of attack, is not quite clear. They are far better fitted, by natural aptitude, to shine in the pulpit and at the bar. . . . But medicine, whilst demanding physical power no less than other professions, is essentially based upon science. Now . . . there seems to be a natural incompatibility between science and the female brain" (Barnes 1875–76, 294). The writer contends that women would attractively adorn both the pulpit and the bar, whereas the demanding tasks of a medical practice exceed both women's intellectual and physical capabilities.

Barnes was not the only one of his profession to advocate this theory of woman's intellectual and somatic inferiority. In fact, as Thomas Laqueur shows, the nineteenth-century medical understanding of women stressed both their physiological differences from the male organism and the importance of their reproductive functions, thus creating a biological argument that rationalized women's disadvantages in the social contest (Laqueur 1992, 142–98). Anatomical theory was used to confirm the existing social hierarchy, which firmly situated women at its lower end. Correspondingly, Henry Maudsley argued in 1874:

When we thus look the matter honestly in the face, it would seem plain that women are marked out by nature for very different offices in life from those of men, and that the healthy performance of their special functions renders it improbable she will succeed, and unwise for her to persevere, in running over the same course at the same pace with him.

For such a race she is certainly weighted unfairly. . . . [Women] cannot choose but to be women; cannot rebel successfully against the tyranny of their organization, the complete development and function whereof must take place after its kind. This is not the expression of prejudice nor of false sentiment; it is the plain statement of a physiological fact. (468)

What Maudsley calls "the healthy performance" of women's "special functions" indeed came under scrutiny.

Going back to "Penelope," we can see that Molly's 1888 illness was only a minor one, possibly physiological leucorrhea, and that an appointment with a gynecologist was likely to be superfluous. However, Molly's encounter with Dr. Collins takes place at a time when gynecological theory had established an economic theory of the female body that advocated the careful balance of body fluids. Doctors now focused their attention increasingly on women's menstrual cycles, their potential suppression, and resulting ailments. Consequently, they identified the retention of the regular flow of the menses as the primary reason for female mental pathologies (Shuttleworth 1990, 47–68; Strange 2005, 102–16).

Medical theory thus created a link between the obstruction of the menstrual blood and insanity, between female physiology and pathology. If the regular flow of the menses was prohibited, blood would be released in the brain causing permanent damage to the nervous system. Maudsley resumes his argument by stating that "at each reoccurring period there are all the preparations for conception, and nothing is more necessary to the preservation of female health than that these changes should take place regularly and completely." He continues: "Hence it is that the outbreak of diseases is so often heralded, or accompanied, or followed by suppression or irregularity of these functions" (Maudsley 1874, 467). The regular event of menstruation is therefore identified as an index of women's mental health.

In its attempt to master the many illnesses connected with menstruation, nineteenth-century medical theory now developed a whole new taxonomy of female disorders. Among those identified were amenorrhea (retention and suppression of the menses), dysmenorrhea (acute pain during menstruation), menorrhagia (morbidly profuse menstruation), and leucorrhea (white vaginal discharges)(Shuttleworth 1990, 61)—this last one being the very illness from which Molly suffered in 1888. And since medical theory suggested that her body functions demand professional attention, it is no wonder that Molly is also worried, in the night of June 16, 1904, if there is "anything the matter with my insides or have I something growing in me getting that thing like that every week" (*U* 18.1149–50) that is "pouring out of me like the sea" (*U* 18.1123). More-over, in the discussions of retention and suppression of the menses, puberty and early adolescence, the times when the reproductive functions start to de-velop, were identified as crucial moments when menstrual blood was supposed to flow regularly to secure women's future health and happiness. Doctors and patent medicine advertisement agreed that obstructions and so-called female irregularities occurring in the years of early adolescence doomed women to a long life of suffering and mental disorders. Viewed in this light, it is not sur-prising that, in 1888, the young Molly Bloom sought medical advice about "that white thing" (*U* 18.1152).

Another of Joyce's characters who is experiencing the authority of this ef-fective medical pathologization of the female organism is Gerty MacDowell. Her "Widow Welch's female pills," which she uses to cure her discharges (*U* 13.85–86), were advertised as a patent remedy for female troubles and for ir-regularities in the female system (Gifford 1989, 385). Both Molly and Gerty are at the crucial age that doctors had singled out as especially dangerous for the occurrence of menstrual irregularities when they seek medical aid. Yet Gerty's case also shows that, in 1904, patent medicine had effectively started to rival orthodox medical practices. Although quack remedies and patent medicines were hardly new markers in the turn-of-the-century cultural landscape, the second half of the nineteenth century witnessed an increased interest in the different patent remedies that were then flooding the market. Advertisements could be found in newspapers, medical manuals, and above all in women's fashion magazines (Richards 1991, 168–204). The influence of patent and do-mestic medicine is also visible in "Penelope."

The suggestion to pair gynecology and patent or domestic medicine in the analysis of Joyce's "Penelope" might be unexpected. Clearly, it must seem as if the two medical discourses represent fundamentally different aspects of nine-teenth-century medical philosophy. Obviously, medical practitioners fought an unrelenting battle against the "irregulars" that threatened to undermine their authority. Nonetheless, these two medical modes are unexpectedly linked by a shared starting point in midwifery and obstetrics. Obstetrical practice fo-cused on the delivery of infants and the subsequent medical treatment of both mother and children. In other words, the obstetrician emerged as a general practitioner or family doctor. As the title of Molly's medical manual, *The Fam-ily Physician*, illustrates, nineteenth-century domestic medicine also identified the family unit as the prime target for its products. Gynecology can therefore be seen as the "official" academic variety of its patent counterpart, domestic medicine. As we shall see, Joyce ingeniously used the two complementary discourses as subtexts for the discussion of gender roles in "Penelope." And since domestic medicine had a far wider reach than its academic sister discipline, its impact on Molly's thoughts exceeds that of official nineteenth-century gynecology. As Stephen Dedalus accurately observes in "Circe," Joyce's characters live in "the age of patent medicines" (*U* 15.4470–71).

Given the omnipresence of patent medical advertisements at the turn of the century, it seems not at all remarkable that Bloom owns a prospectus of "The Wonderworker, the world's greatest remedy for rectal complaints" (*U* 17.1819–20). Yet because they were regarded as more enthusiastic consumers than men, women formed the target market for patent medicine's advertising campaign. Consequently, fashion journals such as Molly's *Gentlewoman* sprinkled their pages with countless patent advertisements, and Molly is, unquestionably, susceptible to the seductions of patent medicine's campaigns. When she worries that her "belly is a bit too big" (*U* 18.450), she recalls the advice publicized in *The Gentlewoman*: "breathing exercises" (*U* 18.455) and "that antifat" (*U* 18.455–56). These methods, masquerading as medical advice, seem far more attractive and palatable than the more obvious solution: "knock off the stout at dinner" (*U* 18.450).

Many of the patent medical advertisements emphasized professional medical approval of the remedies offered and consumed. Doctors' testimonies were quoted extensively in patent medical advertisements in the attempt to underline a product's respectability. Paradoxically, however, while patent medical advertisements and manuals looked to official medicine for approval in order to legitimize the use value of their products, they simultaneously tried to defy the authority of medical practitioners in promoting the woman's agency and independence in the administration of patent medicine products. The full title of Molly's medical manual is *The Family Physician: A Manual of Domestic Medicine by Physicians and Surgeons of the Principal London Hospitals* and the reference to the medical establishment, the "Physicians and Surgeons of the Principal London Hospitals," illustrates that the book represents medical authority. Medical authority that is absent and present at the same time. Although a direct confrontation with a medical practitioner is avoided, the manual's status as a medical bible still authorizes its reader to administer the advocated medical remedies. It therefore seems to promote the creation of a medical empire for women, in which they are independent from their male medical advisors.

By reading domestic medicine manuals, women are able to replace the doctor as medical authority. Equipped with the knowledge provided by the handbook, women take over his position and cure not just their own but also their family members' ailments. Thanks to this new medical education, the woman becomes a second Florence Nightingale, able to perform the doctor's duty—a superior role, explicitly defined as such by the medical manuals. As *The Family Physician*, in a passage describing the use of the thermometer, states: "With [the thermometer] [the woman] will give the doctor a trusty account of the condition of his patient. During his absence her hand will be his hand, her eye his eye, and more than that, seeing a sudden rise or fall of temperature when he is away, she foresees the peril that thermometry predicts several hours in advance, as the barometer does the storm, her mind becomes his mind, she hastens his return, and enables him to ward off a deadly exacerbation or collapse, truly herself saving the life of the patient" (Anonymous 1894, 156). The passage endorses the importance of the woman or mother in medical care. It is now she who is "truly herself" responsible for the patient's recovery.

It is probably fairly obvious, though, that the image of the devoted, altruistic nurse reinforces reactionary gender politics in turning the mother into the doctor's handmaiden. Though a handful of women were admitted to specialized medical knowledge, their role, in general, remained that of a subaltern who replaced the doctor only during his absence. Women in general did not achieve the same knowledge and authority that studies and a degree guaranteed men. Further, this allegedly new role of the woman as a medical administrator was not really a radical breakthrough. Women had since antiquity been responsible for the administration of their family's health (Lane 2001, 2). But late nineteenth-century medical rhetoric recreated the image of the woman healer, identified it as progressive, and thus signposted the dawn of modernity and its ostensibly shifting social roles. However, in spite of this reformist undertone, the woman's domain remained the home. Within its walls she was allowed to share the medical knowledge generally reserved for men—a suggestion amply underlined by the title of Molly's medical manual, *The Family Physician*. All this happened at a time when medicine reinvented itself as a crucial advocate of modernization, emphatically promoting progress and improvement. But as the medically promoted position of women indicates, despite the suggestive label "modern," medicine was hardly complicit in facilitating female emancipation. Instead, the nurse image served to strengthen the gender dynamics that gynecological theories had resolutely established.

Naturally, the woman's role as nurse was accentuated when children were involved, especially in a time that was obsessed with public and national health.

The *Report of the Inter-Departmental Committee on Physical Deterioration* in 1904 was the inevitable result of growing alarm regarding national degeneration. As might be expected, one of its major concerns was infant mortality. The exorbitant numbers of child deaths were conveniently explained by the lack of maternal care (Anonymous 1904, 55). Accordingly, the report states that "very little knowledge is moreover found among mothers of the slighter ailments to which children are prone, and precautionary measures are rarely taken until they have reached an aggravated stage" (56). However, if maternal ignorance was one reason for the failing health of the nation's offspring, neglected breast-feeding was a second explanation for the ill health of infants. Campaigns for children's welfare followed, which tried to reestablish a domestic ideal with an improved form of motherhood at its center. A Ladies' National Association for the Diffusion of Sanitary Knowledge had already been established in 1857, and it extensively distributed guides with titles such as *Health of Mothers*, *How to Rear Healthy Children*, *How to Manage a Baby*, and *The Evils of Wet-Nursing* (Porter 1999, 641). This campaign was, of course, part of the nineteenth-century preoccupation with public and preventive medicine.

Yet in women's cases, medical and social debates crucially interacted. In the medical propaganda for public health the mother, as the incarnation of an idealized form of Victorian femininity, emerged as the pivot for domestic happiness and family welfare. Milly Bloom is one of the many daughters who profited from this reformed understanding of motherhood. Accordingly, Molly proudly announces her profound knowledge of children's diseases. Undoubtedly, it is knowledge that she has obtained from medical guides such as *The Family Physician*. For instance, the book devotes a long section to discussing the examination of children's urine. This is done with the help of a urinometer, which ascertains the gravity of the urine and diagnoses potential diseases such as ringworm (Anonymous 1904, 179–86). Similarly, Molly reports that she "always used to know by Millys when she was a child whether she had worms or not" (*U* 18.1167–68).

By thus showing domestic medicine's influence in "Penelope," Joyce effectively underlines the workings of modern medical imperialism. Its unchallenged position at the turn of the century is also illustrated by Molly's reference to *Aristotle's Master-Piece*. Her slip of the tongue transforms it innovatively into "Aristocrats Masterpiece" (*U* 18.1238). Joyce therefore comments humorously on the medical profession's self-image as impending new social elite. But Molly's remark also becomes, as Stephen E. Soud argues, "a feminist critique of a treatise for midwives perverted by its male author(s)" (Soud 1995, 202) and shows that although Molly's social role is to the highest degree influenced by modern medical prescriptions, she is in no sense unconditionally yielding to its dominant influence. Indeed, Molly's soliloquy develops into an energetic response to medicine's confining recommendations. Interestingly, though, her reactions continue to be intertwined with medicine's cultural prescriptions. But it is precisely through this blend of medicine's didactic suggestions and Molly's conflicting responses that Joyce aims his critique at modern medicine's cultural authority in "Penelope."

Molly's open rebellion against this "chaining me up" (*U* 18.1391), as she calls it, is central to her sexual escapade with Boylan, which blatantly violates the image of domestic bliss and motherhood. But even the subversive image of the adulteress becomes entangled with medical propaganda. When Molly remembers Boylan caressing her breasts, she notices the unmistakable "marks of his teeth" (*U* 18.569). The sexual image is instantly interlaced with that of the infant sucking its mother's breast. In fact, it accentuates Molly's opinion of male dependence on women: "they wouldnt be in the world at all only for us they dont know what it is to be a woman and a mother how could they where would they all of them be if they hadnt all a mother to look after them" (*U* 18.1439–42). Yet if Boylan, through this comparison, regresses to a state of childish dependency, then Molly metamorphoses from lover into mother, claiming that she "had a great breast of milk with Milly enough for two" (*U* 18.570–71)—a fact that makes Bloom want to "milk [her] into the tea" (*U* 18.578). With the emphasis of the biological function of Molly's breasts, we are back in the realm of medically propagated motherhood.

After the *Committee for Physical Deterioration* had expressed its concerns about infant rearing, mothers were encouraged to breast-feed. It was generally regarded as the promise for children's health and physical growth. Accordingly, Molly's *Family Physician* contains detailed instructions for wet nurses to achieve maximum success in breast-feeding. In an extraordinary passage, the manual even suggests that "brunettes make better nurses and give better milk than blondes" (Anonymous 1904, 2). But we can see very vividly in "Penelope" that Molly's thoughts are influenced by this omnipresent turn-of-the-century medical discourse. Even the consideration of her adultery brings her back to the medically promoted role of the mother, creating a blend of incompatible self-representations in her soliloquy. While she hovers between many potential roles—Milly's confidante (*U* 18.1021) or the unbridled adulteress—Molly's conflicting portrait distinctly underscores the crux inherent to one of modernity's most significant medical theories.

Within its progress-orientated mission lies another message: the promotion of a reactionary image of femininity.

Joyce uses an intriguing textual design to underline the argument developed in "Penelope." It is worth remembering that Molly's image is, until we hear her own voice at the end of *Ulysses*, thoroughly constructed by Joyce's male characters. An imaginary reader of Joyce's text encounters her only through the masculine and misogynist comments of characters such as Simon Dedalus in "Sirens" (*U* 11.496–97) or the Nameless One in "Cyclops," who calls her a "fat heap" (*U* 12.503). Yet things change with the opening of the last episode of *Ulysses*. Molly Bloom's voice emerges at a very remarkable moment in Joyce's work. It is, like the final word in an argument, the long-expected "clou of the book" (*LI* 170). Accordingly, it recalls and reexamines people and situations described throughout the text. For instance, Molly vividly remembers Simon Dedalus's alcoholic affliction (*U* 18.1291). She reveals that Bloom is unaware of the secret of his bed (*U* 18.1212–14) and she even refutes his assumption that all her Spanish is forgotten (*U* 4.60–61 and *U* 18.1471–72). And it is not only the world of *Ulysses* that finds its way into Molly's thoughts. Dante Riordan (*U* 18.4) is recalled and Kathleen Kearney (*U* 18.376) and Tom Kernan (*U* 18.1264) are only two of the Dubliners who reappear in Molly's nocturnal thoughts. Molly's is also the last voice a reader hears before diving in to the world of fragmented identities and characters in *Finnegans Wake*. "Penelope" is, therefore, a recapitulation and reevaluation of the so-far unchallenged patriarchal viewpoints presented in the rest of Joyce's book.

But "Penelope" is also Joyce's response to medicine's restrictive notions of women and female social roles. We see this critique in Joyce's representation of Molly as a cultural investigator and critic. Apart from her occasional urge for medical knowledge, "I often wanted to study up that myself what we have inside us in that family physician" (*U* 18.180–81), Molly possesses all the diagnostic talents she needs for medical analysis. If *The Family Physician* underlined the doctor's function as medical detective, then Molly also shows remarkable investigation skills when she tries to find out about Bloom's love affairs or the remaining French letters in his pocket (*U* 18.1235). In "Nausicaa" Bloom also has to acknowledge her sharp eyes: "When I said to Molly the man at the corner of Cuffe street was goodlooking, thought she might like, twigged at once he had a false arm. Had, too" (*U* 13.914–16).

Molly's soliloquy further shows that she is aware of medicine's dominating influence in women's lives. She confidently identifies the medical subtext dominating her environment and its gender roles. Accordingly, her thoughts linger for a long time over male attitudes toward maladies. Bloom, if not a hypochondriac, is certainly not particularly good with pain or ill health. Molly remembers domestic dramas about bleeding noses (*U* 18.24) and Bloom's fear of blood poisoning (*U* 18.31–32). As Molly suggests, he shares this attitude with the rest of his sex: "theyre so weak and puling when theyre sick they want a woman to get well" (*U* 18.23). Men simulate or exaggerate pain, and women attend to them. As Molly recalls, Bloom used a simulated illness to gain Dante Riordan's attention during their stay in the City Arms Hotel: "pretending to be laid up with a sick voice doing his highness to make himself interesting" (*U* 18.3–4).

Astutely observing this phenomenon, Molly identifies the sexual politics that dominate the behavior on both sides by referring to "Miss Stack bringing him flowers . . . anything at all to get into a mans bedroom with her old maids voice trying to imagine he was dying on account of her" (*U* 18.26–29). Women respond to exaggerated illness with a mistaken sense of romance suggested by the nurse image. Molly, who is aware of the underlying sexual dynamics, fails to be romantic when considering Bloom's illness: "if ever he got anything really serious the matter with him its much better for them to go into a hospital where everything is clean" (*U* 18.17–19). But Molly's remark is not misanthropic. Instead it is a response to medicine's sustained dominance in women's lives. As the pronoun "he," referring to Bloom, changes to "them" in the second half of Molly's statement, her comment is to be understood as a political observation on contemporary gender roles. Following from that, Molly admits that she is tired of the role of the nurse: "besides I hate bandaging and dosing" (*U* 18.31). No doubt, this weariness is also the motive for her unsentimental comments about Bloom's potential terminal illness: "yes and then wed have a hospital nurse next thing on the carpet have him staying there till they throw him out" (*U* 18.20–21).

A critical evaluation of idealized motherhood also finds its way into Molly's thoughts. Although she is herself clearly influenced by medicine's authority, Molly nevertheless rightly identifies the model of domesticated womanhood, Mina Purefoy, as its eventual outcome: "Mina Purefoys husband give us a swing out of your whiskers filling her up with a child or twins once a year as regular as the clock always with a smell of children off her . . . the last time I was there a squad of them falling over one another and bawling you couldnt hear your ears supposed to be healthy" (*U* 18.159–65). We know for sure that *Ruby: The Pride of the Ring* is Molly's bedside book. Otherwise, I would suggest the presence of another text, a text with which Joyce was allegedly familiar: Friedrich Engels's

1884 *The Origin of the Family, Private Property and the State* (Brown 1985, 27). In this late work, Engels argues that the "modern individual family is founded on the open or concealed domestic slavery of the wife, and modern society is a mass composed of these individual families as its molecules" (Engels 1972, 137).

Engels's statement reappears in a tortuous version also in Molly's soliloquy: "whoever suggested that business for women what between clothes and cooking and children" (*U* 18.1129–30). As Engels identifies prostitution and the wife's adultery as the two main social consequences of the modern monogamous and patriarchal family (Engels 1972, 131–34), both take up a prominent place in Molly's thoughts. While she is reflecting on her sexual encounter with Boylan, she also suspects Bloom's and other husbands' loitering about the red light district. Strikingly, however, the assumed role of the adulteress, which Molly appropriates to liberate herself from the monotonous existence of wife and mother, fails to meet expectations. If, as Engels suggests, adultery is the product of the modern capitalist society, then Molly's affair with Boylan is in no way liberating. Instead it represents a confirmation of the society that produced the operating cultural and sexual politics.

In commenting on the nature of men, women, and the sexual and social dynamics between them, Molly nevertheless exceeds the role allocated to her. She confuses the gender roles suggested by modern medicine's discourses, and Joyce smuggles in a socialist cultural critique at the least expected place of his text. Molly even has a final prescription to offer: "I dont care what anybody says itd be much better for the world to be governed by the women in it you wouldnt see women going and killing one another and slaughtering when do you ever see women rolling around drunk like they do or gambling every penny they have and losing it on horses yes because a woman whatever she does she knows where to stop" (*U* 18.1434–39). It is an ironic allusion, of course, since Molly has only on that day lost money on horses (*U* 18.423–25) and, at another point, calls women "a dreadful lot of bitches" (*U* 18.1459).

Finally, it should not be forgotten that Boylan is not the only person experiencing gratification and pleasure from Molly's body. Her comments display an evident autoerotic tendency. Her breasts excite her (*U* 18.1379) and she congratulates herself on the whiteness and smoothness of her "pair of thighs" (*U* 18.1144–45). Whereas nineteenth-century doctors suggested a pejorative interpretation of woman's physiology, Molly's positive identification with her body and its functions reconsiders the notion of an innate female pathology. Although she is clearly troubled by the occurrence of what Maudsley calls the "tyranny of the organization"—"O Jamesy let me up out of this pooh" (*U* 18.1128–29)—Molly's affirmative reevaluation of the physical experience exhibits the incompleteness of medical constructions of womanhood.

With Molly Bloom and the intricate representation of modern femininity in "Penelope," Joyce closes another case study on modern medicine's dignostic practices. The last episode of *Ulysses* unmistakably emphasizes that Molly's behavior and comments are influenced by modern medical propaganda and its constructions of idealized femininity. At the turn of the century, both gynecology and its nonacademic sister discourse domestic medicine effectively controlled the interpretations of acceptable female social conduct. Their combined efforts created a significant cultural milieu that determinedly monitored women's lives in a time when the suffragette movement was threatening to overthrow the social status quo. In Joyce's text Molly's miscellaneous and often contradictory images complicate notions of male and female discourses. Cheryl Herr and Kimberly Devlin have both argued that "Penelope" accumulates various guises of traditional femininity in order to undermine conventional representations of womanhood (Devlin 1994, 63–79 and Herr 1994, 80–102). Yet Molly's representation is not just a collage of feminine constructions. Instead, these feminine aspects are contrasted with Molly's engagement in ostensibly male-dominated discourses, especially that of the cultural critic whose analytical work so conspicuously resembles that of the male medical practitioner.

Joyce was aware of the social and cultural consequences of medically propagated theories of women. These theories gave him the opportunity to build into the image of voluptuous femininity a more complex image of womanhood. The result is Molly Bloom, whose image points to and criticizes the arbitrariness of culturally constructed concepts of women and gender and effectively identifies medicine's scientific evaluation of women as fictional interpretations of the social context. In "Penelope" Joyce therefore offers his most vigorous critique of modern medicine's demand for cultural authority.

·

In the *Scribbledehobble* notebook Joyce asks laconically: "Are Ulysses' adventures 12 diseases" (Connolly 1961, 90). *Joyce, Medicine, and Modernity* has offered six detailed case studies on medicine, diseases, and debility in Joyce's works from *Dubliners* to *Ulysses*. As we have seen throughout this book, medicine was an authoritative force emerging in modern society, one to which Joyce responded with fascinated interest, analytical force, and subversive creativity. However, my analysis of this topic is by no means conclusive. There are, of course, many other medical subjects, debates, and references that are incorporated into Joyce's texts (especially into *Finnegans Wake*). Obviously, Joyce's obsession with his failing health could again be taken as a starting point. Among the topics that deserve more detailed examinations in future scholarship on Joyce's *Ulysses* and medicine might be heart diseases in "Hades" or digestive concerns in "Lestrygonians."

Moreover, *Finnegans Wake* is an extremely rich site for future medical readings. In spite of the many references to medicine, doctors, and illnesses— "neurasthene nympholept"; "endocrine-pineal typus" (*FW* 115.30–31); "Remarkable evidence was given, anon, by an eye, ear, nose and throat witness" who has his abode "at Nullnull, Medical Square" (*FW* 86.32–35); "post-wartem plastic surgeons"(*FW* 263.11–12)—critics have focused their attention predominantly on the text's connections to mental illnesses such as hysteria and schizophrenia (Benstock 1982, 169–96; McBride 1996, 145–75; Shloss 2003). But the *Wake*'s unmistakable awareness of its medical contexts could become the focus of many other critical surveys on very diverse topics such as anatomy— "that's pectoral, his mammamuscles most mousterious" (*FW* 15.32–33); neurology, linguistic disorders, and aphasia—Joyce was apparently very interested in "the physiological basis of speech . . . and in Paris attended the lectures of the Abbé Jousse, a proponent of a theory that speech had its origin in gesture" (Lyons 1973, 176); HCE's scopophilia that is discussed at length in the trial in chapter 1.4; public health in chapter 3.3; respiratory disorders—"Just press this cold brand against your brow for a mow. Cainfully! The sinus the curse" (*FW* 374.32–33); or even radiology since *Finnegans Wake* references an "X ray picture" (*FW* 530.8). More work could also be done on Joyce's complex attitude towards Darwinism and eugenics. I hope that *Joyce, Medicine, and Modernity*, in renewing critical interest in Joyce's ongoing debate with medicine, physiology, and the sciences, can clear space for such future studies.

Notes

Introduction

1. In *Joyce's Iritis and the Irritated Text: The Dis-lexic Ulysses*, Roy Gottfried compellingly suggests that "writing, biography, and optics are connected" in Joyce's case (Gottfried 1995, 23).

2. Since Joyce offered to send excerpts of the "Scylla and Charybdis" episode to Ezra Pound in April 1917, it is likely that he had written drafts of the first nine chapters of *Ulysses* before his iridectomy in August 1917 (see Groden 1977, 6).

Chapter 1. Joyce and Modern Medicine

1. Robert H. Bell has suggested that the medical student Buck Mulligan, through his "satiric bias" that becomes the dominant principle in the later chapters of the novel, indeed plays a very central role in *Ulysses*. However, only in passing does Bell link Mulligan's sardonic nature to his status as a medical student (Bell 1991, 14–15).

2. How much Joyce relied on science, scientific debates, and the development of a scientific perspective can be seen in Mary Colum's comments about *Ulysses*. Colum suggests that the book "shows the amazing inroads that science is making on literature." She then continues her critical assessment of *Ulysses* by expressing the fear that science might overshadow the achievements of art and literature: "Mr Joyce's book is of as much interest as science as it is as literature; in some parts it is of purely scientific and non-artistic interest. It seems to me a real and not a fantastic fear that science will oust literature altogether as a part of human expression; and from that point of view *Ulysses* is a dangerous indication" (Deming 1970, 234). The numerous references to medicine and medical lore in Joyce's works might also have prompted Dr. Joseph Collins, a physician and admirer of Joyce, to write a critical assessment of Joyce's work in 1923 (*The Doctor Looks at Literature: Psychological Studies of Life and Letters*).

3. See the Linati schema and Gilbert-Gorman plan reproduced in Ellmann 1984, 190–97.

4. Joyce's *Ulysses* gives credit to Koch's scientific stardom in the "Nestor" episode. In his letter to the press, Mr. Deasy insists that the current epidemic of foot and mouth disease is treated with "Koch's preparation" (*U* 2.332). However, Mr. Deasy (or Joyce) is surprisingly ignorant about the scientific details in the cattle disease's treatment. Although Koch developed a serum to treat anthrax in 1882, he never investigated possible cures for the foot and mouth disease. For more information on Joyce's use of Koch and germ theory see Bock (2007, 23–46).

5. One of the most distinguished advocates of the miasmatic theory of disease was the German cellular pathologist Rudolf Virchow. However, with the general acceptance of Robert Koch's germ theory in the 1880s contagionism (the belief that individuals not places are infectious) replaced miasmatism as predominant disease theory (see Otis 1999, 9–11).

6. The passage in "A Little Cloud" is reminiscent of the description of Dickens's slum, Tom-all-Alone's, in *Bleak House*, one of the most characteristic condition-of-England novels that criticized institutional neglect. Tom-all-Alone's is here described as "a black, dilapidated street, avoided by all decent people; where the crazy houses were seized upon, when their decay was far advanced, by some bold vagrants. . . . As, on the ruined human wretch, vermin parasites appear, so, these ruined shelters have bred a crowd of foul existence that crawls in and out of gaps in walls and boards; and coils itself to sleep, in maggot numbers, where the rain drips in" (Dickens 1996, 257).

7. Rowntree's book offered an extensive study of the living conditions of York's working classes. Rowntree also tried to determine the nutritional balance required to prevent a person from becoming ill from malnutrition.

8. Enda Duffy further examines the medical photograph of an Irishman in order to show how "the Irishman" was pathologized as a cultural "Other" (Duffy 1994, 93–95).

9. For more information on Dublin's nineteenth-century sanitary conditions see O'Brien (1982, especially 3–36).

10. It should be noted though that Joyce seemed to have questioned medicine's valence as a modern progress narrative in the 1912 essay "The Universal Literary Influence of the Renaissance" when stating that "[a]ll modern conquest, of the air, the land, the sea, disease, ignorance, melts, so to speak, in the crucible of the mind and is transformed into a little drop of water, into a tear" (*OCPW* 190).

Chapter 2. "Alcoh alcoho alcoherently"

1. The first neuropathological descriptions of *paralysis agitans* were published in James Parkinson's 1817 study *An Essay on the Shaking Palsy*. In the course of the nineteenth century, paralysis was then increasingly associated with *tabes dorsalis* and syphilis. See Porter (1999, 545–46).

2. A critical evaluation of alcoholism in Joyce's work can also be found in Lilienfeld (1999). However, Lilienfeld concentrates on *A Portrait* without considering "Counterparts."

3. Of course, in spite of this analogy between the two diseases, it should be noted that hysteria allegedly afflicted mainly women, whereas doctors regarded alcoholism as the archetypal disease of the working-class man.

4. Joyce was, of course, not the only writer whose fiction absorbed Lombroso's degeneration theories. Norman Sherry (1971) has shown that Joseph Conrad also incorporated elements of "Lombrosianism" in *The Secret Agent*, which was published in 1907—two years after Joyce finished "Counterparts."

5. The letters to Stanislaus were written in 1906. "Counterparts" was finished in July 1905 (*LII* 92).

6. This conflation of mental illness and alcoholism is, in itself, not a product of the nineteenth century. In the fifth century BC the pre-Socratic philosopher Heraclitus had already

linked all forms of mental derangements, whether they happened to be insanity or a form of intoxication, to the god of wine, Dionysus. Nineteenth-century medical practitioners simply provided the worshipper of the Dionysian cult with an unmistakably pathological label (Sass 1992, 2).

7. Although John Paul Riquelme convincingly argues that the "essentially anti-realist character of Gothic writing from the beginning creates in advance a compatibility with modernist writing" (Riquelme 2000, 586), surprisingly little work has been done on Joyce and Gothic literature. Notable exceptions are James F. Wurtz (2005, 102–17) and Jeff Wallace (2001, 111–28). Sebastian Knowles also has a chapter on the connections between "Penelope" and Mary Shelley's *Frankenstein* in *The Dublin Helix* (Knowles 2001, 104–14).

8. How much Joyce knew about Janet's psychological theory is unclear. According to Mary Colum he was "cross and amused" when she "attended the lectures of Pierre Janet, the greatest of the French psychologists" and suggested that: "'You could learn as much psychology from yourself as from these fellows'" (Colum and Colum 1959, 134). However, Adaline Glasheen has shown that Joyce used Morton Prince's 1905 casebook *The Dissociation of a Personality* for the development of Issy's character in *Finnegans Wake* (Glasheen 1954, 89–96). Prince was a Boston neurologist who was strongly influenced by Pierre Janet's hysteria concept. By the time Joyce was writing *Finnegans Wake*, he was therefore familiar with Janet's and Prince's personality dissociation concept.

9. Many of Janet's results and theories had been discussed and even anticipated by his colleague Alfred Binet although Binet did not formulate them in such an extensive study as *L'Automatisme psychologique*.

10. "[J]'ai dû admettre, pour le délire en général, une nature psychologique, non pas seulement analogue, mais *absolument identique* avec celle de l'état de rêve." [My translation; Moreau (de Tours)'s emphasis.]

11. "[S]ous l'influence croissante de l'excitation alcoolique, l'ivrogne passe du monde réel dans un monde imaginaire, de l'état de veille dans l'état de rêve. Et c'est lorsqu'une sorte de fusion s'est opérée entre des deux états, lorsque l'individu ne sait plus distinguer les phénomènes qui sont exclusivement propres à l'un ou à l'autre, qu'il doit être considéré comme aliéné." [My translation.]

12. "C'est *l'activité humaine dans ses formes les plus simples, les plus rudimentaires*, qui fera l'objet de cette étude." [My translation; Janet's emphasis.]

13. Janet already developed this concept of "doubling" in a shorter and earlier text. (See Janet 1886, 577–92.)

14. "[L]'un constituait la personnalité ordinaire, l'autre, susceptible d'ailleurs de se subdiviser, formait une personnalité anormale, différente de la première et complètement ignorée par elle." [My translation.]

15. Parallel to my own interpretation of Farrington's uncontrollable muscular movements Patrick McCarthy has suggested that they could be read as conditioned reflexes. He points out that "Counterparts" was written a year after Ivan Pavlov was awarded the Nobel Prize in Physiology or Medicine for his work on conditioning and involuntary reflex actions (McCarthy 1997, 448).

16. "En un mot, l'émotion a une action dissolvante sur l'esprit, diminue sa synthèse et le rend pour un moment misérable." [My translation.]

17. "[L]es lois de la maladie sont les mêmes que celles de la santé et qu'il n'y a dans celle-là que l'exagération ou la diminution de certains phénomènes qui se trouvaient déjà dans celle-ci." [My translation.]

18. "Certains empoisonnements comme l'alcoolisme, le saturnisme, l'empoisonnement par le sulfure de carbone . . . amènent des symptômes que l'on peut confondre avec ceux de l'hystérie." [My translation.]

19. This illusionary invasion of the sufferer's bed by rats and mice is by no means unusual for the alcoholic's clinical picture. According to Maudsley, it is an acknowledged symptom of delirium tremens (Maudsley 1886, 484). In general, medical theory associates visual hallucinations with alcoholism and intoxications. Conversely, other forms of sensory hallucinations belong into the clinical picture of separate illnesses. For example, auditory hallucinations can be found in people who suffer from schizophrenia.

20. "L'ivresse de l'alcool . . . rend un homme plus suggestible et plus automatique qu'une somnambule." [My translation.] It is worth pointing out that Janet, in a later article, fundamentally revised his alcoholism concept. In 1915 he understands alcohol as a stimulant used by individuals who suffer from low physical tension (a form of mental energy necessary to keep an organism mentally healthy) (Janet 1915, 476–85).

21. Richard Ellmann reports, for instance, that W. B. Yeats's doubts about his late marriage to Georgie Hyde-Lees evaporated instantly when he discovered his wife's unusual gift (Ellmann 1987, 223).

22. Obviously, Joyce seems to be evoking the commonplace stereotype of the drunken, vivacious, and witty Irishman in many of the cited cases. Postcolonial critics such as David Lloyd have dealt with the problematic aspects of using drunkenness as "a metonym for Irishness" and Irish masculinity (Lloyd 2000, 132). Such postcolonial readings of Joyce have, of course, a lot of valence. My argument, however, aims to draw attention to another so-far unobserved facet of Joyce's treatment of alcoholism, one that is less concerned with the national politics played out in "Counterparts" but with the story's responsiveness to contemporary medical debates.

23. A further reading of the economic and ideological undercurrents that inform alcohol consumption in Joyce can be found in Delany (1995, 381–93).

24. When reconsidering the event later on Farrington also asks himself: "Could he not keep his tongue in his cheek?" (*D* 88). This indicates, once again, that he temporarily lost control over his own body when standing up to Mr. Alleyne.

Chapter 3. "The Heinous Sin of Self-Pollution"

1. Recently Andrew Gibson has written informatively on the different and conflicting formative forces that determine Stephen's upbringing in Catholic Ireland (Gibson 2006, 85–103).

2. Richard Brown states that Joyce's fascination with "self-pollution" is endorsed by a particular book found by Richard Ellmann in the Trieste library: Paul Garnier's *Onanisme* (1885), a medical treatise that was less concerned with masturbation's harmful consequences for the individual than with its implications for procreation (Brown 1985, 55).

3. Especially Thomas Laqueur (2003) has recently offered an informative and original study of masturbation's cultural history.

4. That the book had a strong impact on eighteenth-century culture can be seen by its many

reprints. By the time Voltaire included the entry "onanism" in his *Dictionnaire Philosophique* in 1764, *Onania* had reached its eightieth edition and the formerly slim pamphlet had swelled into a substantial book including an extensive appendix that gathered letters from sufferers, opponents, and supporters (MacDonald 1967, 425; Hare 1962, 2).

5. Neither the anonymous author of *Onania* nor Tissot distinguished between onanism and masturbation. This distinction is a later medical specification. In the eighteenth century, masturbation would have been regarded as a subform of sexual disorders belonging to the group of sex practices that thwarted procreation, either willingly (masturbation) or unwillingly (nocturnal emissions or spermatorrhea).

6. See, for instance, Acton (1857, 39); Howe (1883, 60–61); and Jimison (1912, 13).

7. While Tissot condemned all forms of sexual excess and appealed for strict continence, the dangers of "self-abuse" apparently exceed all other forms of "genital overindulgence." For this hypothesis Tissot offered two explanations: first, sexual intercourse is in harmony with the natural order of things; "self-gratification," by contrast, is intensively unnatural and consequently less satisfying and more strenuous for the human economy. Second, the sexual act is reciprocal and the energy lost in copulation is compensated by the sexual partner's appeal. Tissot even argues that the presence of a beautiful conjugal partner is especially beneficial (Engelhardt 1974, 236).

8. This model of nineteenth-century "spermatic economy" is also connected to contemporary ideals of economic caution, advocating the accumulation of wealth and denouncing the habitual spendthrift (Barker-Benfield 1978, 374–402).

9. It was widely assumed that habitual "self-abuse" would lead to other forms of irregular sexual practices. This, it seems, is the case with Stephen. Not only does he succumb to the evils of "self-pollution," but also this unfortunate practice initiates other unauthorized sexual practices. See, for example, his first encounter with the prostitute at the climax of *A Portrait*'s second chapter.

10. However, when Mulligan suggests in "Circe" that Bloom is "prematurely bald from self-abuse" (*U* 15.1780–81), the "solitary vice" is once more connected to irregular hair growth.

11. Derek Attridge has persuasively argued that Stephen, even if he is not consciously responsive to the sexual meanings of the words "cock" and "suck," might well be subliminally aware of them. According to Attridge these words have a troubled fascination for Stephen because they "possess for him an aura of the forbidden, the sinful, the unclean" (Attridge 2000, 61).

12. Mullin has already suggested that Stephen's reasons for choosing such an uncomfortable sleeping position might well indicate his familiarity with the rhetoric of antimasturbation pamphlets (Mullin 2003, 101).

13. This passage from *A Portrait* echoes the sexually suggestive passage from "Sirens" that sees Lydia Douce operate the beerpulls: "On the smooth jutting beerpull laid Lydia hand, lightly, plumply, leave it to my hands . . . Fro, to: to, fro: over the polished knob . . . her thumb and finger passed in pity: passed, reposed and, gently touching, then slid so smoothly, slowly down, a cool firm white enamel baton protruding through their sliding ring" (*U* 11.1112–17). Derek Attridge also notes that Eileen Vance is "associated from the very beginning of the novel with both sexuality and sin" (Attridge 2000, 63).

14. Interestingly, Stephen's suspicious reading habits are censored by schoolfellows, who promote the spokesman of Victorian morality, Lord Tennyson, and who seem troubled by Stephen's

preference for the immoral, romantic Byron. As a result they cane him for his support for the "heretic and immoral" "bad man" (*P* 85–86). This incident could, of course, be nothing but a schoolboys' squabble in which sexuality is no topic whatsoever. Significantly, though, a second confrontation between Stephen and the ringleader Heron forces Stephen to admit his emotional involvement with Emma Clery. Sexuality and sexual matters are thus firmly on the agenda when the two "rivals" (*P* 80), Stephen and Heron, meet. Moreover, sexuality seems somehow connected to heresy in the schoolboys' imagination. Heron's suspicion that "the model youth" Stephen, who "doesn't smoke and . . . doesn't go to bazaars and . . . doesn't flirt and . . . doesn't damn anything or damn all" (*P* 80), has a darker side is confirmed by Stephen's dissident preference for Byron. It remains unclear if Heron and the other schoolboys really suspect Stephen of any solitary sexual practices. However, both a depraved attraction to romantic literature and a blatant interest in the other sex are part of the clinical picture of the chronic adolescent masturbator and function as a synecdoche for his invisible secret. It seems also significant that Stephen's second encounter with caning parallels, to a certain extent, the incidents at Clongowes in the novel's first chapter with its hushed-up references to "smugging" and schoolboy masturbation.

15. Stephen's dreams are equally vivid: "A figure that had seemed to him by day demure and innocent came towards him by night through the winding darkness of sleep, her face transfigured by a lecherous cunning, her eyes bright with brutish joy. Only the morning pained him with its dim memory of dark orgiastic riot, its keen and humiliating sense of transgression" (*P* 105).

16. The vividness of Father Arnall's hell sermon is probably responsible for producing Stephen's equally graphic depiction of "the hell reserved for his sins: stinking, bestial, malignant, a hell of lecherous goatish fiends" (*P* 149).

17. See also Maudsley (1868, 153).

18. It should be noted at this point that in Maudsley's argument the teenage masturbator's artistically futile attempts are thought to be very different from the productive scholarship of Acton's bachelor who practices spermatic economy.

Chapter 4. "The True Purefoy Nose"

1. For discussions of medical intertexts in the novel's early episodes, see Ellmann (1999, 51–66) or Plock (2007b, 30–42).

2. Many of the episode's intertextual references can be traced with Robert Janusko's helpful "A List of Joyce's Borrowings from his Sources" (1983, 93–155).

3. A lot of thought-provoking work has already been done on the episode's reliance on contemporary medical discourses. Andrew Gibson (2002, 150–82), Mary Lowe-Evans (1989), and Susan Cannon Harris (1998, 373–99) have written illuminatingly on how Joyce critically evaluates medicine's cooperation in sustaining imperialist British politics in "Oxen." As these examples illustrate, most work on Joyce's episode has, to date, focused on medicine's political imports and consequences. And since this is already very well-trodden ground, I want to propose a different reading of medicine's importance for Joyce's "Oxen"—one that illustrates how significantly the medical imagery used in the episode is tied to its aesthetic practice of copying and cribbing from literary precursors.

4. Andrew Horne was elected as Joint Master of the new National Maternity Hospital in 1894 (Farmar 1994, 10). In 1904 the hospital had sixty-nine beds (Gifford 1989, 410). For more information on the National Maternity Hospital's organization see also Gibson (2002, 165–66).

5. The Protestant-run Rotunda, Dublin's oldest lying-in hospital, had opened its doors in 1745 as the first maternity hospital in the British Isles. Although designed as a charitable institution, which attended to poor patients, the Rotunda was also a thriving site for obstetrical and gynecological training. However, continuous population growth in Dublin and the religious antagonism between Protestants and Catholics led, on March 17, 1894, to the opening of a new National Maternity Hospital on Holles Street. This new lying-in hospital had a twofold aim, "to meet the needs of poor women having babies in the thickly populated district in and around what is now Dublin 2 and Dublin 4, including Ringsend, Irishtown and Sandymount" and "to create a Catholic maternity facility for a largely Catholic population" (Farmar 1994, 8 and 9).

6. That a most unlikely place such as the National Maternity Hospital was indeed the location for such unceremonious events can be seen in Oliver St. John Gogarty's semiautobiographical novel, *Tumbling in the Hay* (1982, 169–81).

7. In 1853 the physician John Snow administered chloroform during Queen Victoria's labor. This event helped significantly to fuel the debate about anesthetics in gynecological surgery and obstetrical practice. "Twilight sleep," an amnesic condition induced by morphine during childbirth, became exceedingly popular in the 1920s (Porter 1999, 367 and 692).

8. Miss Grissel Steevens, who is in "Oxen" suspected to be "swineheaded" was the sister of Dr. Richard Steevens, the founder of Ireland's most distinguished eighteenth-century medical establishment, the Dublin Steevens Hospital (Gifford 1989, 430).

9. The sepsis problem was a fiercely debated issue in the nineteenth century until Joseph Lister developed antiseptic treatments in 1867 (Porter 1999, 368–72).

10. It is not clear which of the four different textbooks Joyce used when writing *Ulysses*. Stephen E. Soud suggests an 1855 version as the most likely source, whereas Robert Janusko uses the 1704 version. See Soud (1995, 196) and Janusko (1983, 27–28).

11. Obviously, there are some notable conceptual differences between the two texts, regarding, for instance, the sequence of events. Most crucially the obstetrical "discursiveness" (*U* 14.954) in "Oxen" follows the announcement "that an heir had been born" (*U* 14.945), whereas most of the obstetrical debate in *Tristram Shandy* precedes the eponymous hero's birth.

12. Arthur H. Cash has meticulously analyzed the medical particulars of Tristram's problematic birth. See Cash (1968, 133–54, 152).

13. See *Aristotle's Book of Problems with other Astronomers, Astrologers, Physicians and Philosophers* (1776, 14) for a comparison with the Sternean text.

14. In *Tristram Shandy* Dr. Slop's mighty attempts to deliver the hero are, of course, preceded by those of "a thin, upright, motherly, notable, good old body of a midwife" (Sterne 1998, 11).

15. H. G. Wells, in his 1917 review of *A Portrait of the Artist as a Young Man*, first compared Joyce to Sterne. See Deming (1970, 86–88). Ezra Pound pointedly stated, in 1922, that "Ulysses is, presumably, as unrepeatable as Tristram Shandy" (Read 1967, 196). Michael Hart, who compares Joyce and Sterne exclusively in terms of aesthetic similarities without giving much thought to resemblances on the content-level, suggests that the Sternean parody in "Oxen" can be "read as Joyce's most sustained criticism of Sterne" (Hart 1996, 77). See also David Pierce's chapter on Joyce and Sterne in *Joyce and Company* (2006, 19–37).

16. Sterne's exposure as a plagiarist occurred posthumously. John Ferriar, a medical doctor, provided an extensive analysis of Sterne's literary sources, first in 1791 in his "Comments on Sterne," a paper read at a meeting of the Literary and Philosophical Society of Manchester and published in *Memoirs*, iv (1793), 45–86 and then in his *Illustrations of Sterne* (1798). On Sterne and plagiarism charges see also Howes (1958, 81–110).

17. Such economically motivated arguments help to explain why cribbing from dead authors was regarded as less offensive than "stealing" from contemporary sources (Groom 2002, 41).

18. For more on Alexander Pope and plagiarism allegations, see Terry (2005, 593–608).

19. In "Scylla and Charybdis" Buck Mulligan develops, in an almost Sternean manner, this particular analogy: "I am big with child. I have an unborn child in my brain. Pallas Athena! A play! The play's the thing. Let me parturiate!" (*U* 9.875–77). Of course, Sterne was by no means the first writer to use this analogy. The discussion among Stephen and the librarians in "Scylla and Carybdis" identifies Socrates's dialectics as being based on "midwife's lore" (*U* 9.238) since it assisted him "to bring thoughts into the world" (*U* 9.235–36).

20. Kimberly Devlin has already made the connection between the artist figure and fraud in Joyce (Devlin 2002, 1–36).

21. In his reading of the episode's response to contemporary copyright law, Paul Saint-Amour challengingly suggests that "'Oxen' is interested not in plagiarizing the work of other writers but in testing the boundaries between fair use and infringement" (Saint-Amour 2003, 170).

22. In responding to Beaufoy, who calls him a plagiarist and accuses him of not having been "to a university" (*U* 15.838), Bloom retorts: "(indistinctively) University of life. Bad art" (*U* 15.840). Interestingly, Joyce seemed to have copied Bloom's retort to an accusation of plagiarism from a letter he received from Ezra Pound, who used the expression "bad art" twice in his criticism of "Calypso" (Read 1967, 131). Like Sterne's *Tristram Shandy*, Joyce's text here responds to an allegation of plagiarism by borrowing someone else's words. I would like to thank Ronan Crowley for drawing my attention to this passage in "Circe."

23. Since Stephen recycles textual passages rather than "invent" or "create" his own artwork in the library chapter, the Shakespeare theory can very well be seen as another examples of Stephen's sterile artistic productions that were discussed in the last chapter.

24. See Schutte (1971) for the most substantial analysis of Stephen's verbal borrowings.

Chapter 5. "Nerves Overstrung"

1. Letter from James Joyce to Harriet Shaw Weaver, dated October 30, 1916.

2. The mechanistic understanding of human psychology is also suggested by the popularity of the much-used expression "nervous break-down," a term with an obvious technical connotation and origin. The OED lists, under the entry "breakdown," an early reference to an 1838 manual entitled *Railway Casualties*, whereas the first entry with a reference to health is recorded for the year 1858.

3. See, for instance, the following articles in *Household Words* and *Belgravia*: Anonymous (1857, 522–25) and Wilson (1881, 346–66).

4. As John Gordon notes, Joyce's *Scribbledehobble* notebook includes references such as the following: "depleted nerve centres" and "neural paths" (Gordon 2004, 292). The reference to "neural paths" is complemented by a note about "osmosis" (Connolly 1961, 121, 161). Stanislaus

Joyce also records his brother's interest in his own "highly specialized central nervous system" in 1904 and thus suggests that Joyce was susceptible to the developing discourse of neuroscience (Joyce 1962, 51).

5. Rudolph Virag, Bloom's father, changed his foreign-sounding last name to Bloom on converting to Christianity in 1865 (*U* 17.1636–38, *U* 17.1869–72).

6. An appropriate medical term for the Eumaean prose could be ataxia or ataxy—a neurological ailment characterized by the inability to coordinate voluntary movements; a constitutional unsteadiness in the use of the legs and arms (OED). Although Joyce does not use this term in "Eumaeus," "[l]ocomotor ataxy" appears in "Circe" in the list of the many afflictions that trouble Virag, Bloom's grandfather (*U* 15.2592).

7. Critics, who disagree with such mimetic readings of "Eumaeus" are, among others, Hugh Kenner and Fritz Senn. Senn refers explicitly to the "nervous oscillations" of the Eumaean style (Senn 1984, 109). See also Kenner (1978, 38).

8. Articles on neuroscience and turn-of-the-century literature are indeed still sparse. An exception is Laura Otis's essay "Howled out of the Country: Wilkie Collins and H. G. Wells Retry David Ferrier" in Stiles (2007, 27–51).

9. See also this pertinent 1880 statement: "Nervous acts are now spoken of in physiology as being founded on the grand principle of 'reflex action,' with the name of which every schoolboy is familiarized by his physiology-primer" (Wilson 1880, 170).

10. Not only was Ramón y Cajal a pioneering neurophysiological researcher, he was also a talented artist and prolific writer. In 1905 he published, under the promising pseudonym "Dr. Bacteria," a collection of short stories. See Ramón y Cajal (2001).

11. Ramón y Cajal had already made his revolutionary discovery in 1888 but since Spanish was not read by leading scientists at the turn of the century, it took more than ten years until the scientific world recognized the impact of his neuron doctrine. Hence it was only in 1906 that he was, in conjunction with Camillo Golgi, offered the Nobel Prize. Interestingly, the joint awarding of the 1906 Nobel Prize to Golgi and Ramón y Cajal was by no means uncontroversial. Golgi, in spite of receiving international acclaim for developing his famous tissue-staining technique, was a fervent defender of the reticular theory, stubbornly adhering to his opinion even after Ramón y Cajal's research had proved him wrong. Golgi, unfortunately, used his 1906 Nobel Prize speech as an opportunity to criticize the work of his Spanish colleague and to ridicule the neuron doctrine (Rapport 2005, 163–65).

12. It should be noted here that Wilkie Collins's presence in *Ulysses* is indeed considerable. Boylan's secretary, Miss Dunne, reads *The Woman in White* in "Wandering Rocks" (*U* 10.368–72) and Molly seems to have read *The Moonstone* (*U* 18.653).

13. During the proceeding of the Phoenix Park Murders Peter Carey, one of the suspects, indeed turned queen's evidence (Gifford 1989, 141).

14. Osteen also argues convincingly that the episode because of its stylistic inaptitude "violates most of the strategies realism uses to encourage referential reading" (Osteen 1995, 360).

Chapter 6. "On the Hands Down"

1. See, for instance, Ferris (1995). A much more compelling analysis can be found in Schneider (2001, 453–74), who meticulously examines Joyce's medical records and comes to the conclusion that Joyce, in all probability, suffered from an attack of syphilis in Trieste.

2. The letter, in which Joyce complained about "Hexenschuss" (sciatica) is addressed to Ezra Pound and is dated August 20, 1917 (*SL* 226).

3. In a 1928 letter to Harriet Shaw Weaver, Joyce further comments on having "a large boil on my right shoulder" (*LI* 266).

4. Another Joycean character with a distinctive liking for physical exercise is Gabriel Conroy, who makes his son Tom "do the dumb-bells" in "The Dead" (*D* 180).

5. See also *U* 15.199–200: "Must take up Sandow's exercises again. On the hands down."

6. Although the book's title is misquoted as "*Physical Strength and How to Obtain It* by Eugen Sandow" (*U* 17.1397), the narrator in "Ithaca" comments explicitly on the publication's external appearance: "red cloth" (*U* 17.1397).

7. It has been suggested that, in adopting the pseudonym "Eugen Sandow," Müller simply germanized his mother's maiden name, Sandov (Chapman 1994, 6).

8. Unsurprisingly, given Sandow's ideal and idealized physique and celebrity status, speculations about his sexual orientation mushroomed during his career. He became the object of desire for many gay men. And although Sandow himself had the reputation of being a notorious womanizer, his close friendship with the Dutch pianist Martinus Sieveking gave way to all sorts of rumors about his sexual preferences (Chapman 1994, 51–53).

9. See Schwarze (2001, 113–35) for more information on Joyce's use of the "muscular Christianity" theme in *Ulysses*.

10. Robert Martin Adams was, I think, the first critic to point out that Bloom's physical proportions in "Ithaca" are "absurd and impossible" (1967, 184). Hugh Kenner (1979, 505–8) has since then argued persuasively that Bloom's corporeal measurements must be read in relation to the episode's passion for providing the reader with faulty information. However, it is worth remembering that Bloom is, in "Circe," described as "*pigeonbreasted*" (*U* 15.957, *U* 15.3316). In spite of this, he had some success in gymnastics in school. The Ithacan narrator asserts that although "ringweight lifting had been beyond his strength and the full circle gyration beyond his courage," Bloom "had excelled in his stable and protracted execution of the half lever movement on the parallel bars" (*U* 17.520–23). This athletic achievement was, as the text suggests, due to "his abnormally developed abdominal muscles" (*U* 17.523–24).

11. Stephen's attack on eugenics and social Darwinism in *A Portrait* (*P* 226) shows that Joyce seemed to have remained unimpressed by the eugenic movement's racial sermons.

12. Quoted most often in order to support this view is Joyce's statement: "That's all very well, but believe me, a warship with a captain named Kanalgitter and his aide named Captain Afterduft would be the funniest thing the old Mediterranean has ever seen" (Ellmann 1983, 396).

13. See Davison (1998, 144) for more information on Joyce's interest in this analogy. A very good discussion of Zionism in Trieste and Joyce's interest in the paralleled political quests of the Irish and the Jewish people can also be found in McCourt (2000, 233–38).

14. Interestingly, Herzl's *Der Judenstaat* opens with the author's attempt to prove that his plan "should not be called a 'fantasy.'" Herzl then continues his argument by stating: "I must defend my plan against the charge of being utopian" (Herzl 1997, 123). Herzl thus tries to fend off exactly the kind of criticism Bloom is voicing in *Ulysses*.

15. For a more extensive analysis of Joyce's use of the Kathleen ni Houlihan figure in *Ulysses* see Plock (2007a, 119–30).

16. Nordau is, of course, best known for writing the controversial 1892 study *Entartung* (*Degeneration*). Joyce's use of this particular aspect of Nordau's work has been well-documented by Marilyn Reizbaum (1999, 89–117).

17. "Ruben erhob sich, aber er dachte kaum daran, sich zur Wehr zu setzen, er, der schmalbrüstige, bleiche, schwächliche Stubenmensch, dem an Kraft strotzenden Naturkind gegenüber, dessen schönes Gesicht die Sonne mit einem wildfremden Indianerbraun überzogen hatte und dessen blaue Augen drohend blitzten." [Translation mine.]

18. "Unsere Muskeln sind hervorragend entwicklungsfähig. Man kann ohne Uebertreibung sagen: niemand braucht sich mit den Muskeln zufrieden zu geben, die er hat. Jeder kann vielmehr die Muskeln haben, die er selbst wünscht. Methodische, ausdauernde Uebung ist alles, was dazu nötig ist. Jeder Jude, der sich schwach glaubt oder schwach ist, hat es also in der Hand, sich eine Athletenmuskulatur zuzulegen." [Translation mine.]

19. But Herzl did try to refute the hostile claim that "Jews are not suited to manual labor or are unwilling to perform it" (Herzl 1997, 128).

20. "Und wer ist mehr dazu berufen, die hilflos chaotische jüdische Masse im Osten zu organisieren, als der Zionismus?" [Translation mine.]

21. Of course, in relying heavily on horticultural imagery in "Ithaca" Joyce's text diverts significantly from Herzl's *Der Judenstaat*. Herzl prefers to talk about the industrial rather than the agrarian organization of the new Jewish state. However in speaking about the resettlement of Jews he repeatedly makes use of pastoral and agrarian metaphors: "We, however, want to give the Jews a home country. Not by tearing them forcibly out of their present land. No, by lifting them carefully with all their roots and transplanting them into a better soil" (Herzl 1997, 175).

22. This is certainly why Joyce decided to allocate the organs "skeleton" or "juices" to the "Ithaca" episode.

Chapter 7. Jack the Ripper and *The Family Physician*

1. The sociotechnological implications of the forceps's acceptance in medical scholarship are discussed in more detail in chapter 3 in relation to Laurence Sterne's *Tristram Shandy*.

2. Although Sir William was commonly known as an eye doctor and not a gynecologist, his 1853 book *Medico-Legal Observations upon Infantile Leucorrhoea, Arising out of the Alleged Cases of Felonious Assaults on Young Children* indicates that he was also something of an expert on the manifestation of "female diseases" in young children.

3. The case is discussed in Kent (1987, 116–19).

4. Curiously, while these particular gynecological practices were demonized in the popular opinion at the fin de siècle, doctors also took other extreme albeit rather unusual measures to "correct" alleged female pathologies such as hysteria. Rachel Maines (1999) has shown how gynecologists patented a range of electro-therapeutic devices such as the vibrator—a machine first designed in the early 1880s by the English physician Joseph Mortimer Granville for electric or vibratory massages—to bring about orgasms in their female patients and cure them of their hysterical symptoms. Mary Lowe-Evans (2008, 106–9) has explored how the medicalization of the female orgasm is debated in Joyce's *Ulysses*.

5. Sophia Jex-Blake's battle for a medical education is vividly described in Virginia Woolf's *Three Guineas* in 1938. See Woolf (1992, 246–48 and 347–50).

Bibliography

Ackerknecht, Erwin H., and Esther Fischer-Homberger. 1977. "Five Made It—One Not: The Rise of Medical Craftsmen to Academic Status During the 19th Century." *Clio Medica* 12: 255–67.

Acton, William. 1857. *The Functions and Disorders of the Reproductive Organs in Youth, in Adult Age, and in Advanced Life*. London: Churchill.

———. 1875. *The Functions and Disorders of the Reproductive Organs in Childhood, Youth, Adult Age, and Advanced Life*. Sixth edition. London: Churchill.

Adams, Robert Martin. 1967. *Surface and Symbol: The Consistency of James Joyce's Ulysses*. New York: Oxford University Press.

Amar, Jules. 1920. *The Human Motor or the Scientific Foundations of Labour and Industry*. London: Routledge.

Andresse, Wilhelm. 1847. *Von den Ursachen der einseitigen Aufregung des Wollusttriebes und der Selbstbefleckung; mit Angabe der zweckmäßigen Art und Weise, die Onanie bei der Jugend zu verhüten, und sie, wenn sie bereits vorhanden ist, bald und sicher zu erkennen*. Berlin: Leopold Schlesinger.

Anonymous. 1772. *Aristotle's Compleat Master Piece in Three Parts; Displaying the Secrets of Nature in the Generation of Man. . . . To which is Added, a Treasure of Health; or, the Family Physician: . . .* London: n.p.

———. 1776. *Aristotle's Book of Problems with other Astronomers, Astrologers, Physicians and Philosophers*. London: n.p.

———. 1823. Preface to the *Lancet* 1.1: 1–2.

———. 1857. "The Nerves." *Household Words: A Weekly Journal* 15.375 (May): 522–25.

———. 1867. "Obstetrical Society of London." *Lancet* (April 6): 425–41.

———. 1894. *The Family Physician: A Manual of Domestic Medicine by Physicians and Surgeons of the Principal London Hospitals*. London: Cassell and Company.

———. 1895. "Tea Drunkards." *Irish Homestead* (May 18): 174.

———. 1904. *Report of the Inter-Departmental Committee on Physical Deterioration. Vol. 1: Report and Appendix*. London: Wyman and Sons.

———. 1922. "The Higher Physiology." *Times* (September 7): 9.

Ashe, Isaac. 1868. *Medical Education and Medical Interests*. Dublin: Fannin.

Atherton, James. 1974. *The Books at the Wake: A Study of Literary Allusions in James Joyce's Finnegans Wake*. Carbondale: Southern Illinois Press.

Attridge, Derek. 1988. *Peculiar Language: Literature as Difference from the Renaissance to James Joyce*. London: Methuen.

———. 2000. *Joyce Effects: On Language, Theory, and History.* Cambridge: Cambridge University Press.

Austin, Alfred. 1874. "The Vice of Reading." *Temple Bar Magazine* 42: 251–57.

Baines, Paul. 2003. "Theft and Poetry and Pope." In *Plagiarism in Early Modern England*, edited by Paulina Kewes, 166–80. Basingstoke: Palgrave.

Bankier, William. 1900. *Ideal Physical Culture and the Truth about the Strong Man.* London: Greening.

Barker, James. 1888. *A Secret Book for Men.* Brighton: n.p.

Barker-Benfield, G. J. 1978. "The Spermatic Economy: A Nineteenth-Century View on Sexuality." In *The American Family in Social-Historical Perspective*, edited by Michael Gordon, 374–402. New York: St. Martin's Press.

Barnes, Robert. 1875–76. "An Address on Obstetric Medicine and its Position in Medical Education." *Obstetrical Journal of Great Britain and Ireland* 3: 289–99.

Bell, Robert H. 1991. *Jocoserious Joyce: The Fate of Folly in Ulysses.* Ithaca, N.Y., and London: Cornell University Press.

Benstock, Shari. 1982. "The Genuine Christine: Psychodynamics of Issy." In *Women in Joyce*, edited by Suzette Henke and Elaine Unkeless, 169–96. Urbana: University of Illinois Press.

Benzenhöfer, Udo. 1989. "Joyce and Embryology: Giulio Valenti's 'Lezioni Elementari di Embriologia' as a Source for 'Oxen of the Sun.'" *James Joyce Quarterly* 26.4: 608–11.

Blackwell, Elizabeth. 1914. *Pioneer Work in Opening the Medical Profession to Women.* London: J. M. Dent.

Blair, Kirstie. 2006. *Victorian Poetry and the Culture of the Heart.* Oxford: Clarendon.

Bock, Martin. 2007. "James Joyce and Germ Theory: The Skeleton at the Feast." *James Joyce Quarterly* 45.1: 23–46.

Boscagli, Maurizia. 1996. *Eye on the Flesh: Fashions of Masculinity in the Early Twentieth Century.* Boulder, Colo.: Westview Press.

Brodie, R. J. 1845. *The Secret Companion.* London: The Author.

Brown, Richard. 1985. *James Joyce and Sexuality.* Cambridge: Cambridge University Press.

Brunton, Deborah. 2004. *Health, Disease and Society in Europe 1800–1930: A Source Book.* Manchester: Manchester University Press.

Budd, Michael Anton. 1997. *The Sculpture Machine: Physical Culture and Body Politic in the Age of Empire.* New York: New York University Press.

Burton, John. 1751. *An Essay towards a Complete New System of Midwifery.* London: James Hodges.

———. 1753. *A Letter to William Smellie, M.D. Containing Critical and Practical Remarks Upon his Treatise on the Theory and Practice of Midwifery.* London: W. Owen.

Burton, Robert. 1977. *The Anatomy of Melancholy.* New York: Vintage.

Bynum, W. F. 1984. "Alcoholism and Degeneration in 19th Century European Medicine and Psychiatry." *British Journal of Addiction* 79: 59–70.

Cash, Arthur H. 1968. "The Birth of Tristram Shandy: Sterne and Dr Burton." In *Studies in the Eighteenth Century*, edited by R. F. Brissenden, 133–54. Canberra: Australian National University Press.

Cason, Hulsey. 1935. "The Organic Nature of Fatigue." *American Journal of Psychology* 47.2 (April): 337–42.

Chadwick, Edwin. 1965. *Report on the Sanitary Condition of the Labouring Population of Great Britain.* Edinburgh: Edinburgh University Press.

Chapman, David L. 1994. *Sandow the Magnificent: Eugen Sandow and the Beginnings of Body-building.* Urbana and Chicago: Illinois University Press.

Cobbe, Frances Power. 1878. "The Little Health of Ladies." *Contemporary Review* 31: 276–96.

Cohen, Ed. 1987. "(R)evolutionary Scenes: The Body Politic and the Political Body in Henry Maudsley's Nosology of Masturbatory Insanity." *Nineteenth-Century Contexts* 11.2: 179–91.

Collins, Joseph. 1923. *The Doctor Looks at Literature: Psychological Studies of Life and Letters.* New York: G. H. Doran.

Colum, Mary, and Padraic Colum. 1959. *Our Friend James Joyce.* London: Victor Gollancz.

Connolly, Thomas, ed. 1961. *James Joyce's Scribbledehobble: The Ur-Notebook for Finnegans Wake.* Evanston, Ill.: Northwestern University Press.

Curtis, Lewis Perry, ed. 1935. *Letters of Laurence Sterne.* Oxford: Clarendon Press.

Davison, Neil R. 1998. *James Joyce, Ulysses, and the Construction of Jewish Identity: Culture, Biography, and the "Jew" in Modernist Europe.* Cambridge: Cambridge University Press.

Delany, Paul. 1995. "'Tailors of Malt, Hot, All Round': Homosocial Consumption in *Dubliners.*" *Studies in Short Fiction* 32.3: 381–93.

Deming, Robert H., ed. 1970. *James Joyce: The Critical Heritage. Vol. 1: 1902–1927.* London: Routledge.

Dettass, J. 1898. "Physical Culture Among the Jews." *Physical Culture* 1: 126–30.

Devlin, Kimberly. 1994. "Pretending in 'Penelope': Masquerade, Mimicry, and Molly Bloom." In *Molly Blooms: A Polylogue on "Penelope" and Cultural Studies*, edited by Richard Pierce, 63–79. Madison: University of Wisconsin Press.

———. 2002. *James Joyce's "Fraudstuff."* Gainesville: University Press of Florida.

Dickens, Charles. 1996. *Bleak House*, edited by Nicola Bradbury. London: Penguin.

Didi-Huberman, Georges. 1982. *Invention de l'hystérie: Charcot et l'iconographie photographique de la Salpêtrière.* Paris: Macula.

Doyle, Arthur Conan. 1890. "Dr Koch and His Cure." *Review of Reviews* 2: 552–56.

Duffy, Enda. 1994. *The Subaltern Ulysses.* Minneapolis: University of Minnesota Press.

———. 1999. "Interesting States: Birthing and the Nation in 'Oxen of the Sun.'" In *Ulysses—En-Gendered Perspectives: Eighteen New Essays on the Episodes*, edited by Kimberly Devlin and Marilyn Reizbaum, 210–28. Columbia: University of South Carolina Press.

Dyer, Alfred S. 1884. *Facts for Men on Moral Purity and Health Being Plain Words to Young Men Upon an Avoided Subject With Safeguards Against Immorality and Facts that Men Ought to Know.* London: Dyer Brothers.

Eliot, T. S. 1976. *Selected Essays.* London: Faber and Faber.

Ellenberger, Henri F. 1970. *The Discovery of the Unconscious: The History and Evolution of Dynamic Psychiatry.* New York: Basic Books.

Ellmann, Maud. 1999. "Skinscapes in 'Lotus-Eaters.'" In *Ulysses—En-Gendered Perspectives: Eighteen New Essays on the Episodes*, edited by Kimberly Devlin and Marilyn Reizbaum, 51–66. Columbia: University of South Carolina Press.

Ellmann, Richard. 1983. *James Joyce.* Oxford: Oxford University Press.

———. 1984. *Ulysses on the Liffey.* London: Faber and Faber.

———. 1987. *Yeats: The Man and the Masks.* London: Penguin.

———. 1988. *Oscar Wilde.* London: Penguin.

Engelhardt, H. Tristam. 1974. "The Disease of Masturbation: Values and the Concept of Disease." *Bulletin of the History of Medicine* 48.2: 234–48.

Engels, Friedrich. 1972. *The Origin of the Family, Private Property and the State*. London: Lawrence and Wishart.

———. 1999. *The Condition of the Working Class in England*. Oxford: Oxford University Press.

Farmar, Tony. 1994. *Holles Street 1894–1994: The National Maternity Hospital: A Centenary History*. Dublin: A. and A. Farmar.

Fee, Elizabeth, and Dorothy Porter. 1993. "Public Health, Preventive Medicine and Professionalization: England and America in the Nineteenth Century." In *Medicine in Society: Historical Essays*, edited by Andrew Wear, 249–75. Cambridge: Cambridge University Press.

Ferriar, John. 1798. *Illustrations of Sterne*. London: Cadell and Davies.

Ferrier, David. 1876. *The Functions of the Brain*. London: Smith, Elder and Co.

Ferris, Kathleen. 1995. *James Joyce and the Burden of Disease*. Lexington: University of Kentucky Press.

Fishberg, Maurice. 1911. *The Jews: A Study of Race and Environment*. London: Walter Scott Publishing.

Fissell, Mary E. 2003. "Hairy Women and Naked Truths: Gender and the Politics of Knowledge in *Aristotle's Masterpiece*." *William and Mary Quarterly* 60.1: 43–74.

Fleetwood, John. 1951. *History of Medicine in Ireland*. Dublin: Brown and Nolan.

Foucault, Michel. 1994. *The Birth of the Clinic: An Archaeology of Medical Perception*. New York: Vintage.

Fowke, Ernest C. n.d. *Addresses to Boy Scouts*. Birmingham: n.p.

Fox, Fortescue. 1885. "Stimulants and Narcotics: Their Use and Abuse." *Nineteenth Century: A Monthly Review* 18.106 (December): 923–39.

Froggatt, Peter. 1999. "Competing Philosophies: The 'Preparatory' Medical Schools of the Royal Belfast Academical Institution and the Catholic University of Ireland, 1835–1909." In *Medicine, Disease and the State in Ireland 1650–1940*, edited by Greta Jones and Elizabeth Malcolm, 59–84. Cork: Cork University Press.

Garnier, Paul. 1885. *Onanisme seul et à deux sous toutes les formes et leur conséquences*. Paris: Garnier Frères.

Gasquet, J. R. 1880. "Recent Research on the Nerves and Brain." *Dublin Review* 3.34.2 (April): 373–81.

Geary, Lawrence M. 1996. "'The Late Disastrous Epidemic': Medical Relief and the Great Famine." In *Fearful Realities: New Perspectives on the Famine*, edited by Chris Morash and Richard Hayes, 49–59. Dublin: Irish Academic Press.

Gibson, Andrew, ed. 1996. *Joyce's "Ithaca."* Amsterdam: Rodopi.

———. 2002. *Joyce's Revenge: History, Politics, and Aesthetics in Ulysses*. Oxford: Oxford University Press.

———. 2006. "'That Stubborn Irish Thing': *A Portrait of the Artist* in History: Chapter 1." In *Joyce, Ireland, Britain*, edited by Andrew Gibson and Len Platt, 85–103. Gainesville: University Press of Florida.

Gifford, Don. 1982. *Joyce Annotated: Notes for Dubliners and A Portrait of the Artist as a Young Man*. Berkeley and Los Angeles: University of California Press.

———. 1989. *Ulysses Annotated: Notes for James Joyce's Ulysses*. Berkeley and Los Angeles: University of California Press.

Gilbert, Arthur N. 1980. "Masturbation and Insanity: Henry Maudsley and the Ideology of Sexual Repression." *Albion* 12.3: 268–82.

Gilbert, Stuart. 1955. *James Joyce's Ulysses*. New York: Vintage.

Gilman, Sander. 1993. "'Who Kills Whores?' 'I Do,' Says Jack: Race and Gender in Victorian London." In *Death and Representation*, edited by Sarah Webster Goodwin and Elisabeth Bronfen, 263–84. Baltimore, Md.: Johns Hopkins University Press.

Glasheen, Adaline. 1954. "*Finnegans Wake* and the Girls from Boston, Mass." *Hudson Review* (Spring): 89–96.

Gogarty, Oliver St. John. 1982. *Tumbling in the Hay*. London: Sphere Books.

Gordon, John. 1979. "The Multiple Journeys of 'Oxen of the Sun.'" *English Literary History* 46.1: 158–72.

———. 2003. *Physiology and the Literary Imagination: Romantic to Modern*. Gainesville: University Press of Florida.

———. 2004. *Joyce and Reality: The Empirical Strikes Back*. Syracuse, N.Y.: Syracuse University Press.

Gottfried, Roy. 1995. *Joyce's Iritis and the Irritated Text: The Dis-Lexic Ulysses*. Gainesville: University Press of Florida.

Granshaw, Lindsay. 1993. "The Rise of the Modern Hospital in Britain." In *Medicine in Society: Historical Essays*, edited by Andrew Wear, 197–218. Cambridge: Cambridge University Press.

Groden, Michael. 1977. *Ulysses in Progress*. Princeton, N.J.: Princeton University Press.

Groom, Nick. 2002. *The Forger's Shadow: How Forgery Changed the Course of Literature*. London: Macmillan.

———. 2003. "Forgery, Plagiarism, Imitation, Peglegery." In *Plagiarism in Early Modern England*, edited by Paulina Kewes, 74–89. Basingstoke: Palgrave.

Hall, Charles A. 1907. *Self-Control: A Booklet for Boys and Young Men, as well as for Girls. Deals Delicately yet Plainly with Secret Vice and its Moral and Hygienic Treatment*. London: Fowler and Co.

Hall, Lesley A. 1991. *Hidden Anxieties: Male Sexuality, 1900–1950*. Cambridge: Polity Press.

Hall, Marshall. 1850. "On a New and Lamentable Form of Hysteria." *Lancet* 1: 660–61.

Hare, E. H. 1962. "Masturbatory Insanity: The History of an Idea." *Journal of Mental Science* 108.452: 1–25.

Harris, Ruth. 1989. *Murders and Madness: Medicine, Law, and Society in the Fin de Siècle*. Oxford: Clarendon.

Harris, Susan Cannon. 1998. "Invasive Procedures: Imperial Medicine and Population Control in *Ulysses* and *The Satanic Verses*." *James Joyce Quarterly* 35.2 and 3: 373–99.

Harrison, Mark. 2004. *Disease and the Modern World: 1500 to the Present*. Cambridge: Polity Press.

Hart, Michael. 1996. "'Many Planes of Narrative': A Comparative Perspective on Sterne and Joyce." In *Laurence Sterne in Modernism and Postmodernism*, edited by David Pierce and Peter de Voogd, 65–80. Amsterdam: Rodopi.

Hawley, Judith. 1993. "The Anatomy of *Tristram Shandy*." In *Literature and Medicine during the Eighteenth Century*, edited by Marie Mulvey Roberts and Roy Porter, 84–100. London: Routledge.

Hensley, Brendan. 1988. *The Health Service of Ireland*. Dublin: Institute of Public Administration.

Herr, Cheryl. 1994. "'Penelope' as Period Piece." In *Molly Blooms: A Polylogue on "Penelope" and Cultural Studies*, edited by Richard Pierce, 80–102. Madison: University of Wisconsin Press.

Herring, Phillip F., ed. 1972. *Joyce's Ulysses Notesheets in the British Museum.* Charlottesville: University Press of Virginia.

Herzl, Theodor. 1997. *The Jews' State: A Critical English Translation.* Northvale, N.J.: Jason Aronson.

Hoffmann, E.T.A. 1815. *Die Elixiere des Teufels: Nachgelassene Papiere des Bruders Medardus eines Capuziners.* Berlin: Duncker and Humblot.

Howe, Joseph W. 1883. *Excessive Venery, Masturbation and Continence: The Etiology, Pathology and Treatment of the Diseases Resulting from Venereal Excess.* New York: Birmingham and Company.

Howes, Alan B. 1958. *Yorick and the Critics: Sterne's Reputation in England, 1760–1868.* Hamden, Conn.: Archon Books.

———, ed. 1974. *Sterne: The Critical Heritage.* London: Routledge.

Hunt, Alan. 1998. "The Great Masturbation Panic and the Discourses of Moral Regulation in Nineteenth- and Early-Twentieth-Century Britain." *Journal of the History of Science* 8.4: 575–615.

Janet, Pierre. 1886. "Les Actes inconscients et le dédoublement de la personnalité pendant le somnambulisme provoqué." *Revue philosophique* 22: 577–92.

———. 1889. *L'Automatisme psychologique: Essai de psychologie expérimentale sur les formes inférieures de l'activité humaine.* Paris: Alcan.

———. 1915. "L'Alcoolisme et la depression mentale." *Revue internationale de sociologie* 23: 476–85.

Janusko, Robert. 1983. *The Sources and Structures of James Joyce's "Oxen."* Ann Arbor, Mich.: UMI Research Press.

Jex-Blake, Sophia. 1886. *Medical Women: A Thesis and a History.* Edinburgh: Anderson and Ferrier.

Jimison, John. 1912. *Solitary Vice and its Cure.* Scholes, Yorks.: The Author.

Jolas, Eugene. 1948. "My Friend James Joyce." In *James Joyce: Two Decades of Criticism*, edited by Seon Givens, 3–18. New York: Vanguard Press.

Joyce, Stanislaus. 1962. *The Complete Dublin Diary of Stanislaus Joyce.* Ithaca, N.Y.: Cornell University Press.

Kellogg, J. H. 1894. *Man, the Masterpiece or, Plain Truths Plainly Told about Boyhood, Youth, and Manhood.* Battle Creek, Mich.: Modern Medicine Publishing.

Kenner, Hugh. 1955. *Dublin's Joyce.* London: Chatto and Windus.

———. 1978. *Joyce's Voices.* London: Faber and Faber.

———. 1979. "Bloom's Chest." *James Joyce Quarterly* 16.4: 505–8.

Kent, Susan Kingsley. 1987. *Sex and Suffrage in Britain 1860–1914.* Princeton, N.J.: Princeton University Press.

Kershner, R. Brandon. 1993. "'The World's Strongest Man': Joyce or Sandow." *James Joyce Quarterly* 30.4: 667–94.

Keymer, Tom. 2000. *Sterne, the Moderns, and the Novel.* Oxford: Oxford University Press.

Kinealy, Christine. 1997. *A Death-Dealing Famine: The Great Hunger in Ireland.* London: Pluto.

Knowles, Sebastian D. G. 2001. *The Dublin Helix: The Life of Language in Joyce's Ulysses.* Gainesville: University Press of Florida.

Lamb, Jonathan. 2002. "Sterne's System of Imitation." In *Laurence Sterne*, ed. Marcus Walsh, 138–60. Harlow: Longman.

Lambert, Royston. 1963. *Sir John Simon, 1816–1904 and English Social Administration.* London: MacGibbon and Kee.

Lamos, Colleen. 1999. "The Double Life of 'Eumaeus.'" In *Ulysses—En-Gendered Perspectives: Eighteen New Essays on the Episodes*, edited by Kimberly Devlin and Marilyn Reizbaum, 242–53. Columbia: University of South Carolina Press.

Landry, Donna, and Gerald Maclean. 1990. "Of Forceps, Patents and Paternity: *Tristram Shandy*." *Eighteenth-Century Studies* 23.4: 522–43.

Lane, Joan. 2001. *A Social History of Medicine: Health, Healing and Disease in England, 1750–1950*. London: Routledge.

Lansbury, Coral. 1985. "Gynaecology, Pornography, and the Antivivisectionist Movement." *Victorian Studies* 28: 413–37.

Laqueur, Thomas. 1992. *Making Sex: Body and Gender from the Greeks to Freud*. Cambridge: Harvard University Press.

———. 2003. *Solitary Sex: A Cultural History of Masturbation*. New York: Zone Books.

Latham, Sean. 2003. *Am I A Snob? Modernism and the Novel*. Ithaca, N.Y.: Cornell University Press.

Lawrence, Karen. 1981. *The Odyssey of Style in Ulysses*. Princeton, N.J.: Princeton University Press.

Levenson, Michael. 2003. "Stephen's Diary in Joyce's *Portrait*—The Shape of Life." In *James Joyce's A Portrait of the Artist as a Young Man: A Casebook*, edited by Mark A. Wollaeger, 183–205. Oxford: Oxford University Press.

Lilienfeld, Jane. 1999. *Reading Alcoholisms: Theorizing Character and Narrative in Selected Novels of Thomas Hardy, James Joyce, and Virginia Woolf*. New York: St. Martin's Press.

Lin, Paul. 2001. "Standing the Empire: Drinking, Masculinity and Modernity in 'Counterparts.'" In *Masculinities in Joyce: Postcolonial Constructions*, edited by Christine van Boheemen-Saaf and Colleen Lamos, 33–57. Amsterdam: Rodopi.

Lloyd, David. 2000. "*Counterparts*: *Dubliners*, Masculinity, and Temperance Movement." In *Semicolonial Joyce*, edited by Derek Attridge and Marjorie Howes, 128–49. Cambridge: Cambridge University Press.

Lombroso-Ferrero, Gina. 1911. *Criminal Man According to the Classification of Cesare Lombroso*. New York: Knickerbocker.

Loudon, Irvine. 1993. "Medical Practitioners 1750–1850 and the Period of Medical Reform in Britain." In *Medicine in Society: Historical Essays*, edited by Andrew Wear, 219–47. Cambridge: Cambridge University Press.

———. 1995. "Medical Education and Medical Reform." In *The History of Medical Education in Britain*, edited by Vivian Nutton and Roy Porter, 229–49. Amsterdam: Rodopi.

———, ed. 1997. *Western Medicine: An Illustrated History*. Oxford and New York: Oxford University Press.

Lowe-Evans, Mary. 1989. *Crimes Against Fecundity: Joyce and Population Control*. Syracuse, N.Y.: Syracuse University Press.

———. 2008. *Catholic Nostalgia in Joyce and Company*. Gainesville: University Press of Florida.

Lyons, J. B. 1973. *James Joyce and Medicine*. Dublin: Dolmen.

MacDonald, Robert H. 1967. "The Frightful Consequences of Onanism: Notes on the History of a Delusion." *Journal of the History of Ideas* 28.3: 423–31.

Maines, Rachel P. 1999. *The Technology of Orgasm: "Hysteria," the Vibrator, and Women's Sexual Satisfaction*. Baltimore, Md.: Johns Hopkins University Press.

Marcus, Steven. 1967. *The Other Victorians: A Study of Sexuality and Pornography in Mid-Nineteenth-Century England*. London: Weidenfeld and Nicolson.

Maudsley, Henry. 1859. "Edgar Allan Poe." *Journal of Mental Science* 6: 328–69.

———. 1868. "Illustrations of a Variety of Insanity." *Journal of Mental Science* 66.14: 149–62.

———. 1874. "Sex in Mind and Education." *Fortnightly Review* 15: 466–83.

———. 1886. *The Pathology of Mind*. New York: D. Appleton and Company.

McBride, Margaret. 1996. "*Finnegans Wake*: The Issue of Issy's Schizophrenia." *Joyce Studies Annual* 7: 145–75.

McCarthy, Patrick. 1997. "Reading *Dubliners* in *The Lost Weekend*." *Studies in Short Fiction* 34.4: 441–48.

McCourt, John. 2000. *The Years of Bloom: James Joyce in Trieste, 1904–1920*. Dublin: Lilliput Press.

McGeachie, James. 1999. "'Normal' Development in an 'Abnormal' Place: Sir William Wilde and the Irish School of Medicine." In *Medicine, Disease and the State in Ireland, 1650–1940*, edited by Greta Jones and Elizabeth Malcolm, 85–101. Cork: Cork University Press.

McLaren, Angus. 1994. "'Not a Stranger: A Doctor': Medical Men and Sexual Matters in the Late Nineteenth Century." In *Sexual Knowledge, Sexual Science*, edited by Roy Porter and Mikuláš Teich, 267–83. Cambridge: Cambridge University Press.

Miller, Karl. 1985. *Doubles: Studies in Literary History*. Oxford: Oxford University Press.

Miller, Tyrus. 2006. "Futurism." In *A Companion to Modernist Literature and Culture*, edited by David Bradshaw and Kevin J. H. Dettmar, 169–75. Oxford: Blackwell.

Moreau (de Tours), Jacques-Joseph. 1845. *Du Hachisch et de l'aliénation mentale*. Paris: Ressources.

Moscucci, Ornella. 1993. *The Science of Woman: Gynaecology and Gender in England 1800–1929*. Cambridge: Cambridge University Press.

Mullin, Katherine. 2003. *James Joyce, Sexuality and Social Purity*. Cambridge: Cambridge University Press.

Murphy, James. 1891. "The Influence of Surgery on Gynaecology." *Provincial Medical Journal* 10: 403–4.

Nicolson, Malcolm. 1993. "The Art of Diagnosis: Medicine and the Five Senses." In *Companion Encyclopedia of the History of Medicine*, edited by W. F. Bynum and Roy Porter, vol. 2, 801–25. London and New York: Routledge.

Norburn, Robert. 2004. *A James Joyce Chronology*. Basingstoke: Palgrave.

Nordau, Max. 1901. *Generalreferat über Fragen der körperlichen, geistigen und wirtschaftlichen Hebung des Judentums*. Basel: Birkhäuer.

———. 1909a. "Muskeljudentum." In *Max Nordau's Zionistische Schriften*, 379–81. Köln and Leipzig: Jüdischer Verlag.

———. 1909b. "Was bedeutet das Turnen für uns Juden?" In *Max Nordau's Zionistische Schriften*, 382–88. Köln and Leipzig: Jüdischer Verlag.

O'Brien, Joseph. 1982. *"Dear, Dirty Dublin": A City in Distress, 1899–1916*. Berkeley and Los Angeles: University of California Press.

O'Neill, Christine. 1996. *Too Fine a Point: A Stylistic Analysis of the Eumaeus Episode in James Joyce's Ulysses*. Trier: Wissenschaftlicher Verlag.

Osteen, Mark. 1995. *The Economy of Ulysses: Making Both Ends Meet*. Syracuse, N.Y.: Syracuse University Press.

Otis, Laura. 1999. *Membranes: Metaphors of Invasion in Nineteenth-Century Literature, Science, and Politics*. Baltimore, Md.: Johns Hopkins University Press.

Parry, Noel, and José Parry. 1976. *The Rise of the Medical Profession: A Study of Collective Social Mobility*. London: Croom Helm.

Pierce, David. 2006. *Joyce and Company*. London and New York: Continuum.

Plock, Vike Martina. 2007a. "Why Does Gerty Limp?" In *Joyce in Trieste: An Album of Risky Readings*, edited by Sebastian Knowles, Geert Lernout, and John McCourt, 119–30. Gainesville: University Press of Florida.

———. 2007b. "Modernism's Feast on Science: Nutrition and Diet in Joyce's *Ulysses*." *Literature and History* 16.2: 30–42.

Poovey, Mary. 1989. *Uneven Development: The Ideological Work of Gender in Mid-Victorian England*. London: Virago Press.

Porter, Roy. 1987. "'The Secrets of Generation Display'd': *Aristotle's Master-piece* in Eighteenth-Century England." In *'Tis Nature's Fault: Unauthorized Sexuality during the Enlightenment*, edited by Robert Purks Maccubbin, 1–21. Cambridge: Cambridge University Press.

———. 1999. *The Greatest Benefit to Mankind: A Medical History of Humanity from Antiquity to the Present*. London: Fontana.

———. 2001a. *Bodies Politic: Disease, Death, and Doctors in Britain, 1650–1900*. Ithaca, N.Y.: Cornell University Press.

———. 2001b. "Medical Science." In *The Cambridge Illustrated History of Medicine*, edited by Roy Porter, 154–201. Cambridge: Cambridge University Press.

———. 2006. *Madmen: A Social History of Madhouses, Mad-Doctors and Lunatics*. Stroud: Tempus.

Porter, Roy, and Lesley Hall. 1995. *The Facts of Life: The Creation of Sexual Knowledge in Britain, 1650–1950*. New Haven, Conn.: Yale University Press.

Rabaté, Jean-Michel. 2001. *James Joyce and the Politics of Egoism*. Cambridge: Cambridge University Press.

Rabinbach, Anson. 1992. *The Human Motor: Energy, Fatigue, and the Origins of Modernity*. Berkeley and Los Angeles: University of California Press.

Ramón y Cajal, Santiago. 1988. *Cajal on the Cerebral Cortex: An Annotated Translation of the Complete Writings*, edited by Javier DeFelipe and Edward G. Jones. New York: Oxford University Press.

———. 1995. *Histology of the Nervous System of Man and Vertebrates*, translated by Neely Swanson and Larry W. Swanson. 2 vols. New York: Oxford University Press.

———. 2001. *Vacation Stories: Five Science Fiction Tales*, edited by Laura Otis. Urbana and Chicago: University of Illinois Press.

Rapport, Richard. 2005. *Nerve Endings: The Discovery of the Synapse*. New York and London: Norton.

Read, Forrest, ed. 1967. *Pound/Joyce: The Letters of Ezra Pound to James Joyce, with Pound's Essays on Joyce*. New York: New Directions.

Redfield, James. 1853. *Comparative Physiognomy or Resemblances between Men and Animals*. New York: The Author.

Reizbaum, Marilyn. 1999. *James Joyce's Judaic Other*. Stanford, Calif.: Stanford University Press.

Richards, Thomas. 1991. *The Commodity Culture of Victorian England: Advertising and Spectacle, 1851–1914*. New York: Verso Press.

Riquelme, John Paul. 2000. "Toward a History of Gothic and Modernism: Dark Modernity from Bram Stoker to Samuel Beckett." *Modern Fiction Studies* 46.3: 585–605.

Rothfield, Lawrence. 1992. *Vital Signs: Medical Realism in Nineteenth-Century Fiction.* Princeton, N.J.: Princeton University Press.

Rylance, Rick. 2000. *Victorian Psychology and British Culture 1850–1880.* Oxford: Oxford University Press.

Sacher-Masoch, Lepold von. 1881. *Neue Judengeschichten.* Leipzig: E. L. Morgenstern.

Saint-Amour, Paul. 2003. *The Copywrights: Intellectual Property and the Literary Imagination.* Ithaca, N.Y.: Cornell University Press.

Sandow, Eugen. 1897. *Strength and How to Obtain It.* London: Gale and Polden.

Sass, Louis A. 1992. *Madness and Modernism: Insanity in the Light of Modern Art, Literature, and Thought.* New York: Basic Books.

Schneider, Erik. 2001. "'A Grievous Temper': Joyce and the Rheumatic Fever Episode of 1907." *James Joyce Quarterly* 38. 3 and 4: 453–75.

Schutte, William. 1971. *Joyce and Shakespeare: A Study in the Meaning of Ulysses.* Hamden, Conn.: Archon Books.

Schwarze, Tracey Teets. 2001. "'Do You Call that a Man': The Culture of Anxious Masculinity in Joyce's *Ulysses.*" In *Masculinities in Joyce: Postcolonial Constructions,* edited by Christine van Boheemen-Saaf and Colleen Lamos, 113–35. Amsterdam: Rodopi.

Senn, Fritz. 1984. *Joyce's Dislocutions: Essays on Reading as Translation,* edited by John Paul Riquelme. Baltimore, Md.: Johns Hopkins University Press.

———. 1995. *Inductive Scrutinies: Focus on Joyce,* edited by Christine O'Neill. Baltimore, Md.: Johns Hopkins University Press.

———. 1996. "'Ithaca': Portrait of the Chapter as a Long List." In *Joyce's "Ithaca,"* edited by Andrew Gibson, 31–76. Amsterdam: Rodopi.

Shaw, George Bernard. 1950. *Doctors' Delusions, Crude Criminology and Sham Education.* London: Constable and Company.

Sherrington, Charles. 1947. *The Integrative Action of the Nervous System.* Cambridge: Cambridge University Press.

Sherry, Norman. 1971. *Conrad's Western World.* Cambridge: Cambridge University Press.

Shloss, Carol Loeb. 2003. *Lucia Joyce: To Dance in the Wake.* New York: Farrar, Straus, and Giroux.

Showalter, Elaine. 1991. *Sexual Anarchy: Gender and Culture in the Fin de Siècle.* London: Bloomsbury.

Shuttleworth, Sally. 1990. "Female Circulation: Medical Discourse and Popular Advertising in the Mid-Victorian Era." In *Body/Politics: Women and the Discourses of Science,* edited by Mary Jacobus, Evelyn Fox Keller, and Sally Shuttleworth, 47–68. New York: Routledge.

Sibbald, Andrew T. 1885. "The Brain and the Mind." *Dublin Review* 3.13.2 (April): 381–92.

Simon, John. 1887. *Public Health Reports by John Simon,* edited by Edward Seaton. London: Offices of the Sanitary Institute.

Sontag, Susan. 1978. *Illness as Metaphor.* New York: Farrar, Straus, and Giroux.

Soud, Stephen E. 1995. "Blood-Red Wombs and Monstrous Births: *Aristotle's Masterpiece* and *Ulysses.*" *James Joyce Quarterly* 32.2: 195–208.

Sournia, Jean-Charles. 1990. *A History of Alcoholism.* Oxford: Blackwell.

Spivak, Gayatri Chakravorty. 1988. *In Other Worlds: Essays in Cultural Politics*. New York: Routledge.

Stall, Sylvanus. 1897. *What a Young Boy Ought to Know*. Philadelphia, Pa.: Vir Publishing Company.

Sterne, Laurence. 1994. *A Sentimental Journey and Other Writings*, edited by Tom Keymer. London: Everyman.

———. 1998. *The Life and Opinions of Tristram Shandy, Gentleman*, edited by Ian Campbell Ross. Oxford: Oxford University Press.

Stevenson, Robert Louis. 1998. *The Strange Case of Dr Jekyll and Mr Hyde*, edited by Emma Letley. Oxford: Oxford University Press.

Stiles, Anne, ed. 2007. *Neurology and Literature, 1860–1920*. Basingstoke: Palgrave.

Strange, Julie-Marie. 2005. "'I Believe It To Be a Case Depending on Menstruation': Madness and Menstrual Taboo in British Medical Practice, c. 1840–1930." In *Menstruation: A Cultural History*, edited by Andrew Shail and Gillian Howie, 102–16. Basingstoke: Palgrave.

Swift, Jonathan. 1993. *Selected Poems*, edited by Pat Rogers. London: Penguin.

Terry, Richard. 2001. *Poetry and the Making of the English Literary Past 1660–1781*. Oxford: Oxford University Press.

———. 2003. "In Pleasing Memory of All He Stole: Plagiarism and Literary Detraction 1747–1785." In *Plagiarism in Early Modern England*, edited by Paulina Kewes, 181–200. Basingstoke: Palgrave.

———. 2005. "Pope and Plagiarism." *Modern Language Review* 100.3: 593–608.

Tissot, S. A. 1985. *Onanism or A Treatise u-pon the Disorders Produced by Masturbation*. New York: Garland Publishing.

Varley, Henry. 1884. *Lecture to Men, Delivered to 3000 Men, in Exeter Hall, London. Containing Invaluable Information for Young Men and Those Who Are Married*. Fourth edition. London: Christian Commonwealth.

Walkowitz, Judith R. 2000. *City of Dreadful Delight: Narratives of Sexual Danger in Late-Victorian London*. London: Virago Press.

Wallace, Jeff. 2001. "'The Stern Task of Living': *Dubliners*, Clerks, Money and Modernism." In *Gothic Modernisms*, edited by Andrew Smith and Jeff Wallace, 111–28. Basingstoke: Palgrave.

Walzl, Florence L. 1984. "Dubliners." In *A Companion to Joyce Studies*, edited by Zack Bowen and James F. Carens, 157–228. Westport, Conn.: Greenwood Press.

Watt, Ian. 1974. *The Rise of the Novel: Studies in Defoe, Richardson and Fielding*. London: Chatto and Windus.

Wilde, William. 1853. *Medico-Legal Observations upon Infantile Leucorrhoea, Arising Out of the Alleged Cases of Felonious Assaults on Young Children*. Dublin: Fannin.

Wilson, Andrew. 1880. "Coinages of the Brain." *Belgravia: A London Magazine* 43.170 (December): 168–86.

———. 1881. "The Mind's Mirror." *Belgravia: A London Magazine* 45.179 (September): 346–66.

Wohl, Anthony S. 1984. *Endangered Lives: Public Health in Victorian Britain*. London: Methuen.

Woolf, Virginia. 1992. *A Room of One's Own and Three Guineas*, edited by Morag Shiach. Oxford: Oxford University Press.

Wurtz, James F. 2005. "Scarce More a Corpse: Famine Memory and Representations of the Gothic in *Ulysses*." *Journal of Modern Literature* 29.1: 102–17.

Index

The Florida James Joyce Series
Edited by Sebastian D. G. Knowles

Vike Martina Plock is a Lecturer in English Literature at Northumbria University. She has published articles on James Joyce and Edith Wharton and is currently guest-editing a special issue of the *James Joyce Quarterly* on Joyce and physiology. She is also working on a monograph on fashion, women writers, and literary modernity.

Lightning Source UK Ltd.
Milton Keynes UK
UKHW022154021020
370937UK00003B/167

9 780813 042268